The Ministry of Miracles:

A Complete Guide To Developing Your Creative Thinking

Learning is consciously entertaining an idea.
You get emotionally involved in the idea,
and stepping out to act on the idea, to change results.

'A Leadership Think-Tank'

A complete survival guide for the 21st century.

Part of 'The Mountains Are Calling' series

ISBN 978-1-78222-936-0

Book design, layout and production management by Into Print
www.intoprint.net
+44 (0)1604 832149

Acknowledgments

This writing is meant to help anyone manifest the life they desire and navigate through the dark days with a torch light in hand. This book is for the seekers, those want to grow and evolve by the development of their minds. Millions around the world have used this knowledge to shape their own destinies over the last century.

The wisdom shared in this book was inspired by both methods of creative imagination and synthetic imagination, drawn from the works of personal development legends like Napoleon Hill, Jim Rohn, Bryan Tracey, Bob Proctor and many more mentors. The three latter philosophers, I have had the pleasure of meeting in person, but I have had many mentors and teachers who have been a tremendous source of wisdom. I have befriended them through their audios, videos, and books. I am grateful for their contribution to my life, growth, and career. They have had a deep impact in my adoption and development of accurate thinking.

My father and the rest of my family have been gracious in giving me the personal freedom to make my own choices and peruse my own dreams while instilling the belief in myself in my soul. My mother has been my biggest supporter, cheerleader, and inspiration in my life. Through war, illness, and painful challenges of life, whenever I ask her, "How are you, Mom," the answer has always been the same: "I am doing wonderful, my son. God bless you." Talk about a positive mental attitude. She never learned to read and write, but she has a simple positive within her nature that is simply beautiful.

At age of thirteen my brother handed me a book called Uncle Tom's Cabin that inspired me to choose Canada as a home country to raise my family.

I also feel that Canada – the country I love and admire so much – must be represented from my unique perspective. The Canadian values of peace, harmony, tolerance, respect, cooperation, and kindness must be spread throughout the world.

My two kids have been an inspiration, and my own personal reasons to become a better human being by pursuing the person development knowledge. The reason I never gave up on my dreams through all the struggles, was the joy of witnessing them grow up to be outstanding individuals.

As a son, brother, husband, father, coach, and teacher, I do not take the responsibility bestowed on me lightly. I hold myself to a higher standard and responsible for my own actions and behavior.

I have put together the best of my research, discoveries, and revelations on human behavior – after twenty-five years of research – in this book. For our mutual benefit, I've recorded my wide exposure to many cultural settings around the world and a personal study of psychology of human behavior, and how it can help you achieve YOUR miracles.

Enjoy reading…

Arif Gilany.

Foreword

Paul D. Lowe – CEO & Founder Of World Game-Changers

To the change-seeking readers of this book…

Have you ever experienced a situation where you have only recently met someone, and yet you feel you have known them so much longer; to the point where it feels you have actually grown up together?

In the case of Arif, I am truly pleased to say that really has been my own experience. What immediately hit home with me, was Arif's deep respect and love of humanity – under-pinned by an unswerving authenticity.

Having personally been on the personal development pathway all of my life, I have come to gain and understand many invaluable insights about this voyage of self-discovery most of us are on.

Oftentimes, taking those first uncertain steps can be perceived as having to climb a mountain; the self-doubt that creeps in as we progress along our path, can temporarily derail us, without the guidance of a mentor.

This book is a superb mentorship companion; with many tried-and-tested strategies highlighted, galvanised by a very heart-felt and honest sharing of a multitude of Arif's own personal life experiences.

It is often said there is no substitute for experience. Well, if that cliché is true, Arif's work here certainly embraces a very wide range of colourful experiences – all combining to inspire the reader.

As a best-selling co-author myself, I humbly suggest I am well-placed to assess what makes a 'good book', and this collection of inspirational insights certainly falls into the category of being a good book.

Today's ever-changing world necessitates much more than just having credibility though; the expectation and focus is that you take responsibility for applying continuous improvement to your own personal brand.

Not only does Arif lead from the front with that responsibility, he goes further by skillfully knitting together theory and practice, effectively producing a blueprint for enhancing one's own reputation in life.

Taking everything into account, you can (hopefully) now appreciate why would-be readers need to invest in these life-enhancing reflections from Arif. Not by purchasing one book though – invest in more!

I endorse that you buy 10, and send copies to your most valued top ten relationships in life, as well as in business. After all, what better investment is there, than helping people grow?

THANK YOU Arif for your compassion, your friendship, and most of all, your love and service dedicated to serving humanity. You are without doubt, a beacon in a world that can oftentimes appear devoid of light.

Paul D. Lowe

CONTENTS

Introduction

Marco Polo, the 13th century Italian explorer, was the first person to record all his findings, experiences, customs, and systems he had learned along the Silk Road to China, in a written format. Europeans studied and used his findings to develop their society for the next millennia. Similarly, I have been seeking the specific knowledge in creative thinking and the use of imagination for over twenty-five years, learning from some of the top minds in today's world.

The chapters in this book will paint a clear picture of the social fabric, religious beliefs, and causes of many of today's personal, domestic, and international problems. There will be sound advice, solid strategies, and simple practical routines that you can help improve your thought process and improved quality of your life regardless of your location or circumstances.

In this book we will talk about creative vision, the success principle that's responsible for the building of all our plans, aims, and purposes. It has been said that imagination is the workshop wherein we fashion the purposes of our brains and the ideals of our souls. That is the true definition of imagination. We will explore the possibilities of the creative mind and what holds us back from creating miracles in our lives; as well as providing insights into real mind hacks and simple-to follow instruction on how to unlock your own potential with imagination.

There are two forms of imagination. Firstly, there is synthetic imagination which consists of organizing and putting together recognized ideas, concepts and facts arranged in a new combination. Very seldom does anyone create an idea or anything else that is new. Nearly everything known to civilization is but a combination of something old. Secondly, there is the creative

1

imagination that operates through the sixth sense and has its base in the subconscious section of the brain and serves as the exclusive medium thought which new facts and ideas are revealed.

There are many examples of synthetic imagination that we enjoy today. It is safe to assume that millions of people have reassembled old ideas through synthetic imagination that have made fortunes, while living lives of purpose.

Creative imagination is responsible for receiving new ideas that have never been thought of previously. This is where one draws ideas from outside of one's education or experience. Consciously entertaining an idea, you get emotionally involved in that idea and step out of your comfort zone to act on the idea to change results.

Sometimes people tune into their creative imagination and come up with ideas that benefit a great number of people and make themselves popular and rich.

I am going to give you some suggestions solely as inspiration intended to introduce you to your faculty of creative imagination. I believe the best ideas are yet to be revealed and put into service of mankind.

Imagination is a trait that becomes active by constant learning based on the principles described in this book. You are the one who must supply this activity. The rules of accurate thinking and imagination are so clear and simple that I often wonder why so few people ever take the time to learn the rules since accurate thinking and imagination are the very foundation for all achievement. Albert Einstein famously said, "Imagination is more important than knowledge."

A mentor of mine said, "Science is organized knowledge, while wisdom is organized life." Completing the lessons in this book will help you organize your life according to your own principles. This takes imagination and accurate thinking.

A Planned And Organized Life

If you let people's perception of you, rather than accurate thinking, dictate your behaviour, you will never grow as a person. The aim of this book is to reveal the possibility for personal growth and attainment of your most intimate desires for a planned and organized life. If you leave yourself open to experience and experiment with life despite what others may think, then you will learn to grow and evolve.

I have had the privilege to learn from the wisdom and the experiences of many of mentors & coaches and applied the principles in my own life. When the pandemic lockdown happened, I started to organize these ideas because I felt that I owe something to those who will follow me. My children, my family, my community, my country, and my nation should be aware of the wisdom that was so painstakingly accumulated. Those who have inspired me to live a phenomenal life and pursue my own passions should have the benefit of my research and experiments with the wisdom shared here. The journey I began was not easy, but it has been worth every challenge that I have faced and overcome.

My goal is to equip you with the skills to handle the crisis of life and to develop abilities to create your own peace of mind and personal freedom. The freedom to choose your own path despite tragedy, loneliness, disaster, and any other disappointing moments of life require a certain mindset that we will discuss here. We all face challenges and struggles in our lives, but how we respond to them is what makes the difference.

When Covid-19 crippled the world, having recovered from two near-death experiences enabled me to build a strong mindset based on personal development wisdom. I thought about authoring a book about developing a strong mindset and manifestation of health and prosperity during the uncertainty we all faced. I asked myself:

'What does it truly take to change the future for the better?" 'Is there a formula that we can demystify the process of building a better life?'

I thought about the problems we all face and the wild spread of the fear in the world, its causes, and its effect on mental health. The only problem we all have in this lifetime is, of course, ignorance. The so-called experts poured even more fuel on the fire and caused even more fear while governments imposed stricter restrictions to contain the pandemic.

In this age of the literate, ignorance is spreading effortlessly, but in the age of information, ignorance is only a choice. We need to stop this plague that has contaminated the lives and consciousness of multitudes of people. The aim of this book is to help one gain control over one's own thinking mind and life.

I am not naïve about the fact that most people never read another book after they finish their formal education. It is sad that even in country like Canada most people would only read books or manuals related to their work and only if it is required by their company or workplace. In other parts of the world, most do not even read one single book for the rest of their lives after getting a job or graduating from school.

Self-help books and resources have only become available to the public in the past century. Its founding fathers were some of the mentors who have inspired this writing. Over the last hundred years such material has helped millions of people transform their own lives by gaining control over their own mental faculties, going from rags to riches or creating more harmony in their lives.

Future In Canada

Making a lifestyle change, can be hard, especially when you are stuck in adversity. For example, I was living in the middle of war in a third world country. I was not born into a wealthy family, but rather an educated family. My father, who was orphaned at age seven and took on the family responsibility at a very early age to help raise six sisters and two brothers, had a deep passion for learning. I had wonderful role models in my life. We had the respect of our people and a beautiful simple life in a small village of less than fifty households, but all we ever we had was gone in the war and years of struggle followed.

As mentioned earlier, when I was thirteen years old and lived in the middle of the Iran-Iraq war, my older brother, a poet and writer, handed me a translated copy of a book called Uncle Tom's Cabin. I have never stopped reading but when I read that book by Harriet Beecher Stowe, an idea filled my head that changed the course of my life.

I fell in love with the concept of Canada, a country in which anybody could become anything. One night after finishing the book, I wrote in my notebook, "One day I will live in Canada and write books." At the time, I was a not aware of the laws of the universe that I discovered later as discussed in this book, but I was inspired to make a change in my life.

It seemed like an impossible dream for a teenage boy from a war-torn country in a small village in the most geopolitically sensitive region in the world to be able to move to Canada. Years later when I finally made Canada my permanent home,

I read other books about the laws that governed the human mind, personal development, mindpower and manifestation.

I have personally met many challenges in life besides surviving the war, refugee camps, and years of homelessness yet eventually I was able to build my life and business travelling the world and living in many first world countries including Canada, United States of America, Sweden, and Australia, and travelled all over the world. This is because I met mentors and attended seminars that altered my life once again. From their instruction, I realized that everyone has a conscious mind which is our thinking mind and subconscious mind that acts as a operating system that guides our actions and directs our paths in life.

A Purposeful Life

I have seen all sides of the world, its good, bad and the ugly. We are always most powerfully positioned to serve the people whom we once were in their position. I feel that there are many people in the many situations that I have experienced; therefore, I am here to challenge you to put these principles to the test and experiment with the results. I am also familiar with the opportunities the new world represents, and I will give you glimpse into both sides of the equation.

Let me ask you two questions:

- ❖ What if we could prepare the life you dream up while living in the now?
- ❖ What if you could live a purpose-driven life and build your own legacy?
- ❖ When was the last time you broke a big bad habit or built a better one?

We do not always realize that we are the authors of our own stories. You can change the way you tell your story. Your life is not just a list of events that happen. You can plan, edit, interpret, and retell your story even as you are constrained by the many facts of life. Many years later, I have revisited my old settings and see that so many friends and family have not grown, but rather have regressed from where they were, and their ambitions have died inside.

Friends and family may say that you tell great stories but allow me to remind you that the story you tell yourself about yourself is the most important story you will ever tell. Creating a narrative from the events of your life brings clarity to life. It helps you understand how you became you.

Be gentle and kind to yourself if your parents did not know any better and could not teach you. Oftentimes, parents and politicians enter their roles unprepared for the task ahead. They are expected to have acquired the fundamental skills, knowledge, and insight into the hierarchy of human needs before they are entrusted with their significant responsibility. Every person only understands based on their own personal capacity to comprehend the circumstances of life.

I want to sell you on the idea of the better version of your story through a vision we can craft together for your future. I have recorded the steps I took in creating my own version of an ideal life. I wanted to author a book with the formula that anyone could use to reinvent themselves and manifest their dreams whatever they may be.

Most of this book is based on my personal findings and the application of the wisdom and philosophies in my own life. The lessons learned from all the mentors and teachers mentioned have been put to real test in life. You will have the benefit of learning from some leading world experts on self-help and personal development research. I am only a messenger.

If you can adopt some ideas and apply them to your own daily life to improve your result or build new habits, the purpose of this writing will have been served. Principles shared in this book have the potential to change your life.

I have read hundreds of books on life transformation and mental growth. I know when I have my hands on a good book that is enjoyable and informative from the beginning to the end. I wanted to author such a book. I just love the wisdom shared here so much, I had to get it out of my system as it may be of help to someone else.

Life presents challenges to all of us, that is part of the journey of life. We can prepare ourselves by acquiring the skills to navigate through these challenges. Each of us as individuals can take the responsibility to build our own lives based on proven up to date scientific research, ancient wisdom, and shared testimonials. The aim of this book is to prepare you for such an undertaking.

Most people wait for disease, trauma, diagnosis, and tragedy, when they reach the lowest point of their lives, to make up their mind to change. The message of this book: is why wait? If you can start the process of progressive change today, you should. The fact is you need to be your own hero and you need to be the difference in an indifferent world. You will never be younger, smarter, or wealthier than you are today unless you make a deep decision to do it.

We change under difference circumstances. We can change in the state of joy and inspiration; we could be forced to change in the state of pain and suffering, or we can learn to change in our current state. Change is the only constant in this world, and we are living in the new era of information where change is happening faster than any other time in history. In the age of information, ignorance is only a choice made by those who are unaware of their own abilities.

Awakening To Learning

Today the Internet has made it possible to connect with an unlimited number of people and make an even bigger impact. We do not need a doctor, a teacher, a priest, a rabbi, a minister, or a governor to obtain information any longer. Technology has enabled all of us to access all the information that was not available before. People all over the world are awakening to this newfound wisdom and taking their destinies in their own hands. There is a new movement of awareness that we all need to join now.

Technology has made it affordable for all of us to research anything we want to learn. We can learn something new anytime we decide to pursue a new direction or choose to change course of action. When we learn new things, we are making new synaptic connections in our brain, using more of our brain power. In fact, learning is making new connections by activating of the dormant cells in our brains.

Research shows that when people learn one new bit of information and concentrate on it for an hour, they double the number of relevant connections in their brain. If they do not review new information if they do not think and talk and about it, those connections prune apart within hours or days of learning it. In other words, we forget what we do not practice.

You have heard that "repetition is the mother of learning." Therefore, the lack of repetition means the loss of information and weakening of our brain powers. What we are taught in the school system is to memorise facts and figures and apply them to life and business. However, real learning is consciously entertaining an idea. You get emotionally involved in the idea and step out to act on the idea to change results. The aim of this book is to provide some new learning opportunities which becomes installed in the circuitry of the brain that reveals new ways of doing things.

A great question to ask is: What do you do with new information? If we can take the new information, personalize it, demonstrate it, and apply it to initiate some new behaviour, we can change our results. If we can get our behaviours to match our intentions, thoughts, and actions, then change becomes automated and we can change our paradigm.

If we can make our mind and body to work together, we are creating a new experience, and that is where change starts to happen. New experiences enrich the philosophical circuits in our brain, laying down a network of neurons. The minute those neurons string into place, the brain makes a chemical, and that chemical is what creates feelings or emotions. Good or bad feelings are the results of the chemical that the brain produces.

The moment you feel grateful, inspired, or unlimited because of some new experience, you are teaching your body chemically to understand what the mind has understood intellectually. Knowledge is intelligence for the mind and experience is education for the body. When we are embodying the truth of this philosophy for a moment, the body and mind are aligned to create a new existence preparing us for a new destiny.

If we begin to think differently, make new choices, and do things in a new way, we can create new experiences. Creating new experiences can change our genetic destiny, because the chemicals our brain produces can inspire us to act in the new direction. If we learn to do this once, then we should be able to do it again. When we repeat an experience repeatedly, we begin to condition the mind and body to work together as one.

When you do something so many times that your body knows how to do it, as well as your mind understands its benefits, it becomes second nature. It gets easy, it becomes familiar, it gets automated, so we begin to master the philosophy of change.

For instance, waking up early in the morning and running for fitness could be challenging for those who love to sleep in, but once you discipline your body to follow a certain routine, as soon as your mind is awake, the body follows. That is how new routines are built which we will talk about in detail in this book. Routines can unlock creativity.

The Power Of Creativity

Do you think human creativity matters? I love poetry, but most people do not spend a lot of time thinking about poetry. We have busy lives, so we are not that concerned about poetry until someone close to us dies, we go to a funeral, trauma happens, somebody breaks our heart, or something unpredictable happens to us. Suddenly, we are desperate to make sense of it, thinking, "Has anybody ever felt this bad before?" We think of poetry to relate our experience to someone or something outside of our own experiences.

Emotion may lead to self-expression as well. You meet somebody and fall in love. Your heart explodes, and you love them so much you cannot see straight. You cannot get them out of your mind. You feel desperate to express yourself, thinking, "Did anybody ever feel this way before?" Those are the moments when art and creativity are not luxuries anymore; rather, they are sustenance. We seek refuge in our own creativity to give meaning to how we feel.

Writing is sustenance for me. I love expressing new and unique ideas through the written word to give and to guide. Writing is therapy and it is transcendence to me, as is reading. I believe the person who is disciplined to read will never be without a friend. I intend to make some best friends through this writing. Perhaps, if I am blessed, one day my name may appear in your testimonial.

In the meantime, I invite you to write. Writing down what you bear witness to or what you are passionate about, captures the wisdom in what happens.

There are three steps I use in my writing:

1. Brainstorm and write down ten things that you have born witness to or are passionate about.
2. Narrow it down in focus: pick the three most important things including details, and how they made you feel.
3. Pick one to tell your story. We are natural storytellers. Stories stay in our memory bank better than facts and figures because of the narratives and timelines we create in our brains.

Why I Wrote This Book

This book, which involves more than ten things I'm passionate about, is the labour of love and a deep passion and understanding of our deepest of the human desires and needs. We are here on this star in space to help one another; to understand each other's pains and to guide and comfort one another. We are here to uplift each other through shared wisdom. As we go forward, you will read why and how we can do this together.

Our deepest passion is what we love to do even without expectation of any compensation. If we could find our deepest passions, develop them, and stick with them long enough and learn how to adjust to varying circumstances of life, we could create miracles in our lives. Our purpose is our main pursuit in life that anyone can find and pursue.

After we are born into life and survive childhood, we are encouraged to thrive though life, and to be this, that or the other. We are taught to give life meaning through our careers and express ourselves through what we do. We are not taught how to find our passions and pursue what makes us truly happy.

It would be most useful to find out what we are here for at an earlier age. If we commit, we could excel, but we need to find out what we want to do with our lives first. It could sustain our joy and happiness throughout our lives and give us peaceful outcomes. The sooner we find our purpose, the sooner we find happiness in our lives.

To develop a sharp vision constructing an intentional course of action to lead us to an ideal future would almost guarantee the best outcomes in our lives. When we begin to select a new idea of the future and emotionally embrace what it feels like, we begin to feel an elevated emotion because we are so caught up in our inner visions.

When you feel an emotion like gratitude, inspiration, or motivation, in that instant the heart starts to respond differently. It acquires a more rhythmic pattern and is in harmony with the mind. In contrast, living by the emotions of fear, resentment and frustration causes the heart to beat in irregular patterns.

Unfortunately, most people spend a lot of time consumed by these stress indicators. Those are the survival mechanisms not a pastime or self-consumption routines.

The question becomes:

- ❖ Can we teach ourselves how to build or rebuild a more coherent brain function?

Can we regulate the heart patterns and how it responds to what happens to us?

The answer is yes, it is possible. Throughout this book you will learn how to respond purposefully to what happens to you instead of reacting to the circumstances of life. Failures, disappointments, and setbacks are inevitable in life, but we can prepare, respond, and overcome them accordingly.

I used the setback of the COVID-19 pandemic lockdown to organize this writing to follow my long-term passion of writing books that make an impact.

There is huge need for improvement of the physical and mental health as well as financial well-being of my fellow men which I am to address in this writing. The aim is to equip entrepreneurs, individuals, and organizations with the tools to prepare for the unpredictable future ahead.

Thank you for reading, and enjoy.

Chapter 1

Your Why

"Find your why, and you will find your way."
(John Maxwell)

The Why – The Reason We Do What We Do.

Every person on this planet knows what they do or how to do it, but very few know why they do it. We often assume that we know why we do what we do. For example, we work to provide basic human needs for ourselves and our dependents, but why do we choose a certain career path or start a particular business? Is it just to make money or make more money, or is there more to it? Why do we work all day long and get home exhausted to repeat it again the next day?

When you have a great idea or a program that can integrate your life with your passion, you rarely know where to start.

There is a simple step... you start with "Why'"

Write down why you want to do what you are planning to do, because clarity of purpose is the beginning of all successful achievement. "Why" is not about profits or money, that is the result of what we do. Your why is more about your purpose, your cause, your beliefs, and the grand outcome of what you do.

I remember sitting in front of the guidance counselor in the City Adult Learning Center in Toronto, Canada after finishing my high school diploma, upgrading my high school education to Canadian standards. I was there to ask for some direction for applying to college or university.

15

The counselor asked me, "What are you passionate about?" I thought about it for a moment, then I said, "I am passionate about people, I am passionate about health care. I am passionate about the environment. I am passionate about business, and I am passionate about my family."

She knew my background. She knew I was alone here, that perhaps I was tired working a full-time job to support myself and going to school full-time.

She asked me a few more questions, then suggested a survey to see my academic qualifications. Then she suggested that I take business as a career path. She said, "You could work in the corporate world and when you gain the experience, you could eventually start your own company. Once you build a strong foundation, you can visit your family back home as often as you want and for as long as you wish while raising your own family here."

I thought about it, then I said, "Okay, let's apply."

My "why" was explained clearly but the "how' and the 'what" were still unknown to me. "You can figure those out later on," she added.

The Art Of Creative Thinking From Inside Out

My favorite topic at DeVry University was the course called "The Art of Creative Thinking." Looking back at my life, it seems like it all unfolded as it was planned except the few bumps on the road that I call divine intervention that led me here.

If you just work at a company or a job for the money alone, you will have a short-lived unhappy career at the company. We rarely stick around for the money alone. When you work at a place where you believe in the vision of what they do, you may stay there a lifetime.

People don't buy what you sell beyond necessities; they often buy why you sell it. Similarly, people don't buy what you do, they buy why you do it. What you do proves what you believe. When I started marketing camel wool products, nobody had heard that camels even have fur, let alone knowing about its many health benefits.

When I told them my mother's story of recovery from her heart attack and the relief she found in wearing the garments, everyone that needed the products became a client and started bringing friends and family over to us.

All the inspired leaders think from inside-out. They think about why they do what they do first then they figure out what or how to do it. This explains the correlation between our human brain function and the use of the faculty of reason.

The core of the human brain is called the limbic brain which controls our feelings, behaviors, and decision-making. If you look at the human brain you will see three distinct layers. The core of the brain controls behaviors, feelings and decisions which allows us to rationalize our decisions and the tangible things we say and do. It rationalizes our "why."

As it turns out, there is a pattern to the behavior of all strong leaders and why they do what they do. It's the opposite of how everyone rationalizes their decisions. The goal of strong leaders is not to sell people what you have or what they create, but to sell people on their belief of why they do it. The school counsellor sold me on what she believed was the best course of action for me, based on her assessment of my desires and she knew my overall goals and dreams.

If you are the type of person who likes to have total control over every aspect of your life, then I have a great message for you...

"If you find your why, you will find your way."

Let me give you an example of this philosophy. In the summer of 1963, two hundred and fifty thousand people from all over the USA gathered in Washington, D.C to hear Dr. Martin Luther King speak. He was not the only man in America that suffered from civil rights injustice, and he was certainly not the greatest speaker of his time. He did not send out any invitations and there was no website to check the date and time. How did he bring out masses to hear him speak?

Dr. King did not go around telling people what was wrong with America. He went around telling people what he believed.

"I believe, I believe, I believe," he repeated, and the people who believed what he believed spread his message. Nobody showed up just for him. They showed up for themselves. It was what they believed for themselves, not for what he believed for them.

By the way, he gave the "I have a dream" speech, not the "I have a plan" speech.'

We follow servant leaders not for them, but we follow them for ourselves. Those who lead and inspire us are those we want to follow not because we must follow. All those who start with "why" are the leaders that inspire the people around them. They love what they do.

If you love what you do, you may be on-track to finding your purpose in life because knowing your "why" could be the key to a happy life. Your "WHY" could keep changing, expanding, and continuously growing throughout your life. Purposeful living is not for everyone, of course, because it's not an easy path. For me it has been a long hard journey but through trial and error I discovered some facts that have helped find my own path in life.

Why Am I Here?

Throughout my journey I kept asking myself, "Why am I here on this planet?" Then I was enlightened that I am here to take care of my family, help those I love, and be of service to people who are looking for guidance and answers to their problems.

I found out that the more people I help, the easier and more driven my life becomes. I figured if I could help others find solutions to their problems, I could overcome all my own challenges. My father was my hero and I learned from him that he never even ate breakfast alone. He always had people over discussing some idea or a solution over a meal.

I find joy and happiness in seeing other people happy as he did.

When I arrived in Canada in my early twenties, I was trying to find my way in my new country. Like many newcomers, I did not know anyone, and I had no friends or family. I started to look for organizations to join in my unique new environment. I thought I could find opportunities for myself through being a member of the community and of service to others.

After graduating from DeVry University, I was hired right out of college and began my professional career at FedEx Corporation in Pittsburgh Pennsylvania, travelling across North America to manage various teams to peak performance and production. In 2006, using these skills we were able to build the third largest organization within one of the top financial services companies in North America.

After working in the corporate world for nearly a decade, I had reached a stagnation point in my journey. I had the chance to settle in that life, but I did not migrate here to settle for the average life. I wanted to contribute, to build, and to play a bigger role in my new country because I came here with a vision and a dream.

A year later I started my own company in the financial services business on a part-time basis. I thought it was a great service to help protect the future for families like mine who had no one to depend on in case of the unforeseen or premature death.

A few years later, I found out that my parents' health was deteriorating at a fast rate: heart problems, specifically my mother's heart attack, arthritis, and multiple surgeries. The emotional burden was too heavy to bear and the responsibility too sacred to ignore. After a long visit with my parents, I changed paths again and focused on seeking solutions for healthy aging and developing products that could provide comfort for health problems.

Comfort is a good word. I wanted to find some comforting products for my aging parents that provided relief. I thought if I am lucky enough to live as long as they have, I need to learn the process of healthy aging for myself and others. I started to research and learn all that I could about the healthy aging process. It became my passion leading to development of unique natural fiber products for health and wellness and relieving arthritis pain. It took me places I had never been. I met people I would never meet otherwise. It led to the birth of a new company, The Camel Company Of Canada.

Right after a great start, I was a victim of a hit-and-run accident resulting in a ten-day long coma, sustaining a trauma that totally wiped my memory, in 2013. I added another line of research to my course. After a two-year long recovery, I focused my research on understanding the brain and its complex unlimited potential and functions. Suddenly, it became an obsession; furthermore, I could not escape from the interesting world of the mind.

The learning helped me regain my own memory and accelerated my personal recovery. I found out that our thought process was the key to solving most of our human problems. The brain is the most interesting organism in the body and the central command for all our health, wellness, our behaviours, and human achievements.

These remarkable experiences helped me realize that we are always most powerfully positioned to serve people when we once were in their positions. For instance, if you were a hundred pounds overweight and now you are in the best shape of your life, you would be best positioned to help the people that are in that very condition.

I had to go through so many personal challenges and professional metamorphoses that have positioned me to help others who are seeking to find solutions to their many challenges. The wisdom I share in this book can help anyone reclaim their health and wellness, rebuild, and create business opportunities that could transform their lives.

Through this writing I get the opportunity to teach how to create a strong mindset, overcome mental and emotional challenges that we all face today. I am in a place where opportunities are presented to me in multiple ways on daily bases. I am manifesting my new path by the practice of the principles shared here. Perhaps my experiences and research can help you forge your own way forward and find your own why. It just takes creativity.

The Struggle For Creativity

Many people struggle to be creative because they are consumed by daily challenges of survival. We struggle to rebuild, recreate, and grow ourselves when we face difficulties. We become our own worst critics and suspicious of our own talents and abilities, so we stick to the familiar and get stuck where we are planted. Without using our creative faculties to make necessary changes, we will have a tough time overcoming many of our health and life challenges.

If history has taught us anything, the world is an extremely unfair critic, so it is up to us to decide what we want to do or whether it any good or not. All we can do is to perform at our best, where we feel we are most productive. All of us can have a bigger impact on each other by sharing what we learn throughout our careers and our lives. I believe that most of us really want to offer the world something of great value. We want to offer something that the world will consider noble or important.

When we are younger, we think that life is infinitely long, and we have dreams but no plans. We think five or ten years are too long. The truth is that we rarely think or plan ahead, and time flies. Life is too short for all we want to accomplish; therefore, we must learn to plan and act on our written plans immediately.

How we spend our days is very important because our time here on this star in space is limited. Are we spending our time doing what we love where we can make the most impact? Most of us do not ask ourselves this question because we never think about it. I know that change is hard because the trap of habit is so huge. I am here to challenge the status quo.

We are all governed by forces of habit. Changing habits takes time, consistency of action and real determination. We are most impactful when we learn, unlearn, and relearn new skills quickly repeatedly. That is changing the paradigm. We will talk about changing paradigms at the conclusion of this writing.

What makes children so beautifully creative is that they have not developed any habits yet. They do not care if what they create is any good or not. They just do what they are directed to do, having fun in the process. For instance, when a child builds a sandcastle, they do not build it thinking, "I am going to be the greatest sandcastle builder in the world." They just throw themselves at whatever project we put in front of them, dancing, singing, painting, playing games or whatever we direct their minds to do. Any opportunity we give them, they try to use it to impress us with their individual creativity and expression.

If we want to help our families, friends, and our community, we must be able to express ourselves through our work, the way children do. To express ourselves and what we want, we must know ourselves and keep developing our abilities and learning new skills along the way. This can be easy if you love what you do, because when work is like play, the learning becomes interesting. Mind mastery can unlock our creativity.

It All Starts With The Brain

The brain is the most interesting organism that is still being researched and yet to be fully understood by science. In recent years, many professional researchers have dedicated their lives to fully understanding the brain and its complex functions. We know that the brain is the central command that directs every aspect of our lives.

The brain is an organism that can grow, develop, and even repair itself and the entire body through the function of its complex circuits. Just like our cell phone or computers, the brain is made of circuits that are connected and can be turned on and off at will.

Most people do not know how to turn these brain circuits on or off. All spiritual, inspirational, or motivational circuits or the circuits that cause fear, stress, and anxiety can be under our own command. We need to learn, practice, and master our brain function.

Most people are victims rather than captains of their brain functions because the brain is a primarily survival mechanism. Its main job is to protect us from the hazards and dangers that threaten our lives and comfort.

However, our brain is an organism, not an organ or a muscle as is falsely believed; therefore, the brain can grow, develop, and even repair itself. I speak from experience. Mine had been damaged and completely wiped of all memory after the hit and run accident in Toronto, Canada on October 18th, 2013, but I helped it repair and restore itself.

This book was written based on researched data and application of these facts and findings in my personal life and recovery. I do not believe we are our brains, but we have a brain that can heal itself and the body that it lives inside. It can even maintain function as we age!

For most people, the brain function deteriorates with age because of lack of awareness that the brain can help it maintain itself and continue its growth. Brain education is very important because illnesses such as Alzheimer's or excessive stress take control of our brain and impact our health and well-being causing multiple challenges as we age. Once we train our brain and discipline our bodies, we can deliberately and consciously evolve in many ways. We cannot separate our way from our childhood programming, dramas, and wounds but we can reprogram our brains to create new and more exciting patterns.

I'm lucky because I was able to use the principles shared in this book to regain, retrain, and restore my brain function and memory. I rebuilt my physical body and functional strength by developing some simple practices and habits I developed in the process.

After comprehensive research and my individual experiences, I concluded that my sustainable mission throughout my existence would be to help improve the mental, physical, and financial lives of the people around me. This book is written with that purpose and grand vision in mind.

The only viable way to healing from inability, poverty, lack, trauma, illness, or any other condition is by going the extra mile to educate myself. Going the extra mile is a principle that we will talk about extensive in the closing chapters of this book. It has me helped heal from physical and psychological trauma and recover from business failures.

I am authoring this book to give you the secrets to being your best self. The most important relationship that you need to pay attention, improve and maintain is the one you have with yourself. You are the most important person in your life. Your imperfections and personal abilities make you unique. If you are not loving you, if you are not taking care of you, you cannot help anyone else. Your friends, family, coworkers, clients, and potential customers need a healthy you. Life is less about constant joy and more about constant expansion of our personalities. You can be the source of positive energy and help others find health, happiness, and fulfilment in lives and workplace.

We are constantly grinding each other trying to be "better" than the other person. We think we have more fun than our neighbors, we can outsmart our coworkers, our lives are better than others, but we are all wired differently. I discovered that the best version of myself was the one that was in service of others, my family, my community, and the rest of the world. That is how I found mentors, collaborators and even competitors that helped me grow along my own journey. I felt best when I forgot about my problems and pains and directed my focus to be of service to others.

When I took my focus off myself and redirected my efforts to helping others, including my parents, family and friends, things started to shift. I felt much better when I was listening and finding solutions to other people's problems. As much as we want others to listen to what we have to say, I found out that I feel better when I made others feel better about themselves by listening to them.

In words of my great grandfather, "Sit at the door and let your words speak from the podium. Don't be at the podium, let the value of your words be at the door until you earn the right to take your words to the podium with you."

I hope my words will speak from the podium to you. I have put together a collection of life-changing ideas, ground-breaking psychological and behavioural brain research, historic events, unique stories, and personal discoveries that bring a new perspective to work and personal life. I enjoy reading this book because it contains valuable real-life world-class lessons learned from world renowned experts and mentors about the art of creative thinking for everyday use.

Most of these ideas have been used to challenge and change the behaviour of peers, colleagues, teams, and family members over the years. I was able to put these philosophies and ideas to the test in the real world and the results have been remarkable. That is my "why" for sharing these principles with you.

The Challenge Ahead

The so-called *challenge* is presented through two concepts where you are encouraged to think before putting these ideas to practice. This double-edge hurdle of scholarship and relevance makes this book an implicit message for real change in personal and organizational development. A culture is a paradigm, people have cultures and organizations have cultures. We need to challenge and change our paradigm as we go forward and grow through our lives.

In the following chapters you will also learn a bit about the interesting and quite complicated different ways of life in the Middle East, Europe, and North America. Insight is provided into the complicated inner-world of the Middle Eastern belief systems and cultural differences that impact all of us today.

The Internet has made the world a global village and we all need to learn from each other to get along better.

In 2018, after starting the Camel Company of Canada and after my recovery from the hit-and-run accident, I wrote my first book The Mountains Are Calling, while restoring my lost memory which led me to the discovery of my true passion for enlightenment through writing.

Writing has become my therapy and sustainability for my mental and spiritual health, but it's also my sacred duty. I come from a family of writers and that goes back centuries in the history of Middle East, but I discovered writing for my own reasons – as my 'why' – kept changing and my perspective kept shifting.

What do you feel is your sacred duty? What are the things that you would wake up in the morning and fight for all day? That is your "why." You need to find your own sacred obsession. That is the fire that never runs out. I found mine in the hours I spent in authoring this book to be able to make an impact in someone else's life.

I found the courage to come face-to-face with my inner fears and grow through challenges overcoming my own inabilities. I found out who I really was and discovered my purpose in life. I just wanted to feel better about myself and keep growing along the way. I found out that real power to feel good comes from within; hence, any person on a mission can go through any difficulty or hardship.

Let us see how we can create some miracles together and make lasting change for a better future. In the next chapter, we will talk about the workshop of the creative mind.

Chapter 2

The Ministry Of Miracles

"A positive mental attitude will create more miracles than any other drug." (Patricia Neal)

In 1985 scientists conducted extraordinary research in the university of Michigan that was titled, "The most important research in metaphysics." The researchers assembled a village like the 'Pioneer Village" – a tourist attraction attached to York University in Toronto, Canada. That year they built a similar community that was based on lifestyle that was lived forty years prior to the time.

The buildings, the streets, the cars, the clothes, the foods, and everything that was in the community resembled that of four decades previously. Then the researcher went to senior homes and selected a group of seniors over 80 years of ages that had spent a longer time there. One night they were all given sleeping pills and while asleep they transferred the entire group to the reconstructed community.

The next morning when the seniors woke up, they looked around and saw everything that resembled forty years prior: their breakfast, the home and even the morning news was of the 1940s, the bygone era of their youth.

At first, they were shocked, thinking they were dreaming, and had difficulty adjusting. But after a few days they believed that time had reversed, and they were living at the time of their newly reconstructed habitat. They believed their age had reversed and they were younger.

The interesting thing was that there were no mirrors so they could see themselves, but their nurses aided them with their necessities. After three weeks they believed they were younger. They believed that a time machine had taken them back to their younger days.

After one year of the residents living there, the research findings were most astonishing to the scientists. The seniors' physical and mental illnesses had improved miraculously. Their hand and face wrinkles had straightened out visibly and even some of their hair had reversed back to darker colours.

What do you think was the reason for the incredible improvement of health? It was their beliefs. They believed their age had reversed. Your beliefs are so powerful that they can change the physiology of your body. We live with our beliefs and our beliefs build our lives. You can build a powerful belief in yourself and live a strong, rich life. Wealth is not only accumulation of money, but also peace of mind, mental and physical health. Your health is your most valuable asset.

The Miracle Of Small Changes

Our ability to follow through on our best intentions, to get into a new habit or to change our behavior in any way does not depend on reasons we might do it but on the depth of our convictions. It does not depend on our understanding of the benefits of a particular behavior or even on the strength of our willpower. It depends on our willingness to be bad at our desired behaviour until we master it.

Motivation is not something that we can always muster at command, but you can always be the inspirit to act based on your beliefs. A sound physical and mental health is your own responsibility.

When life gets tough will you give up or will you be relentless?

- ❖ Will you be a cynic, or will you be a builder?
- ❖ Will you be clever at the expense of others, or will you choose to be kind?
- ❖ I will hazard a prediction after observing my parents mature to their mid-eighties and having my loving father pass away peacefully in my arms during the writing of this book, at the age of eighty-four.

When you are 80 years old and sit in a quiet moment of reflection, memorizing or narrating the most personal version of your life story; the stories that will be most meaningful will be the series of unusual choices you have made and the kindness you showed others in the most desperate moments of your life.

In the end we are our choices. It is our choices that build our characters and create our outcomes. This book was written to bring you a set of inspirational instruction, fun practices and healthy daily routines that will put you in charge of your life. What direction you take in shaping your own destiny and how you want to live your life is a choice. The aim of this writing is to help you build yourself a great memorable story, a purposeful life, and a solid character.

Life of course, does not come with instructions. We know that life does not get better by chance, but it does gets better by choice. Life gets better by continuous learning and most importantly by making adjustment to our daily activities and habits as we grow older.

We are talking about minor adjustments in our eating, sleeping, and thinking habits, small corrections that can lead to improved physical and mental health and our productivity. Thinking habits because these are the most important habits of all. That is where the magic and miracles happen, inside one's own thinking mind.

Most people think there is nothing they can do about their circumstances, or they think that their life is harder than anyone else's life, so they attempt to take shortcuts in life. Fast food, faster drives to get nowhere and shorter tempers are all the result of looking to shortcut the process of what we really want, our own way in life.

Adding to this unsuccessful mindset, most people depend on luck or misfortune, and misfortune is the one that rules. There are many philosophies one can die by, but we need a real philosophy to live by which I call "**The Compound Effort Effect.**" We ultimately benefit from the compounding effect of our continuous learning, working, and building efforts.

You see, God never puts a real dream inside your heart without giving you the ability to turn it into reality, but you must put forth the effort. We have all been given the six faculties to turn any dream into reality. We are the only species with **faculties of perception, intuition, the will, reason, imagination, and memory** that we can use to create our own favorable circumstances. This does not just mean wealth, as you might think.

In every country and environment there are people who can accumulate money, but to live a life in which you are satisfied with most of your choices is a bit more challenging. A relative of mine is the wealthiest man known in the region, yet when I arrived here, he was suffering from depression and had locked himself in an apartment and was not letting anyone to see him. This to me is proof that money alone does not buy you happiness; rather, it's the depth of our relationships that bring us real joy and happiness.

We have difficulty choosing happiness. We human beings are such worried little creatures. Our poor mangled minds just worry, compare, and become concerned about everything that we do not understand and cannot control.

We fret, seethe and rage in suffering trying to find some sort of comfort in our misfortunes or mangled minds. Occasionally, if we get the idea that we are doing is what we are supposed to do, we feel happy. However, most people are constantly living in misery and crisis of life. They gripe and complain about how tough their life is or how unfairly they have been treated.

I just wonder if this life was not meant to be full of love, joy, happiness, and possibilities. Of course, we know that life is hard and none of us gets out of here untouched or alive; therefore, I suggest minimizing the things that cause suffering while we are here. Things like worry, stress and pity are not healthy; therefore, we must replace them with hope, creativity, and action. I just know when I am eighty years old, I am not going to worry about the things that could not control, all the mistakes I made or chances I did not take. I will have made the best of all my life circumstances.

I Am Getting Better And Better

One of the teachers I read about taught me something I've lived by. The French psychologist Emile Coue gave the world its first simple formula for a sound mental attitude a century ago when he taught his students the simple principle:

"Day-by-day, in every way, I am getting better and better."

Health, happiness, joy, and financial success are the results of what consumes our minds daily. We'll return to this mantra later.

To back up a bit, the physical body is a house that the Creator has provided as a dwelling place for the mind. It is the most perfect mechanism ever built and it is self-maintaining. The brain serves as the command center, operator of the nervous system, and the coordinator of all physical activity. It is also the receiver of all sense of perception, but the brain is yet to be fully understood and explained by science. The brain coordinates all senses of intuition, perception, imagination, knowledge, and memory and the will into new patterns that we call thoughts.

Our brain is the commander of all voluntary and involuntary activity operations carried out by the conscious and subconscious part of the mind. It dictates things such as breathing, heartbeat, digestion, blood circulation, nervous system and much more that we don't consciously control. In contrast, our daily habits and physical life activities are controlled and can be carried out consciously. We can consciously get better and better.

The brain is the storehouse of all knowledge, the interpreter of influences of environment and the source of thought. It is also the most powerful and least understood organ of the body. The brain is the housing place of the subconscious as well as the conscious section of the mind. It is the generator of energy that operates the body.

The energy and intelligence with which thought is produced flows into the brain from great universal storehouse of what author Napoleon Hill, another of my teachers, calls "The Infinite Intelligent," The Universe or God.

The brain is only the receptor and distributor of this energy through our words and actions. Amongst many other duties, the brain runs a first-class department of chemistry through which it breaks up and assimilates the food we consume. It liquefies the food and distributes it to the body through the bloodstream to every part for the maintenance and repair of the individual cells.

All of this is performed automatically, but I've discovered certain simple aids that everyone can give the brain. In this chapter, we will discuss some of these aids I learned through a brain injury and total memory loss, and the subsequent recovery.

First and the most important of the aides that we give our brains to grow, expand even recover from injury is the ability is to maintain a *positive mental attitude*. As much as the brain is the undisputed central command of the physical body, I should mention that a sound mental health demands a positive mental attitude.

A sound physical and mental health begins with a sound and positive health consciousness, just as financial success begins with prosperity consciousness – in other words, being aware of your thoughts regarding that topic of health or money. Let it be known here that no one ever succeeds without a prosperity consciousness, nor does anyone enjoy a sound physical health without health consciousness.

To maintain a health consciousness, one must always think in terms of sound health and never think in terms of ill health, disease, or pity for oneself. Whatever the mind dwells upon consistently, the mind brings into existence. To maintain a positive mental attitude is suitable for development and main-tenance of a sound health consciousness. The mind must be kept free of negative thoughts and influences through self-dis-cipline and established daily habits.

The application of Emile Coue's mantra uses the principle of autosuggestion and is the simplest way to get you on the right mindset. Coue recommended that his students repeat this sentence thousands of times daily until it is picked up by the subconscious mind. Eventually, when it is picked up, accepted, it is carried out to its logical conclusion in terms of sound health or financial abundance.

Many people reading this book will not practice this one simple daily exercise, but those who do will see definite results. I picked up this simple formula from an audio program while in recovery, accepted in good faith and practiced it daily. It has produced marvelous results in terms of sound physical health and creation of opportunities.

I used this simple line every day during my recovery that took two long years. I did not feel great every day, but I put forth effort and made progress each day, making tiny changes. As time passed, I felt better and better until eventually I was fitter and felt better ever before. I made so much progress that I was able to defragment and reprogram my mind that has produced superb powers, which I tapped into to write two books, this one being the second.

Here is another reason a positive mental attitude is essential for the maintenance of sound physical health. All thought energy, whether it is positive or negative, is carried to every cell in your body and deposited there as energy on which the cell operates.

The energy of thought is carried to the body through the nervous system and the blood stream. It is a known fact that the body mixes this energy of thought with every particle of food that is assimilated and made ready for circulation in the bloodstream.

It is also a known fact that any form of worry, fear, anger, jealousy, or hatred that one may experience while eating will cause the food to firm up in the stomach without becoming properly assimilated, resulting in indigestion and internal problems.

While in recovery, when I felt anxious or worried, I walked it off while listening to positive podcasts and audios. I thought grateful thoughts about the remarkable people that I already had in my life. I started the practice of walking at least twenty kilometers a week, and then when my mind and body were more stable, I started the habit of running. Today, I still run routinely to take care of my body and keep this discipline to improve my physical health.

Speaking of digestion, another crucial factor in sound physical health is our eating habits. Eating right alone is worthy of an entire book, but there are many professionally written books on the subject that you can access, so I will confine myself to a few simple recommendations which are on the must-do list if you want to enjoy a sound physical health.

First there must be no overeating because it overworks the heart, the liver, the kidneys, and the digestive system. A straightforward way to control overeating is to get up from the table before one is fully satisfied.

This habit may be a bit difficult to acquire at first, but once you master it, it will pay big dividends saving you thousands of dollars in medical bills and doctor visits. Food is fuel for the body, not a hobby to be exploited.

When we eat a certain amount of food, no matter how delicious, we must make sure that it is followed by equal amount of physical activity otherwise the excess stored in terms of fat in various parts of the body. Being overweight is often the result of stress eating, overeating or lack of physical activity and the beginning of many health problems.

Healthy Or Hypochondriac?

To stay healthy, there must be no complaining, griping or fault-finding because these affect the digestive system, organs and our performance at home and the workplace. There must be no hatred, for hatred upsets the digestive system and causes many problems in our society.

There must be no fear since it indicates friction in the human relationships. Lack of harmony and understanding within one's mind discourages digestion. There must be no talk about illness and disease, for that leads to the development of the worst of diseases. A disease that is known to doctors as **Hypochondriasis**; to the average person it is an imaginary illness.

A hypochondriac is someone who lives with the fear that they have a serious but undiagnosed medical condition even though diagnostic tests show there is nothing wrong with them. Hypochondriacs experience extreme anxiety from the bodily responses most people take for granted. During the Covid-19 pandemic, fear of death has caused more casualties than the pandemic virus itself as I understand and believe it to be true.

I rarely take any pharmaceutical or manufactured drugs. I have observed that while pharmaceutical drugs aim to repair one part of the body, they often destroy other parts or organs. I have built myself a suggestion that "I am a self-healer."

Being a self-healer suggests that our body has the power to heal itself of any illness of disease, if you give it the right nutrition and enough physical activity with the mindset that *"day-by-day, in every way, I am getting better and better."*

To return to the question of diet, one must eat a balanced ration consisting of a fair proportion of fruits and vegetables because they contain many mineral elements that nature demands in the building and maintenance of the physical health. By eating right and thinking correctly, we can go a long way in keeping the doctor away. I learned this from hundred of health experts, nutritionists, psychologists, doctors, and nurses in one of the best health care systems in the world, the Canadian health care system, and its professionals.

I was blessed to have such a unique exposure not because of my unhealthy habits but an accident that almost brought me to total health breakdown and financial devastation. My recovery was nothing short of a miracle, and the result of defragmentation and reprogramming of my mind through habits that keep the body in good health. My recovery was full of valuable lessons, and I will share some of them with you in the following chapters.

Thinking with a right mental attitude regardless of your circumstances is a tough personal responsibility. It is not easy, but no one can do this for you. For example, when it comes to eating properly, there are many resources to find out how to eat healthy, but keeping a *Positive Mental Attitude* is our own individual responsibility.

Our mental attitude is a very powerful determinant for improving our physical health. *What we dwell on eventually develops inside us*. I believe if we dwell only on the positive side of life, eventually positives develop inside of us. A healthy mind lives inside a healthy body and a health consciousness is the source healthy living.

Today more people are following these guidelines and are living longer happier lives all over the world. Eat right, think right, and follow that with enough physical activities. Then, you will always make you feel right.

Old Man On A Lonely Highway

Even when disaster strikes, a positive mental attitude will enable us to pull ourselves out of the pits of life and regain our physical health. When we have superior healthy habits and the right disciplines, we will always look into the future with brighter hopes. We will be able to develop an abiding faith in the future.

Faith in ourselves will give us greater chance of success in our workplace, a happier home life and wonderful personal relationships. Keeping faith will keep you free from fear and worry. We will be able to enjoy the confidence in our abilities to solve life's problems. We will build lasting friendships and we will enjoy a closer relationship with our Creator whom I believe intended that we should be healthy and enjoy the full powers of our own minds.

The road that leads to the happy valley has many fellow travellers on it; thus, we will need their cooperation and they will need ours. Remember that there will be many generations that follow this generation, and their lives will depend on the mindset and kind of intellectual inheritance that we leave for them.

The collaborations we engage in today may make this world a more livable place for our children who have a right to expect something aside from worry and the mountain of public and private debts from us.

I have benefited from the knowledge and experiences of many of mentors those who have come before me, but I owe something to those who will follow me.

For the present generation and the generations that will follow our footsteps, we must become bridge-builders in the spirit of the poet who wrote:

An old man travelling a lonely highway,
Came in the evening old and grey,
To a chasm deep and wide,
The old man crossed at the twilight dim,
For the wild steam, had no fear for him.

But he turned, when he reached the other side,
And built a bridge to suspend the tide.
"Old man," cried out a fellow pilgrim nearby,
"You are wasting your strength building a bridge here.

Your journey will end with the ending day,
and you will never again pass this way.
You have crossed the chasm deep and wide,
Why build you a bridge at even tide?"

The builder raised his old grey head,
"Good friend, on the path that I have come" he said,
There follows, after me today,
A youth whose feet must pass this way.

"This stream which has been unkind to me,
To that fairy boy, it may be.
He too, must cross at the twilight dim,
Good friend, I am building this bridge for him.

I identify with the spirit of that old man. My children, my family, my community, my country, and my nation has given me the inspiration to live a phenomenal life despite all the dark days. I feel that our nation must be represented from my unique perspective. The Canadian values of peace, harmony, tolerance, cooperation, and kindness must be spread through out the world.

The Canadian system of free enterprise and social values could be adopted in many parts of the world. Our schools, churches and mosques must be given a firm foundation for inspirational teachings and our financial resources must be secured through fairness in trade and self-education.

As my mentor, the late Jim Rohn, the American philosopher, said, "Formal education will make you a living, but self-education will build you a life." As a service to those who will follow us, we must leave a legacy like the one that was built and preserved by the great generation that preceded us.

Life must go on and our standard of living must be improved with every coming generation, and this is only possible by us becoming the bridge-builders. The Baby Boomer generation that lived in the beginning of the last century was one of the toughest generations that build the foundation for the world that we enjoy today.

Shiny Distractions

We need to equip ourselves and our children with the knowledge that is not taught in our school system but through personal pursuit of such wisdom. We live in interesting times with many fast-moving distractions, apps, gadgets and the contumaciously growing presence of social media and online systems in our living rooms.

The lure of course is quite shiny, and a lot of people fall into this time-wasting vacuum. Time, of course, is much more valuable than money and most people just waste away in what they may perceive as entertainment and in less wholesome pursuits instead of investing in themselves and growing their personal skills and abilities.

No matter what misfortunes we may face individually or as a nation, the burden will fall heavily on the shoulders of each of us to educate ourselves individually and make sure our families and our children are not influenced by the disturbances.

We can counter these influences by acquiring and expressing the spirit of self-discipline and unselfish cooperation in all our relationships. As America's Founding Father Benjamin Franklin said, "We must all hang together or assuredly we will all hang separately."

Until we become inspired by this broader spirit of cooperation, we will not be able to benefit individually and collectively by the principle of cooperative effort. The spirit that recognizes the oneness of all people and the fellowship of all humankind is entirely antithetical to greed, selfishness, and racism. A continuous educational approach to life and the spirit of fairness of open exchange and trade between all nations and races will bind our hearts and minds together. We can all benefit from each other, we all need each other.

Greed is a distraction too. The world is an abundant place, and we can build a pie big enough to share with as many people as possible. You do not have to fight over the same piece of the pie, because the world is an abundant place and there are plenty of resources to be shared to feed everyone on the planet. There are principles you can learn on how to acquire every resource you need including money through your own personal growth and development.

In the spirit of creativity and collaboration with others, imagine your vision giving rise to someone else's freedom, health, and abundance. Imagine your talents and abilities inspire action in one and then another and another giving birth to more visions and ideas. Creating an environment that fosters more innovative thinking, growth and more innovative ideas that can change the world for the better.

Imagine developing new products and services and creating innovative ways to promote hope, health, and happiness. Your passions, your story and your creativity can give someone else the strength, determination, and power to push through their own tough times. You can be the light for someone else in the face of greatest challenges, pains, and adversities.

Just imagine your skills, talents and ideas benefiting not only you but also to your neighbours, your friends, your family, your colleagues, your country, and your nation. Imagine finding one "out of the box idea'" that creates a ripple effect of health, wellness, and prosperity in the lives of thousands of millions of people around the world.

New Awakenings

When Covid-19 almost paralyzed the world, I asked myself:

"What can I do right now to create a ripple effect of hope, health, opportunities during these tough times?"

If we use this time for reflection, analysis, learning and preparation, we can grow our thinking and learn new skills that would be invaluable soon. If we tap into our God-given potential, we will emerge stronger than before. I know we are going through these unprecedented tough times, and for the first time in our lives everyone on a global level has been affected similarly.

Our families, our neighbours, and our communities are affected by a new bitter awakening as we hear news of loss of life daily. It is now time to act individually towards a collectively better future. All I know is we have a short memory and soon everyone will forget that desperate feeling and start tearing at each other.

I wanted to help you in a better awakening by bringing you some peace of mind, joy, and comfort through this unique inspirational writing. I am known to bring happiness to my family, friends, and thousands of our clients in Canada through my words and new and innovative products. I was compelled to draft this book because of personal findings on the subject matter.

After the hit-and-run accident where I was reduced to 150 pounds. I could not remember who I was or where I came from. I was able to rebuild myself back and put my life back together in a situation that, for me, was much worse than my experience of the pandemic. Since then, so many have asked me how I stayed positive I faced dark moments and skeptical future.

Allow me to remind you that the Great American Depression lasting from 1929 to 1939 was one of the worst economic downturns in the history of the industrialized world. It wiped out millions of businesses and many people took their own lives, but it also brought about the conditions for the growth and the prosperity for the next hundred years.

This pandemic reminds one of that historic misfortune as many businesses close and go bankrupt right in front of our eyes. Millions have lost their jobs and even more have spent all their savings to stay afloat and survive the rough ride, but I also see great opportunities rising around the corner.

We can prepare ourselves and our families to take advantage of what is coming next, which I believe is going to be the greatest time of innovation and prosperity for many nations and people of diverse backgrounds. Of course, the lack of direct social interactions and the fear of the unknown has so many people understandably worried, stressed, and anxious about their futures.

However, I believe humanity is creative and we always find ways to survive and make life even better and more exciting. We will move beyond these dark days. We are the kings of the animal kingdom with creative vision and the power of faith that can take us through any misfortune.

No circumstance can be called a failure unless and until it has been accepted by an individual as such. All people meet with adversity, defeat, and failure at some point in their lives, because it appears that these are nature's tools for the refinement of men's character. All great leaders have face great difficulties and overcome unbearable challenges.

Imagination Revisited

My goal is to give you an idea of the inner workings of our mind and how to control your thinking which is the starting point of building of habits that rebuild life. Brain research is new and mind training is not taught in our education systems, but there are researchers who have dedicated their lives to this brand of education. I was fortunate to connect with them and read their work and research.

This knowledge was first released to the public by Napoleon Hill, and Andrew Carnegie through their collaborative work in the past century. Prior to that it was taught only through specialized elite societies and handed down from one generation to the another as a hidden wisdom only known to those who sought such wisdom.

Napoleon Hill and Andrew Carnegie teach that those who want to reach peace of mind, sound health, and prosperity can use this power to manifest their own lives as they imagine it. The control over our own mind is the most powerful tool that we are given as a birthright, and it is given to all of us for free.

If we learn how to use this power, we can turn any situation around. Millions of people have practiced these principles and overcome unimaginable hardships. No, it will not be easy, but if we put in the work required to turn this wisdom to simple practical daily routines the possibilities are overwhelmingly in our favor.

Most people do not use their imagination constructively; in fact, most people use their imaginations destructively. Stress, worry, and anxiety are the real enemies of our happiness. But they can be replaced with thoughts of hope, joy, and happiness by reprogramming our subconscious mind.

Unfortunately, most people think, consciously or subconsciously, about what they do not want all day long and that is exactly what they get. The mind is primary a survival mechanism and fear driven. Thus, we must imagine consciously and deliberately what we want and how to get it. As I stated earlier, I have discovered that the easiest way to achieve our own goals and desires is to be of service of others first. Only through collaboration with others can we achieve beyond the average life.

I have found that most successful people are invariably successful in direct proportion to challenges they have met and the obstacles they overcame, and the way that they consciously decide what they want. We are not just here to follow nature's path of least resistance in our survival efforts.

It is a known fact that nature penalizes people for neglecting the proper use of their minds and physical bodies. If we do not use our mind, it becomes lazy, unreliable, and predictable, just as if we do not take care of our body, it becomes weak, deteriorates, and becomes infested with illness and disease.

Problem-solving forces the mind to develop through use. Just like iron sharpens iron, our minds sharpen through its use. A challenged mind continues to grow and develop while an idle mind seeks laziness, ease, and comfort, deteriorates, and gets wasted. Look at what happens to some of the children of wealthy people, who feel entitled and let the mind go in other directions, and often end up in a different sphere than their self-made parents. Even the best education money can buy does not prepare us for maximum development,

Quiz: Who Am I?

If you take a pen and paper and write down the answer to the following questions, you will see that we are not challenged in formal educational system in this manner. Have you ever asked yourself, "Who am I?" Well, let me answer that you are God's highest form of creation. Every religion in the world says that man was created in the image of his maker, therefore we have the power to create. God created us to think and thinking leads to ideas and ideas can be turned into products and services. But first, I encourage you to ask yourself these questions.

Why am I here? Write down your best answer.

1. What do I really want out of my life? Describe what you want to have in your life.
2. What do I want to be remembered for when I am gone? What do you want people to say about you? Write it down.
3. Would you be able to give a clear picture of your most intimate desires and wants?
4. What do you want out of your life, house, car, family, business, travel? List as many as you can in your own script.
5. This goal-setting exercise has a purpose. I will be explaining the process of goal-setting in the upcoming chapters. As I said, I believe that there is a reason the Creator has given man the ability to think, decide and create, which no other animal has. Our purpose is higher than just to make sure that we have children of our own, and that our life form continues through each of us.

Also, we are not merely here to accumulate all the wealth, money, and things we can get for ourselves and build walls around our assets either. We have a higher purpose, and each of us can find that higher purpose only when we look deep within our own hearts.

Self-analysis in our hearts and souls leads to deep discovery of reasons for our existence. We are the Creator's highest form of creation, so let us not undersell ourselves.

You Are A Miracle, You Are Special

You have the power to learn, change, evolve and get better at anything you put your mind to improving.

Surely, there is a formula for achievement in accumulations of money and material goods. We all have things we want to accomplish, dreams to live and places we want to go, yet we never learn how to seek and find our paths and true purpose. A purpose-driven life is not for everyone, I must add, but I believe those who find their purpose are who live in the minds and hearts of others long after they are gone.

My own major definite purpose is to make a positive impact in health, happiness, and lives of my fellow men. I am happy when I see others happy. My purpose was to travel the world and face unbearable difficulties to bring back knowledge of how to overcome challenges and a message of hope, health, and prosperity.

Our immediate personal health goal should be to keep death and illness at a respectable distance. However, the overall goal of life should be to serve our fellow men through the discovery and cultivation of our own talents and abilities. It is what we are remembered for when we are gone. Some are remembered long after they depart, while others are forgotten right after the funeral is done.

We do not need to have a lot of brains to be successful and

accumulate money in this world, but we do need solid motives to move in a certain direction in life. If we do not know what to do in our lifetime, we must ask ourselves what we do we want to accomplish this year. We can have a one year, five year or ten-year plans, assess and adjust our progress and our direction as we go along.

When an aeroplane takes off for a destination, it is the job of the pilot and the navigation system to keep it on-track for the destination. Likewise, it is our job to keep adjusting our course of action in the direction of our major definite purpose.

Creating Our Own Vision

We can create our own grand vision or major definite purpose in life and live our lives accordingly. When an author drafts a book, he conveys a message to the mental faculties of the readers. Reading causes thinking and thinking creates images; moreover, once you get these images going, you get a vision.

I hope you can take on the mental attitude that I am conveying here because life is short, and we all need to get started living a more abundant and blissful life of purpose. Having an unobstructed vision for our futures and our ideal lives reduces stress, anxiety, and depression. It is the visionaries that changed the world. Everything we see is the result of someone's vision.

Reconnecting with my extended family and taking care of my elderly parents who cannot take care of themselves – while running a business and caring for my children in Canada – was not an easy task. However, it was exactly what I envisioned what I would be doing in the half-time of my life. If I had to do it again, I would not change a thing. I have kept a positive mental attitude throughout all my challenges.

I will share with you how to create your own vision and explain the steps to turn it into reality. You and I have a marvelous imagination that we can use to envision our ideal realistic futures and to create our own reality despite all the personal and collective challenges around us. We just need to apply the steps based on understanding of human psychology. We all know the wise words of famous quote:

"Early to bed, early to rise, makes you healthy, wealthy and wise."

But truly how many of us put these simple wise old words into practice in our daily lives?

I will share the research-based how-to part; all you must do is to apply the formula to your own life as I am doing to mine daily. Anyone interested in living with peace of mind, becoming more productive and finding true purpose in life can enjoy this book.

Simple Answers

Jim Rohn, the great American philosopher, once said, "In the new century we need both life skills and business skills." I have put the answer to most life and business questions in the simplest possible form in the English language. I love the English language because the English language is so rich that you can say something in ten separate ways.

In some other languages there is only one way to say something, or some words have ten different meanings, and you have to guess what they mean, but not in the English language.

You will find simple practical real-life strategies and techniques to help you develop and implement them into our personal and professional life immediately. This knowledge has been used to transform millions of lives around the world over the last century I am only putting it into a new perspective. It can help anyone make a real move in the direction of their written goals and turn them into reality. These ideas are just the tip of the iceberg, there is so much more to come. These are not motivational tips; rather, they are inspirational instructions.

Every single one of us can be the best at something in this world. We have the choice to find out what our uniqueness is and capitalize on it. My own talent is in writing and putting concepts in words to communicate with others, to create an understanding.

Real self-discovery of our uniqueness is hard at first, messy in the middle and beautiful in the end. You can live in such a way that your neighbours feel happy to have you around and you feel happy to be there. You can reflect that with every person that meets you every day of your life. It is time to enjoy the blessing you have and plan for a future, you will love even more.

Here are three tips to create a healthy growing lifestyle.

Join or build a community like-minded people who love to improve and progress daily.

1. Create monthly goals and share them with your master mind group; the people who love and support you.
2. Celebrate your small success and every milestone. Life itself is a celebration.
3. In the next chapter we will look the most important skill in getting the cooperation of other people in our journey of life, communication.

Chapter 3

Communication – Affecting People With Language

"The proper use of language has a God-like power."

Affecting other people with your language is your most powerful personal asset.

Does the language we speak shape the way we think? Research shows that it does. Could this have any consequences on how we think? Yes, it does. Languages also differ in how we describe events in our lives.

People who speak different languages will pay attention to different things depending on what their language usually requires them to do. This gives us the opportunity to ask; Why do I think the way that I do? How could I think differently, and what thoughts do I wish to create?

The use of language is one of the greatest gifts where we affect others by painting a picture with words. Our ability to speak and frame words in such a way that we create images, paint pictures, or tell stories is a powerful tool. We can help someone understand a concept, become educated or see what they could not see with our words.

The proper use of language has a God-like power. I am lucky to speak several languages, but my favorite language in commu-nication is English. It is simple and you can say one thing in so many ways, whereas in some languages there is only one way to express yourself.

Words have multiple meanings, and each word may have

many connotations, just like translating poems, deep cultural settings, and folklore. Translation of writings in many other cultures does not always do justice to the actual meaning of the message communicated in the original text.

Communicating For Success

All the great successes in life start with and come from good communications. It is an expert skill and the most powerful relationship-building tool we possess. Our ability to communicate well with other people counts for 80 percent of our success. Oftentimes it is the lack of social skills, not technical skills, that gets people fired from their jobs. The ability to communicate well is a learned skill that we will discuss here in this chapter.

When you are speaking, whether to one person or a thousand people, you are talking to one person. You have to be in love with helping others with what you are saying. Your self-image has a great deal to do with how you communicate with others. When you are talking to a microphone, imagine that device is one person you are talking to. Talk like you are talking to the most positive person, and if they open their mind for a second, you are there.

There are three parts to any enjoyable conversation. The first part is the character of the person. Credibility and believability are important in a conversation. For instance, Mother Teresa could say a few words and change someone's life, whereas a person with limited character or credibility does not have the same effect.

The second part of a great conversation is connecting with other people's emotions when we communicate. That is when we tune in and focus on the needs, emotions, and feelings of the other person. In our communication, we must remember people are carrying a heavy load, especially during these crises that have been brought on us. When we think we have problems, consider that most people have vastly bigger problems than ours.

The third part of an effective communication is the factual content of the conversation, which is the least important part of an enjoyable conversation. Unless we have a solid character and connect well with others, the facts that we want to convey do not matter.

Words only count for seven percent of our communication. People will forget what you say, but they always remember how you made them feel (Maya Angelou). The tone of voice is very important in communication, as are the words that we use, so choose wisely and speak softly.

Use of language and communication skills are important topics, so we need to expand on them so that we only need to say the least number of words possible to convey a clear message. We can create pictures with our words. We help someone else see something they could not see before by using the best words we know. My goal is to make the message of this book as clear as possible because I know the importance of what is being communicated here.

I cannot think of any line of work in which you are not going to benefit from communicating better, with more clarity and effectiveness. Before you have a meeting or a speaking engage-ment, always take time to think about the way to communicate; furthermore, be a kind, caring and genuine person, choose your words carefully and express them softly.

Oftentimes before going into an important meeting, I will go over the whole communication and prepare a written draft of the main point that I want to talk about in my meeting.

Conversation and public speaking, just like drafting an essay, should be based on a structure to be more effective and allow you to create memorable moments.

The most memorable people in history have used dramatization of language in their speeches and communication. They can tell a compelling story, request something, ask for a favor, give an order, or even reprimand an associate in such a manner that it has a lasting effect on the other person without offending them.

In communicating, you are also sharing something of yourself. Everybody has a story. Some go through war, or overcome trauma, cancer, divorce, unemployment and so on, and still come out happy and satisfied with their overall lives, while others give in at the first sight of difficulty.

So, take the time to think about how you can handle your life challenges and how you can use your story to inspire yourself and others. The story you tell yourself about yourself is the most important narrative of your life.

Every time something unpleasant happens to you, ask yourself:

"What am I supposed to learn from this experience?"

You will always find a lesson in each struggle. Let your struggles be your cooperators, not your conspirators. Many people fear speaking their minds about their challenges. We all want to look perfect or hide when troubles arise, but everybody has a story that can benefit others. Why do you fear telling your story? Your story matters.

Let me ask you a question:

"Do you want to play the supporting or the leading role in your own life story?"

When you pull back, you are playing the supporting role. It is fear and the lack of proper communication skills that hinder people from sharing their story or engaging in constructive conflicts, both of which can increase social connectedness.

Psychologists say that social connectedness is directly related to our longevity and health. As we age, proper communication skills become much more important. Let me first share a small secret for your story…

In social settings, speaking engagement or business meeting, *always be yourself*. You should be the same person in front of your family, your client and everyone else, because people appreciate authenticity.

Smile!

You can tell a great deal about what is going on in a person's mind by the expression on their face. A great lawyer who is clever at questioning a witness in court often can tell if a witness is lying or telling the truth by the expression on his face. Master salesmen follow the same rule, and by careful observation of the facial expressions of the prospective buyers they can detect the clients' thoughts.

You may be able to judge what a dog may be thinking about, based on the expression on his face and the wagging of his tail. A smile produces a line of facial expression while a frown has a different facial arrangement, but each of them clearly and accurately express what is taking place in the mind of a person.

A smile, the tone of voice, and the expression on one's face constitute the three open windows through which you may feel and see what takes place inside a person's mind. A smart person will know when to keep these personality windows closed and he will also know when to open them. This habit, like all others, is directly related to a person's mental attitude. If you are not convinced of the direct relationship of habit of smiling and mental attitude, just try to smile when you are angry. When you receive some good news, you will notice how quickly you will change from a negative to a positive state.

If you want to be more enthusiastic, then walk faster, talk softly loudly, and keep a smile. A sense of humor in our communication helps one to become adjustable and flexible to adopt quickly to varying circumstances of life. It also allows a person to relax and to be more human instead of looking cool and staying distant, a trait that does not attract friends.

When you meet a person for the first time, a smile, friendliness, and a keen sense of humor can be great ice-breakers. It will help one refrain from taking oneself too seriously, a tendency which many people are inclined to have.

The person who cannot relax, laugh at himself, and live lightly is to be pitied because he will miss many of the better benefits of life, no matter what his other assets he may have. We all need a method by which to release stress and escape from our daily routines and mundane habits. A sense of humor helps to break the monotony and acts as a tonic that helps with maintenance of your physical health.

A smile can drive away many of our worries, while a frown is the lack of understanding between man and his Creator. We understand that material blessings in life are gifts from the Creator for the common good of all humankind.

You can get a clever idea of the important part a positive mental attitude plays in your life by considering that it influences your tone of voice, the expression on your face and the posture of your body. It also modifies every word that you express as well as determining the nature of your emotions. Moreover, it effects every thought you release and therefore it affects your outcomes favorably or unfavorably. A positive mindset helps with flexibility as well.

When In Rome...

Flexibility is the habit of adapting oneself to quickly changing circumstance without losing your sense of composure. A man with a flexible personality is like a chameleon, able to quickly change color to harmonize with the pristine environment. Through experiments in all my travels, I have learned to blend in the crowd. I never consider myself an outsider even if I look like one.

I was in Mongolia on a business trip just before the COVID-19 outbreak and I had the greatest time of my life even though I looked different. My attitude was of a local person. I was social and talked with people like I belonged there. The local people loved this attitude because people do not like outsiders who think they are better than anyone or treat others with arrogance.

Part of my job takes me to various places in the world whereby I meet all kinds of people from all counties and communities. If you develop an interest in people, learn their ways, and incorporate them in your communication, they will be more cooperative. When it's upside down or downside up and you can't understand, be patient, and stay calm. Do not make any assumptions but approach life with questions.

You have no doubt heard the proverb that says, "When in Rome, do as the Romans do." What it means is to be adjustable and adaptable to new environments. This way you can adjust yourself to new circumstances without the interruption of any outside force or person.

Flexibility is the one quality that is developed and becomes inbuilt in all the great salespeople. A flexible person can sit down and play a game of marbles with a group of boys and then go right to his office and enter a mastermind meeting to decide about a multimillion-dollar deal.

A person who lacks the quality of flexibility will not be a good leader whether in business, government, or any supervisory position where success depends on the cooperation of others. The manager or executive with a flexible personality in any operation can have the cooperation of all his colleagues, workers and even supervisors because he is able to relate himself to each man according to that man's personality.

For example, when I was a young manager at FedEx Ground Corporation, I was assigned to a permanent location in at the Toronto hub. My first assignment there was to clear up a backlog of thousands of lost and damaged packages in the aftermath the busiest season. The package load was hill-high because of the sheer volume of packages moving through the operation.

My main project was to sort out each package with the help of a team of twenty workers of all races, genders, and backgrounds. The project was supposed to take at least three months to sort, track and ship each package to its rightful owner.

Within two weeks we had everyone working in harmony with each other in an assembly line system where we made great progress. In less than six weeks, we had the huge mountain of packages cleared up, mainly because I was able to closely relate to each person, build relationships, conveying our goal and ask them for the full cooperation. I told them that if we worked together and met or beat the project timeline, we were going to have a big celebration.

When we completed our project, of course, I took them out to have dinner at an excellent restaurant. We celebrated their achievement and the spirit of teamwork and cooperation. Some of those people are still my friends to this day and we often talk about how much fun we had in the process.

Life is a series of experiences in salesmanship through which one must sell himself to every person that he meets in social, occupational, or professional settings. If one lacks a pleasing personality, it will be harder to harmonize his mental attitude with the people he associates with in his endeavours and business dealings.

A Lamp For Your Feet

The man who is on good terms with his own conscience is also in harmony with the Creator and His other creations. He is humble at heart and in excellent communication with others. I have been blessed to have met many such wonderful people who have helped me learn from their good nature and experiences.

They have uncommon knowledge on many subjects and are usually interested in other people and their ideas. Most often they go out of their way to express interest in others by asking open-ended questions, where they inspire appropriate action.

A versatile personality has a clear understanding of the funda-mentals of major religions and belief systems of all other people including a clear concept of his own. A man may be very knowledgeable in his own field, but if he cannot connect with others on their playing field and build quick rapport, he is under a great handicap in his own personality.

A clear knowledge of the subject matter that one speaks on is a very important aspect in any clear communication. The basic rule of communication is to know your topic, understand your message and say it with all the emotional feelings you can muster and then sit down.

I am here to equip you with intangible tools that can help clarify the images in your minds and clarify your message. Thoughts create ideas and expressing ideas in a clear manner is the key to understanding of those ideas. I want to help you clarify your thoughts through the spoken word, so you become a great communicator of your thoughts and ideas. Helping someone see through the darkness is the greatest gift to be bestowed on a person.

Have you ever heard the expression, "It dawned on me!" That is where you can paint a picture so clearly with your words that the darkness disappears, and the picture gets filled with the rising sun at dawn. Teaching is one of the most gratifying feelings because it has such a power.

The best place to start practicing these teaching is at home with your children and family. Teaching them the disciplines and principles that can help them shape their own futures is the best inheritance we can give our children. Helping them take the early step in their lives is the best parenting anyone can do.

Words of wisdom are like a lamp for your feet so you can see where to walk not to fall. Words are also like a pathway to know which direction to go and which one to avoid.

Cards & Flowers

Clarity of communication is the foundation of any relationship. Business relationships, just like personal relationships, need to be decorated with beautiful words of encouragement and love. It is fine to give flowers to those we love, but flowers do not communicate enough.

Flowers have a limited vocabulary; they are limited in the message they can convey. Do not let the flowers do all the talking. All flowers say is that "I am thinking about you," but what you are thinking about is what you put down words on a postcard.

Electrifying words show more than just a gesture or a thought. When you write beautiful words with sincerity and in style, it gives a postcard a whole new value. In the age of texting and quick distractions, a written communication will be very memorable, so make your "Thank you card" or postcard one that they will remember and keep for rest of their lives.

I have sent, received, and kept many such cards in my life and career. I have boxes of thank you cards as a reminder of those I have served. If someone is especially important to you, use words like, "Nobody in the world affects me like you do. Love, Arif."

In the beginning of my career, when I was building my first business, I sent out thousands of "Thank You" cards. When someone was kind enough to trust me with their business, I made a big deal out of it. It was important to me, so I made it a big deal out of it for them as well. Oftentimes when they received my card, they referred me to their friends and family as a friend and a trusted advisor. Word-of-mouth is the best advertising for any new business or the character of a person.

They say that words are no substitute for action but let me tell you that action is also no substitute for the right words either, written or spoken. What you can do with words, you can never accomplish with actions alone.

A Kurdish proverb says:

"A gentle tongue will pull a snake out of its hole."

Meaning you can get anyone to do anything you want if you use the right words.

All the great people can put their visions in such words that others are attracted to them and follow them. We can all start expressing what we are trying to communicate in better words. You can always use more impactful words with your daily language.

Fishing For Good Communications

In clear communication, you need to read your audience whether it's one person or one thousand people by expressing the kind words – written or spoken. Clarity of communication gives you their feedback and reaction, which is a very important part of building rapport with your audience.

Ask yourself, "Is my style, my story, and the way I deliver my content touching those who need to hear my message? Am I making an impact with my words?"

In business meetings, read what is happening around you before you speak so you learn how to respond, not just to react. Know how you are going to direct a conversation before you engage in one. Write down ideas to discuss on the subject so you can stay on track for the ideal outcome in each conversation.

Read your audience's body language, listen to their words, and tune into their facial expression so you know how to proceed in your responses.

Pick up emotional signals. For instance, in sales, if someone is standing by the door facing the road, you better hurry to express some creative words that may resonate with them, because they are ready to leave.

Think about your choice of words and the tone of your language and select the right ones in each situation. Do not be too strong and do adjust your different tone of voice in each situation.

In some other places in the world, people often speak with much higher volume in their daily communication. This tone of voice sounds like they may be arguing, but this is more of a cultural way of interaction. There are social, cultural, educational influences that have a significant impact on our behavior and the use of language.

In my experience in sitting down with thousands of clients from diverse backgrounds, races, religion from all over the world as financial advisor and years of selling camel wool products, women are better at reading the other person's body language and tone of voice. They usually speak in a softer tone which itself is natural survival mechanism to read the environment before they respond to it. Like a mother must read the dangers around the newborn baby, you need to read others when speaking.

Words are impactful when loaded with feelings. Powerful men and women have used language to move nations and change the direction of generations of people throughout history. "I must reduce myself to zero," Gandhi said once, meaning I must adopt a beginner's mindset in my communication to be able to connect with the common man.

Choose your words carefully and express them cheerfully. Touch someone with your kind words every day and uplift your argument, not your tone of voice, as much as possible.

In my early years in customer service and public speaking, oftentimes I was overly enthusiastic. I did not have enough experience or knowledge to read my audience as well as I do today. Sometimes, I only had a few minutes to make a point to a big crowd and drive a point home.

Today I have learned it's not the quantity of the words you put in a speech but the quality of the words that make the most impact. Your mental toolbox makes your responses well-adjusted and memorable. You do not need to be long-winded and go through the whole history of things to make a point. Just get to the point as clear as you can be with the wisest and fewest well-selected words.

I was always learning and prepared the best I could, but most often, I got through my speaking engagements by sheer enthusiasm and most people still thought I did great. I am getting better at becoming more impactful as a speaker and communicator by selecting the right words and expressing them softly and thoughtfully.

I have also learned to read my audience and to look for signs that give me clues on when and how to begin and end a conversation. Watching your audience's body language is a great way of learning how to adjustment to your tone, volume, and the choice of words you choose to communicate. Listening is also key.

My grandmother, a quiet person by nature, used to say, "Son, you have two ears and one mouth. You listen twice as much as you speak."

You learn by listening more than by speaking. So, I learned to be brief and to the point in every conversation and respond only when I am asked a question, but also to be authentic. To achieve clear communication, and to make an impact with your audience, it is wise to have well-chosen words with a great vocabulary.

The intensity of your words can also be important in communication and to make a clear point. Words loaded with emotion can change a nation, help people change direction, and leave a permanent footprint on someone's heart. Well-selected, loaded words can change lives. The most powerful leaders have used loaded words with emotion to make memorable speeches that move nations.

You can heal or hurt someone with your words. It is the words, the tone, and intensity of expression that determines if your message is getting through. Well-chosen words measured with the right intensity of emotion are powerful. You can be brief, yet impactful in your communication, and not belabor the point.

We can learn a lot from children. Sometimes kids have a legitimate objection when you keep repeating yourself to make a point. They say, "Dad (or Mom), you are making it a big deal out of this." And they are right. Our job as an entrepreneur and the CEO of our life and business, is to make a big deal out of a big deal and a small deal out of a tiny deal and we clearly need to know the difference. Do not mix the two and you will flow in your communication without repetition or engaging in unnecessary arguments.

Good communication flow is like fishing with a tackle. When you go fishing in the marina in Istanbul, the veteran fishers tell you that to catch the fish, you must play with the tackle line. Pull easy when you need to and pull harder when must. It's all about the pull and push in your communication just like fishing in the sea. You need to read your audience to know when to pull and when to push and when to use intensity and when to pause to make a good point.

Give people room and time to think and understand what you have just said so it makes sense to them. Interrupting someone to make a point is either an argument or the sign of poor communication skills. I'd rather work with an interested introvert than an interesting extrovert. You can learn how to overcome shyness and poor communication skills, but it's hard to shut up a person who want to be the center piece of every conversation and jump into discussions without an invitation.

Effective communication is an art and a craft, so learn it well and you will ensure the cooperation of others. All people enter our lives or hear what we say from their own level of understanding. We need to adjust to each person's level of understanding every time we communicate. Great ideas and favorable outcomes merge when you adjust your language. Mastering proper communication alone can lay the foundation for life transformation. Adjust your style and craft your communication to the occasion. An enjoyable conversation is like a tennis match; that is, it flows from one person to another effortlessly, and so does kindness.

Greeting The Person In The Mirror

Always have something good to say or give genuine compliments when you can. Have you ever had the experience where someone says things that aggravate you so they can feel better about themselves? How does that make you feel? Remember, only hurting people hurt people. Your unkind words will hurt others and never make you feel good inside.

Some people wake up in the morning and have nothing good to say. It seems like they have been meditating on their problems and negativity all night, so when they wake up their subconscious mind is set for negativity all day long. Others choose to be at peace and wake up every morning with a smile because they have been meditating on the blessings in their lives thus attracting even more of those every day. My mother is such a person and that is why in a country in which the average life expectancy of a woman is about seventy-seven, she has already surpassed that by many blissful years.

You can learn new ways of communication through methods explained here. A simple suggestion would be to say, "Good morning," to the first person you meet each morning. That is, the person you see in the mirror. That way, you are preparing to communicate that day.

The key to excellent communication is preparation, but it seems like all of life is preparation. They send us to school in preparation for the life ahead. The first seven years we go to elementary school to prepare for high school, then we prepare four more years to go to college or university. Upon graduating we prepare for work, and then we prepare to start a family. We prepare to have different experiences in life. Eventually we prepare for our afterlife.

In my estimation the whole of life is just a preparation, so why not prepare for the life ahead of us? When an animal like an antelope is born, it only has one hour to walk and run with the herd because the lions are coming. As soon as it is born the mother nudges it to get up and does not give up until the baby walks. Why such urgency? Well, because the lions or the jackals are coming. So, in less than an hour the antelope is ready to join the herd and run.

Human babies, however, take a little longer. They are different. We learn how to walk, talk, and take care of ourselves before we can join society. Even after eighteen years of preparation, we still do not think our kids have developed the ability to escape all the lions and jackals in society, or to build their own herd or team.

Here Comes The Camel Guy

Proper communication is the key in team-building for your life and your business. We often need to be able to organize people to work together towards a common goal. A purposeful life is the coordination of effort of a group of people without necessarily forcing anyone to do anything. How you get people to do something for you is that you do something for them first. It is easy and that is the base premise of team building. The good news is that you do not even ask people to do something good for them. You do not need anybody's permission to do a good deed.

We have a proverb in Persian that says, "A good deed does not require permission," referring to the principle of going the extra mile. Nobody minds a good deed, and many will reward you for it in multiples.

How would you like to have an army of people or family members to cooperate and collaborate with you when you need them? Well, first you cultivate the goodwill of others. Cooperation of others is indispensable in a home setting, professional environment, social interaction and in organizing of governments.

Building an ardent team of strong independent people of all ages, genders and backgrounds is like herding cats. Unlike sheep where all you need is a little salt in the palm of your hand, give the first one a taste and the rest will follow but if you have eight cats, they are going in eight different directions.

Each person brings their own unresolved issues of life and business with them inside their head. So, we need to be able to focus them on the main goal of what needs to be accomplished by giving them enough motives to act in a certain direction. When we get independent people to work towards common goals, miracles happen.

In team-building communication, you can use humor to your advantage. Humor is a great icebreaker and Winston Churchill was a master at using humor in making a point. A lady in the English parliament was so angry with him that one day in a question-and-answer period she said, "Winston, if you were my husband, I would put poison in your coffee." Churchill being the wit that he was, answered, "Lady Astor, if you were my wife, I would drink it."

Not everyone that asks a silly, stupid question or makes a sarcastic comment deserves an intelligent answer. However, you can sprinkle some salt and paper in your communication with your humor and wit.

When we first started marketing Camel Heal products, some people said:

"What? Camel's fur? Camels have no hair."

They laughed it off, reinforcing…

"I have never heard of that. This does not work for me."

To which I would smile and said, "I bet you did not know that camels are originally from Canada either. It may not work for you, but it works for those who want relief from physical pain and arthritis. If you have not heard it, here is a pamphlet with our research."

I have a childlike fascination and enthusiasm when I talk about camels because their hair is known as "Nature's Magic Fiber" and the products speak for themselves.

My response to those comments were somewhat funny and surprising, but I provoked their curiosity through storytelling, because everybody loves a good story. They would take the information, read it, and often come back and with a wide smile on their face buy the products they needed or ask further questions. When they saw me anywhere, they would say, "Hey, that is the Camel Guy." A few even humored me.

"Here comes Doctor Camel." To which I often smiled and waved in content.

Gathering relevant knowledge, such as about camel hair, pays big dividends.

In the beginning of my life in Canada, I joined clubs and groups and teams to gather knowledge about the way things were done here. I wanted to learn the Canadian ways. I already knew the old ways, but I needed updated information and new knowledge about my country. And I needed to improve my communication and public speaking.

One day I asked a professor in my Critical Thinking class for advice. He recommended that I join Toastmasters International Club. I found a club near me and joined right away. It was the beginning a lot of wonderful memories and great amount of learning. Toastmasters International is a global goldmine for developing business presentation skills and meeting new people and it is available worldwide.

Asking for advice is good but putting the advice in action is the real power. When you have a plan of action and follow through by acting on it, you have the power to change the future. That's the power of communication with a purpose.

Chapter 4

The Definiteness Of Purpose

"The mystery of human existence lies not just in staying alive, but in finding something to live for."
(Fyodor Dostoevsky)

Our reasoning faculty helps us to think about the impact we want to make in the lives of those we care about. In other words, what our purpose is. If you don't know or cannot find your purpose, just follow your passion. Following your passion will lead you directly to your purpose.

Finding your purpose is not the same thing as finding that ideal job that makes you happy. Your purpose is less about what you want and more about what you give back. Your purpose may be raising great children, having a wonderful family life, or providing the best products for your customers and giving the greatest customer service.

The key to finding our purpose is using our strengths to serve others. A definite purpose is the starting point of all individual achievements. Your purpose may be impacting others through your writing, poetry, or communication. You will know when you feel good about what you do, and when you get in the right frame of mind. That is your definite purpose. The possibility of the manifestation of our deepest desires exists but we need to know clearly what those things are before we can acquire them.

A definite purpose must be followed by a definite plan of action. Living with purpose makes us feel whole and satisfied, but we need a definite plan, and it must be followed by appropriate action. Our purpose must be clear, and definite.

Purposeful living is independent of the times we live in and is all about what we do with the time we have for living. My purpose is to present the idea and knowledge that we really can make our lives what we want them to be, not just in the moment but in the long run. If you want to help someone, give them love without an agenda. Sharing my knowledge and experience with those I love and deeply care about is my way of making a difference and living a purposeful life. I have followed through on that ambition. If we think right, plan accurately, and have the stamina to develop the discipline to follow through our ambitions, we can make miracles happen. I am merely a bridge builder; that is, my mission is to help others cross over their fears and see the possibilities for realizing their ideal lives.

Fear is caused by doubt, worry and anxiety of the unknown. To eliminate fear, we must develop a deep understanding of the root of our fears. Understanding requires focused study, and focused study puts us at ease. If I doubt myself, I need to understand myself better, so I became the field of study through which I understand others. I feel the responsibility to teach, offer my experience and research to help others who want to live better quality of life.

Oftentimes we underestimate what we can do today and overestimate what can do in five or ten years. When we think our wishes will come true just by having the thought cross our minds or through some magical divine intervention without taking any action, that's called daydreaming. It makes many people delusional and wasteful of their time and talents.

This is a fast-moving world of action and those who do not move quickly and accurately in the direction of their objectives will only get in the way of those who take action to make daily progress. When you observe people, you will notice that those who dilly-dally trying to make up their mind never get around to doing much. They are never popular and rarely successful in life. They are the procrastinators.

Even after we know all the laws, what the score is and how goals must be achieved, most of us ignore them until we run out of time. I do my best not to wait till the last minute to do things because I have developed the habit of living a proactive life. I can always say I tried, and nobody will accuse me of being lazy or inactive, or not planning.

Our plans do not have to be sound, because we can always change and modify the plan. I have modified, changed, and altered my plans several times during the composition of this writing. We live in fast-changing times and face many uncertainties due to the COVID-19 pandemic crisis and other unforeseen events of life. Even with changing plans, our purpose must be clear, because if we do not know what you are going after, we will never get it. When you begin to put your plan together to work in your daily life, your human relations, and your business interactions you will see a difference.

Selling Your Purpose

All individual achievements are a result of a motive or a combination of motives. We have no right to ask anybody to do anything at any time without giving that person an adequate motive to help us. The basis of all salesmanship is the ability to plant in the mind of the perspective buyer an adequate motive for her purchase.

Most salespeople are not aware that they must plant a definite motive in the mind of the buyer for the purchase because that is where all sales begin. Professionals know and use this principle in the sales process; they know we live in a world that is increasingly technology-oriented and driven by data.

To address the challenges of our modern times, we must understand a phenomenon that is not easily captured by data, nor necessarily affected by technology: our human behaviour.

As an independent researcher I have long been in the spirit of inclusivity and followed the study of psychology and the study of thousands of other high achievers. When I was unable think for myself or to move and lay there on a hospital bed wondering who I was and why I was here, I was challenged by my doctors to recall the past through a series of questions, tests and quizzes that challenged my mind.

They reminded that I had young children who needed their father to be able to grow as good strong individuals. They told me, "Your children want to be able to play with you and take them to places like a normal family again." I could not recall anything because that part of my brain memory was temporary wiped out.

I was challenged to overcome my disability with a definite motive to pull myself out of the emptiness that had overtaken my mind at the time. When the idea was planted in my mind, I was given strong motives and I could not stop thinking about it day and night as I lay in my hospital bed lifeless.

My most pressing and first question was, "How do I do that?"

I was looking for directions. After months, I started to pick up the ideas the doctors planted in my mind that helped me connect the dots and regain my memory and form new habits to move me in this new direction.

My mind started to pick up the answers automatically and I acted upon the instructions given to me in terms of regaining my memory and rebuilding my physical health. As I progressed in my recovery over a two-year period, I continued to ask the question "How do I do that?"

Allow me to remind you that the job of a physician is not to fix us but to inspire and instruct us to fix ourselves.

By the time I was independent and self-sufficient on my own, I had a set of instructions on how to act to repair and maintain my health based on this new programming. I retrained my mind and reset my thinking into a new pattens of processing information and data. I am sharing those instructions and procedures here as I still use them to overcome unhealthy habits and personal inabilities.

I had to tell my mind what I wanted repeatedly through visualization, even when I was physically unable to act upon those ideas. When I read about the Coue formula while in recovery, I kept repeating to myself and I still have this sentence written and posted on my mirror that states:

"Day-by-day, in every way, I am getting better and better."

To everybody that asked me how I was doing, my reply was the same: "I am getting better every day, thank you."

I met other people in the Toronto Rehab Clinic Hospital who had no desire or willingness to improve they dire situations. At the time, I was not able to elaborate ideas for them as I am doing here. In my mind, I had to follow experts, my coaches' and mentors' instructions given to me, including the Coue quote.

It is a wonderful time to remind you that the subconscious mind does not know the difference between right or wrong, truth or a lie. It does not know the difference between positive or negative, and it doesn't know the difference between success or failure. The subconscious mind will accept any statement that we give it through repetition of imagination, visualization, thoughts, spoken words or any other means of reprogramming our higher faculties. One important thing to understand is that we are made from the same perfect spiritual DNA. We are created in the image of the Creators. We have the same gifts. So, we can program our minds to reflect this.

Laying Out Our Purpose

One way to program our mind is to lay out our definite purpose. Simply write down your major definite purpose, which is the grand outcome of your life, what you want to be remembered for or what you want to leave behind. We must go through the physical act of writing our thoughts on paper. In addition to your major definite purpose, you might have many smaller goals or purposes that lead you in the direction of your major definite purpose.

Our whole life should be about carrying out our major purpose in life. Write out your major purpose so it can be understood, accepted, and internalized into your subconscious mind. When we write down a goal, we make it real.

You need to write down a clear outline of your major definite purpose and the time you allow to attain it. Write down what you are willing to give in return for realizing the object of your major definite purpose. I had to make many sacrifices to be able to do what I am doing and develop the perspective that I have developed.

Write out a clear definition of your major purpose, commit it to memory and read it over at least once a day in the form of a prayer or an affirmation to program it into your subconscious mind. We must memorize it by starting to repeat it day and night until our subconscious mind picks it up and automatically acts upon it. Our subconscious mind must have an idea of what we want. The real value of reading any self-help book is to put the instruction and the wisdom to use. We cannot skip this one critical step in finding purpose in life.

This is going to take a little time and persistence. We cannot expect to undo overnight what we have been doing to our subconscious over the years by allowing negative thoughts and crystallization of its patterns.

You will find out that if we emotionalize any plan that we send to our subconscious mind and repeat it in the spirit of faith with enthusiasm, it can materialise. The subconscious mind acts more quickly, accurately, and positively as new doors open to us. You can see this in action when you wake up after a nap and find out the situation has totally changed prior to taking the time to shut your mind down for a few minutes.

Any dominating desire, plan, or purpose backed by the state of mind known as faith is taken over by the subconscious mind and acted upon immediately. That state of mind will produce actions immediately in the direction of our burning desire. When I talk about faith, I am not referring to wishing, hoping, dreaming, or even mildly believing in the Higher Power. I am referring to a state of mind in which we can see our goal already in its finished form before we even begin.

I can truthfully tell you that even when I was on my back in a hospital bed with very little chance of ever bring able to keep a proper balance and walk again, I believed I would. When I got up from the hospital bed for the first time with the help of my nurses and practitioners, I was unable to walk without assistance, but over time I could see myself walking without any help again. My health condition was not permitting such a physical ability in any near future, but in my mind, I could see myself regaining my full health at some point.

We must develop that kind of conviction and faith about our burning desires and plans. Anything that I wanted to do but I did not accomplish was because I was careless in my desire or mental attitude towards what I wanted to accomplish. I have never failed at anything that I made up my mind to do. When I was thirteen years old in the middle of the war in the middle of a chickpea field, I told my sister that one day I was going to live in Canada, then I wrote it in my notebook.

Years later when I was living in Canada and graduated from university, I had a burning desire to travel all over Canada and the USA. I was selected to be the replacement manager trainee with FedEx Corporation, which gave me an opportunity to do exactly as I desired for three years with all expenses paid by the company.

Most times we do not know how our desires will all come about but that is what faith is all about. We must work a plan of action with total faith and be open to divine intervention in our plans instead of underselling ourselves on our abilities, talents, and possibilities.

It is the strangest thing how nature penalizes us with mediocracy when we do not accept and use these principles. Everything that we need to attain or all that we want to accomplish within reason in this world can be ours if we accept them with faith and act on them with self-confidence. Nature always wants things to be in action like the changing seasons but especially it wants the human mind to be in action.

The mind is no different than any other part of the physical body if you do not use it and apply it, it weakens, withers away and becomes a handicap. The Creator has given us unquestionable means of control over our own thoughts. The person who is most successful is the one who taps into this infinite intelligence and puts it in action. Every individual has the power to use this intelligence as he chooses. Results come about only when one keeps faith and puts in the work and uses the subconscious mind to access infinite intelligence to bring about a new reality.

The First Radio Station

Our mind is the receiving station and the broadcasting station for all our thoughts. When the brain and the conscious and subconscious mind are so charged with definiteness of purpose, we attract the physical or intellectual equivalent of that thought. I believe the first radio broadcast and receiving station that was ever invented was the one that is in the mind of man.

This broadcasting station not only exists in the mind of man, it also exists in many animals. You may have experienced this in your own association with domestic animals like dogs, cats, and horses. They can tune into our thoughts without you even saying a word. You have probably heard the proverb, "Be the person your dog thinks you are." So yes, dogs do think and can read your thoughts.

We can tune into animals' and other people's thought through telepathy. That is how you know when someone likes or dislikes you without expressing a word. You can train your own mind to only broadcast positive vibrations as well as receive positive vibrations and ideas that are related to what you want in your life. How you do that is to keep your mind only on the things that you want in your life by repetition of thought and followed up by action.

We can condition our minds so that they do not pick up anything that is not aligned with our definiteness of purpose or what we want in life. We all can recognise a lie from the truth. Similarly, we can educate our brains to only recognise the vibes that are related to what we want and reject or ignore the rest.

If you are going to do anything that requires the cooperation of others, condition your mind so that you know that the other person is going to cooperate. They must be convinced that you are going to offer them something so honest and bring so much benefit to them that they cannot refuse.

This belief was put to the test when presenting our clients with therapeutic camel wool products for comfort and pain relief. No one had even heard of such a thing when we began marketing the products. I had conditioned my mind about the benefits of the products because of my personal experience and the testimony of their benefit from my own parents.

Our clients picked up the idea and gave us a chance to prove ourselves right based on my belief in what we were doing. Today our research has proved it to be true. I have total faith and know that camel's hair is "nature's magic fiber" because extensive research-based health and therapeutic benefits have been proven over time.

For many years I taught salesmen how to sell financial services products. The life insurance business is one of the toughest sales in the world because people rarely buy life insurance on their own; it has to be sold. The first thing I taught my students was that they must make the sale to themselves before they can make the sale to another person. If they were not fully and consciously aware of the benefit of the product, they would never be able to make a sale to another person. Somebody may have bought something from them as a favour or because of a close personal relationship, but they would never be able to make a sale to a stranger. If they were able to master and broadcast the benefits of the product in their own lives, when sitting with a prospective buyer, they would be guaranteed a sale where possible.

Similarly, if we want to make our prayers come true, we must act upon the clues that come back to us. Remember that our whole lives are a constant prayer. Belief in our dignity and the belief in our ability to tune into the Higher Power is a magnificent trait we must develop. We have the ability to create the circumstances for the life that we want to live.

Plan With Self-Confidence

When an opportunity presents itself to you, do you begin to question your abilities or use and improve them? Do you accept the challenges? You matter. Most people do not believe they matter. They don't think that they are worth it. You matter very much, you are worth very much, there is a reason why you and I are here.

We all go through different challenges and obstacles in our lives. It seems to be nature's way to test of our character. We need to face these challenges to complete our growth. They are here to teach us something about ourselves, perhaps to discover our true strengths. Do not run away. Go to the challenges, face the obstacles, and overcome them, sometimes with small steps.

Focus every day on how you can improve a little more so you can feel better and make the people around you better. Purposeful living requires continuous improvement. Small incremental improvement makes miracles happen over time, especially if you are clear in your purpose.

Our definiteness of purpose gives us self-reliance, sparks personal initiative, ignites imagination, and entices enthusiasm. It also promotes self-discipline and concentration of effort which are the prerequisites of successful living. Definiteness of purpose is knowing what we want, having a plan on how get it and being one hundred percent busy on carrying out that plan.

Timing is an especially important part of the whole plan because nature has a way of timing everything. For instance, if you wanted to plant some wheat in the field, we go out and plow the land, then we sow the seeds at the right season and then we wait for nature to do her part. We do not go back and start harvesting the next day. Similarly, there is a universal intelligence that does its part if we do our part first.

Not all plans will work out perfectly, and when you realize your plan is not working, discard it and develop another plan. Keep on keeping on until you find the one that works. If you have a plan that is not working out so well, ask for guidance and you may get that guidance, as I did while authoring this very book during the pandemic quarantine. I believe that the Creator does hear prayers and our thoughts as well.

If we condition the mind to respond when emergencies arise, we will be right there to deal with them. Prayer works the same way. I have learned that if we want our prayers to be effective do not wait until the time of need to utter them. Develop the habit of prayer when we do not need anything; it is a type of preparation for the future. Most people wait to pray until their time of need as a last resort. Of course, that is not how we get results from prayer. Prayer is a lifelong journey of belief and communication with the Creator. The secret to prayer is in acting in accordance with our desired prayers.

Just remember that God may have a better plan for you. It may even be better than the one you have designed for yourself. Be open to divine intervention. When you get a hunch or a gut feeling, it is our subconscious mind trying to get an idea over to us. We must act on such clues immediately before they disappear.

When the pandemic shut down the world, I saw an opening to go and serve my father who was getting up there in age and needed a real companion to care for him. Nurses are incredible people who take care of our loved ones but there is no replacement for the love between a father and son that have been friends for a lifetime. I was blessed to follow my intuition and create some incredibly peaceful moments with my father, who eventually left this world for another in my arms. Now all is well with my soul, and I can focus on my next purpose, which is to serve my fellow human beings.

The definiteness of purpose motivates you to plan your time and recognize opportunities, which can lead to the attainment of the results we seek. We must move with courage, faith, and determination, and be success conscious. When we are health conscious, our thoughts are predominantly about health. Similarly, to be success conscious our thoughts must mostly be about success and greatness.

Greatness is the ability to recognise the power of our own thoughts and use them to our advantage. In my mind every person can become genuinely great at something if they recognize this power, embrace it, and use it to create all we desire in an environment of love and harmony.

Unique Opportunities

Most of my professional life I wanted to bridge the gap between my roots and my children, as I discuss at the end of this book. In addition, I wanted to create opportunities to help people on the global scale. I am doing just that through the writing of this book, with the goal to impact multitudes of lives. So many people reach out to me about my positive mental attitude and express love and kindness. I wanted to create a formula for such an attitude where anyone can adopt and make it their own.

I also see a unique opportunity to represent Canada, its great people, unique values, and morals that have shaped my character, and personality. Elsewhere in the world cultures, attitudes, and behaviours are quite different.

When I arrived in Istanbul at the onset of the COVID-19 pandemic, I knew the attention of the kind of people I wanted to have. I got busy writing my ideas and working my own plan. After ninety days of writing, I had a great foundation, and then I got busy getting things organized.

I kept asking for guidance, and suddenly, I was presented with the opportunity to meet with a self-made CEO, a member of the board of directors of one of the largest companies in Turkey. He knew my roots and was curious to find out what I had been doing over the last twenty-five years.

The night before our meeting I put in all the necessary work and submitted all to my subconscious mind. The morning of our meeting, I strolled into his tightly-guarded office with a notebook and pen in my hand. I was ready to present my ideas within the 30-minute time frame I was given. Three hours later, I had a new best friend, an offer and the opportunity that could potentially impact many lives.

When I was given the opportunity to work with the gentleman, I made sure that he knew that I was not here to waste his time. I even offered to work for free for ninety days just to learn the tricks of the trade from his perspective, and I was loyal. No matter how educated or intelligent we are, we must be loyal to the people we work with. Loyalty is at the top of all the characteristics of the people that I want to work and associate with. I am loyal to the people who trust me, even if things don't always work out the right way.

Not everyone is trustworthy. We need to keep our major definite purpose to ourselves and only reveal to our mastermind group. These are the people in our immediate family or close business associates that we fully trust, and those who fully support us in our mission in life.

The reason to keep your major definite purpose to yourself is that there are lots of idle curious people in this world. Sometimes they would like to stick their toes out especially if they feel you are going further than they are in life. For no reason at all they will stick their toe out just to see you fall. As a mentor of mine once told me, "Keep your cards close to your chest." People will slow us down one way or another because of envy and an abundance of idle minds.

Visualizing The Movie Of Your Future Life

Develop the habit of visualizing your plan as often as possible perhaps before you sleep at night and in the morning when you awake. Those times are when the subconscious mind is open to accepting orders from the conscious mind as per clearly written plans. I close my eyes and play the movie of my future in my mind as if it has already happened.

Dr. Joe Dispenza has done incredible research in this area in recent years and the results are astonishing. We need to believe in our future more than we replay or talk about the past.

Normally, the conscious mind is on guard and does not let anything go by except the things we are afraid of or the things that we are exuberantly enthusiastic about. If we want to plant an idea in our subconscious mind, we must do it with a tremendous amount of faith and enthusiasm. Play the movie as real as possible in our imagination like watching a movie on the big screen. This will take time planning and practice to master.

Often, our minds will only allow the negative thoughts, but when you use deliberate control of your thinking, you will open the gate. The best time when this gate is open is when the brain is on a lower vibration like late at night or early in the morning after you open your eyes.

Those are the times to submit our plan with clarity, enthusiasm, and repetition until it has been accepted by the subconscious mind and becomes part of our daily routine. If you keep repeating something it will be submitted to our subconscious mind. I am sure you have heard that "repetition is the mother of learning" because the mind needs retraining through daily repetition.

Every night just before we go to bed, we should give our subconscious mind some sort of instructions so that it works on it while we sleep. Those are the images we can visualize. Oftentimes you wake up in the morning with some sort of hunch or answer to your deep meditation. The healing of your body happens in the same way. Before you go to sleep submit thoughts of health and healing to your subconscious mind.

Visualize that every organ in your body is healthy, perfectly functional, and that you are as strong as you can possibility be. Of course, this must be followed by physical activity to keep the body in shape through exercise and proper nutrition.

Reprogramming the mind has a certain procedure that must be followed. First try this method for seven days, which primes your subconscious mind to the new ideas. It's a short enough time that you can decide to do it as an experiment. When you enjoy your new practice, extend it for twenty-one days to make it a routine or a habit. After doing this for 90 days it will become a well-run new lifestyle where you cannot sleep before playing your future movie in your mind.

If we do not tell our subconscious mind what we want, by default we end up getting what we do not want because the mind is primarily negative. Everything that you have is what you have been asking for, consciously or by default. In the same token, what you do not want is what has happened by neglect. Most people only play the movie of what they do not want to happen in terms of worry, stress, and anxiety, and that is what they get.

I never go to bed without giving my subconscious mind an order to work on during the night. You can get in the habit of giving your subconscious mind some orders to prepare for the morning, like a factory floor where orders are prepared.

If we tap into the power of our subconscious mind, we can have everything that we want and we can have it in abundance. You are the only one that can qualify or disqualify yourself. You are the only one that can set up limitations for yourself. Nobody else can limit what you can achieve unless you allow them to do it. James Allen, the great American author, in his book As A Man Thinketh, explains these principles clearly.

Each Day Is A New World

There are many gravestones in cemeteries around the world. Unless and until we are aiming at something memorable, we will be joining the crowd both here and thereafter. We were all born with some special gift, talent, and the ability to leave a bigger mark on the hearts and minds of our family, village, community, country, or perhaps the world.

We all have an opportunity to do something special with our lives. I imagine the Creator would be disappointed if we wasted our lives just passing through to the end without discovering the power to create some good with our lives. I fully realized this after my traumatic accident through a near-death experience which left me like a blank white page as a person. I imagine you are a person that aims higher in life, and that is why you are reading this book. I imagine you were sent here to do something special with your life.

You can always start here with the reading of this book to plan out something special for your future. It may be something important to you and your family. It may be a move to another country or study of a certain topic. It is never too late, and you are never too old. It's important to remember not to measure your future by your past.

Each day is a new world, and you are a new person. With every sunrise, you are going to be born again, you are living a day that you have never experienced. Till this moment you may have not realized it but now it's time to be born again physically, mentally, and spiritually. You have nothing to lose and everything to gain by believing in yourself and pursuing what you are passionate about. We should look upon every day and every night with open anticipation of miracles.

Find a new way, write a new purpose, and come to a new realization of your own God-given power. A new realization of our own dignity as we relate to other human beings. The greatest sin of humankind is neglecting to use his greatest asset: the power to control and direct his own thinking which is given to us at birth.

Why not have fun pursuing something substantial, something that will benefit others in some way? Even if only one person picks up an idea from this book and implements it to achieve some goal, the purpose of this book would have been served. You can set a reasonable goal for the remainder of this year, and next year, you can expand it to a bigger one.

Many people have become skeptics and now doubt everything due to the COVID-19 pandemic. I hope you did not shrink into a corner trying to make it out of this pandemic alive, but picked up some skill, interest, or hobby with your extra 8 hours a day to learn, expand and grow through out your life. What a wonderful time to equip ourselves with the skills and tools we need to prosper as things return to some sort of normal.

During the Great Depression Mr. Napoleon Hill, the author of the global best seller <u>Think and Grow Rich</u> was hired by Franklin Roosevelt the great American President, as a private consultant to help turn the public opinion around to a more optimistic outlook. The goal was to get the American people focused and working on recovery efforts. Napoleon and his team started to work on newspaper headlines, took every negative news headline and put a positive spin on them across America.

In about three weeks' time the mood of the American people and the public opinion about the future had shifted in a more optimistic positive way. Many companies were born out of the positive effort as people started to look for opportunities more than to face the challenges they faced. Some of those companies are still here. The turnaround set the pace for the following hundred years and the whole nation made an incredible recovery that lasted until the birth of the Internet at the end of the twentieth century that changed the world forever.

We can look for opportunities and create them during these difficult times. Real viable long-term opportunities are only created through proper education and discipline to follow through with on our plans. Distance learning has become the new way for many educational institutions but if we do not have self-discipline to do what we are supposed to do in our own space, online learning becomes a waste of time.

Our social interactions have changed, and personal account-ability is diminished. Today we have to rely on our own discipline more than ever. If there is only one inheritance that man can leave for his children, let it be self-discipline. It is time to acquire some new disciplines that we can put to work immediately.

Canadian Opportunities

My love for Canada and admiration for its highly educated, hard-working people and its cold climate has been a lifelong love affair. Now I get the chance to represent the Great North in a whole new way.

As I said in my introduction, I was first introduced to the oppor-tunities that Canada offers through the original work of Harriet Tubman, the American author and activist in her remarkable literary narrative <u>Uncle Tom's Cabin</u>. I was only thirteen years old. I was given a translation of the book as a present and I was hooked for life.

I read the book with great enthusiasm. I loved the idea of Canada and I wanted to live in Canada. Right after I finished reading the book, I decided that one day I would be living in Canada. I thought writing books about my own adventures and experiences and sharing them with the rest of the world would be a great honor. Today I realise that honor and lifelong dream through my books.

I remember one day while working on a field of chickpeas with one of my sisters, a passenger plane split the blue skies right open and left a white trail behind. I looked up at the sky with the roar of the jet plane and told her:

"One day I will take a plane like that go to live in Canada."

That very night, I wrote in my notebook, "One day I am going to live in Canada and there I will be writing books."

By the age of twenty-four I was in Canada and started the journey that led to this very moment that we share together.

I had to go through a total personal and professional trans-formation repeatedly to become a true Canadian. You see this 'science' as I call it, has been proven to me personally, and millions of other people around the world have used the to create their own meaningful lives.

When I arrived in Canada my greatest wish was to find a mentor, a guide, a wise friend, someone that could show me the highways and byways of life in my new home country. I came from a great family ancestry and caring parents, nine siblings and the most loving grandmother but here I was alone.

I missed my family and that kind, caring mentorship, one-to-one coaching, and guidance. I did not know one single person, I had to build my life from the very bottom. I had to survive the cold of the Great North and the pain of being lonely, but I used the time to grow through books, social interactions and meeting some incredibility great people.

I had questions to ask and ideas to discuss but nobody to do it with. Fortunately, on a sunny afternoon in late 1995 in while walking the streets, I came across a yard sale. I looked around to see what second-hand item I could buy for my humble apartment. There was not much that I could use or afford but a book titled <u>Unlimited Power</u> by Tony Robbins jumped out at me.

I checked the inside cover it was being sold for $2 with a hand-written note on the back cover. The inside note said:

"Dear …., this book is an incredibly useful in helping overcome your challenges, please read it you will be able to change your own life. Signed…."

I checked my pocket I only had twenty dollars and I bought the book.

I took it home and pulled out my dictionary and read it with great enthusiasm and a lot of difficulty that winter, but I was hooked again. I found my future mentors inside that book; I met Jim Rohn, Bryan Tracey, and many other greats, some of whom passed away, but it set the pace for my upcoming life's attractions.

I heard a wise man say, "Poor people should take the wealthy people out for dinner, pay for it, ask questions and listen." I did just that on many occasions. Learn the ways to communicate and connect with such leaders in your community. In the wise words of Jim Rohn:

"If you want to see further, stand on the shoulders of giants."

Today there are many successful business owners, entrepreneurs and friends from diverse backgrounds that are building phenomenally successful businesses across the world and in Canada. You can reach out to people ahead of you in the game of life and most of them will be happy to lend a hand to like-minded people.

In the age of information and awakening, ignorance is only another choice.

In the early years, you would find me on the field, in the classroom or on the stage of some sort or another. I did not want to miss any chances for learning and getting better. I was and still am an active participant in the adventure of life. Throughout this incredible journey I signed up with clubs, groups, and sport teams to gain firsthand experiences.

I drafted this book to give you the opportunity to connect with your own feelings and emotions on a new level. The chance to learn from ground-breaking research, educational content, and my unique experience to direct your own path in life. After a quarter century of personal growth and development, I have paved the way for the new generation of seeker to take advantage of all the exciting opportunities that one can create for himself.

The knowledge of personal development and growth mindset is new even for most veteran businesspeople, many of whom, when the traditional sources closed their doors due to Covid-19 pandemic lockdowns and restrictions, went online and tapped into this knowledge. Prior to Covid-19 we were attending seminars, workshops, and events that taught business growth, entrepreneurship and much more, all tailored to the pre-pandemic reality. Now, many traditional businesses have closed their doors and there is a desperate need for fresh current ideas and how to deal with present reality.

Restarting Your Life With Purpose

Every time I had to restart my life, for example during my near-death experience being grounded and humbled, I started right from rock-bottom. I went back to basics. This pandemic was no different. It left me with very little choice but to do my very best under the circumstances to use my experiences to make the best of the pandemic crisis and the lockdown. If you learn the principles in this book and apply the laws of nature, you can overcome many life challenges including disasters and crises.

In fact, life is only a series of crises, we are either in one, getting out of one, or getting into one with a period of calm and peacefulness in-between. We may as well learn how to handle them with the only real resource we have, the power of our own thinking minds.

I had to reprogram my mind to see the positive side of every situation including the pandemic. Thinking back, I had to do it this way so I can bring you this particularly important message based on truth and the real-life challenges we are all faced together.

I had to go through unbearable obstacles and use my mind to re-apply the same principles to get back up on my feet. But the man that has a motive can bear almost any circumstance. This time I had many more reasons to do my very best, namely my children, my parents, and the time pressure to fulfil my purpose through sharing these principles. I am not one just to sit around and feel sorry for myself during the worst of the pandemic. I have a mission and a dream.

Overcoming challenges, such as the pandemic, is one of the steps we take in achieving greater accomplishments in life. Challenges are the test of your character and belief systems. Tears are the sweat of the heart and the price we have to pay to go from one level of consciousness to a higher one. Nobody is allowed to attain the higher status in life without being tested. Similarly, nobody can go to a higher position in a company and stay there without going through all the learning and severe testing thereby earning the right to be at the top.

One of the most astounding things that I found was that all the greatest achievers of all backgrounds have reached their heights in direct proportion of the obstacles they have met and overcome. It is not their brilliance nor their intelligence, but their belief that they could do it. Usually, the harder the going got the more they believed that they could do it. Of course, you cannot believe it unless and until you go through it yourself or use someone else's experience.

When you know exactly what you want and clarify your

compelling reasons, they propel you into the future like a magnet. It will open the ways for the construction of our self-fulfilling future. When our reasons are clear we can look beyond day-to-day struggles of life and stay positive in the storms of life, through cold dark long night of winter and the gloomy days. If you can take this attitude towards life, if you can keep faith when you are overtaken by adversity and faced with opposition then you are using the principle of applied faith.

Every adversity carries within it the seed of greater benefit and every defeat carries an equal opportunity. The Higher Power has been within us since birth which helps us go through our challenges. I believe our adversities could be the source of the greatest blessings because they open our eyes to the Higher Power beyond our earthly comprehension.

One of the greatest adversities of my life was the hit-and-run accident on Yonge Street that left me in a coma for ten days in 2013. A near-death experience that helped me understand and never take another moment of life for granted. It gave me the opportunity to reprogram my mind with the principle of faith, clarity of vision and the will power to act. I knew I had to undergo mental, physical, and psychological transformation to be able to come out of my challenges with the ability to make an impact on the lives of other people.

Furthermore, the adversity gave me the opportunity to strengthen my faith and develop the courage and the ability to handle anything that life throws at me. Death is not to be feared but to be understood as a part of the journey of life. We are not from this world; we are only moving through it as energy.

We can learn from other people's stories as well. I witnessed the sacrifices my parents, especially my mother, made to raise all ten of us in a very turbulent world. You can imagine why her heart attack and her arthritic pains is what inspired me to launch extensive research into the healing benefits of camel hair products. I resigned my job at another company as a financial broker to pursue that dream. Her pain, recovery and relief have brought relief and comfort for thousands of our Canadian clients over the years.

My mother inspired all of this despite never being educated. However, her father was a poet and a scholar that wrote many in Persian and Kurdish and Arabic languages. She has his wisdom and that natural simple wit and positivity in her spirit that is admirable. She has always had tremendous faith in me, I am obligated to give back.

She was my compelling reason to change careers and pursue a whole new road that had never been taken before. I believed that I could help her live a longer more comfortable life. She survived her heart attack and pains, and she has had a long-blessed life.

You can learn from her example. Look into your own experiences, challenges, and unpleasant moments, and transmute them into something positive and pleasant. Whenever a negative thought crosses your mind, immediately turn it inside out and think of the exact opposite of that idea for a minute. Try to change your emotions based on those newly reversed ideas. For instance, whenever the idea of "I can't" comes to mind, reverse it to "Yes, I can." Follow it with the question, "How can I do it?"

We choose our own thoughts and our thoughts about ourselves create our reality. Find out what your options are to solve the problem and how you can create a new reality for yourself. And listen to your conscience because it will guide you through adversity.

Self-respect through faith and harmony with one's own consciousness is a marvelous thing. We do not have to ask anybody what is right or wrong. Our own conscience tells us. All you have to do is to tune into that feeling. The Creator has given you enough wit to tell right from wrong. You know the difference between right and wrong, the truth or a lie.

Our conscience will tell us to we follow our intuition unless we become conspirators instead of cooperators with our own conscience. Lots of people use their conscience as conspirators in wicked aims. That is why we have so many brutes on the loose in the world always conspiring to start new wars all the time. They have killed off their conscience and have submitted to the darker side of life. Trust your conscience.

Life Is Iffy & The Search For Meaning

A growth mindset and success-oriented thought process are the most powerful forces that we can cultivate as our personal allies. We can develop written programs for our future and if we have a solid work ethic, take our opportunities, and make early sacrifices, we can manifest real transformation in our lives.

Jim Rohn wisely said, "Life is iffy…"

Life is full of challenges, but if we follow these instructions and formulas, we will have an easier time as an entrepreneur and the CEOs of our lives and businesses. It may take time and overcoming many small and big challenges, but the results will eventually show up. Life requires consistency of action and strength of mind.

Developing this type of strong mindset is a lifelong commitment to learning, training, and growth. It will take focused attention to details because wherever our attention goes, our energy flows. We must make sure our attention and energy are flowing in the direction of our written goals, dreams, and our major definite purpose – this is where real miracles happen, whether it is behind closed doors, in the boardroom, in the library, in the gym, or outside in nature.

Miracles start with a vision – seeing the future with the mind's eye, unfolding based on our written plans. Over 97 percent of people do not have written goals. We need written goals and in the goals program chapter and we will learn how to write them, so they are accepted by our subconscious mind.

Remember that darkness starts in the mind and so does the light of hope. In his book <u>Man's Search for Meaning</u> Dr. Victor Frankl explains this attitude under the most horrifying conditions facing certain death in his meaningful narrative of WWII. Facing the burning human inferno of the Nazi fanatical hate machine, Frankl chose to dream of freedom over the reality of certain death. He chose hope over fear. We lose nothing if we choose to hope over despair, but it could cost you everything if you dread and live with fear in our mind. Eventually Dr. Frankel was freed and moved to the United States of America to become a world-renowned doctor and author who taught his unique mindset to others. He no doubt used preparation to achieve this.

Preparation is the key to a better future, so when full of fear, choose hope, and prepare a little more. When you have written goals you will always have something good to read and remind yourself why you work so hard. Many colleagues and family member know me for my work ethic. I still do put in ten-to-fifteen-hour days because I love what I do. To me it's not work, it's all play in the game of life. It only makes sense to prepare for what we want and even what we do not want way in advance. So, prepare, prepare, and prepare some more because that is how confidence is cultivated. Preparation is laborious and tiresome but winning the game of life takes preparation.

Sport teams prepare the whole season and fight their way to the playoffs for one night of championship and glory. Preparation is the key to winning and the lack of preparation means defeat, disaster, illness, and disappointment. When we are prepared, we feel confident and our chances of winning automatically skyrocket. A prepared person feels full of joy, happiness, and confidence – and gratitude.

In A State of Constant Gratitude & Peace Of Mind

We have many things that can keep us in a state of constant gratitude. We have our lives, our children, parents, family, a home and whatever it is that is valuable to you. There is so much to be grateful for if you pay attention. We utter prayer in applied faith thus by being grateful for what we have, not merely to ask for what we need or want.

If you wrote down a lengthy list of what you have and that you are thankful for, you would find out that it is one of the most calming therapeutic practices of life. Gratitude for all the bless-ings that we already have opens the gateway to our subcon-scious mind for more blessings to pour into our lives. We may not have a lot of things in life that we want, but we do have a lot of things that we do want. You can write down all the things that you can be grateful for and remind yourself of these things every single day of your life. It keeps your mind open for the guidance from within and opens the gateway to miracles in your life.

I am grateful for many blessings in my life. I am also grateful that I am a citizen of a country where I have freedom of thought, freedom of opportunity, and freedom to act in any direction I choose. There are a lot of countries where we do not have those freedoms. I chose Canada to raise my children, but I also wanted to stay connected to my roots, and I had the freedom to do so.

Raising my kids was my first responsibility but spending time with my aging parents and siblings was also important to me. I had to write down goals that would include both motives. I had to create a business and a lifestyle that would give me the freedom to include both of those two separate worlds.

It is not easy to be spread out all over the world, but technology has made it easier than ever before. It is the one of the obligations of a good Kurdish son to take care of his aging parents. My siblings have done a wonderful job helping them in old age, especially before my father died, but I wanted to do my part. I am the last son and one of ten children to proud parents. I could not leave them and pursue my own selfish motives because my children are also watching what I do for my parents.

My parents were married for seventy years, and it was a joy and source of much inspiration to see them reach a mature age where they enjoyed their golden years together. You see, back in Iran they do not have a solid health care system, old age homes or seniors' residences. We have homes where they stay till their last breath. It is the children's responsibility to take care of elderly parents in our culture. I had to honor that way of life. I was received with incredible admiration and respect when I did so, during the Covid-19 pandemic. The resulting peace of mind was priceless.

We need to balance our books in life to have peace of mind. Our state of mind is everything because our thinking mind is the only thing in this world that we can have total control over. The most important of all things is to have peace of mind and a clear conscience.

The Creator must have chosen the most important trait to give us total control over. The most pitiful thing in the world is the man who has nothing but money. I have met many rich men who have an abundance of monetary riches, but they do not have peace of mind. Their riches have become a burden to them instead of a blessing to help others.

We do not have to worship wealth but to create peace of mind in our relationships with our fellow men. I could not tell you with a straight face that I have everything in this world that I need, want, or wish for in abundance but I do have peace in my soul and have lived the life of my dreams. Everything I have done has been achieved through self-discipline and gratitude.

There have been times where I had much more money in the bank than today, but I am much richer today because I have peace of mind, incredible relationships and the love and admiration of my colleagues and family. I have no grudges, no regrets, no worries, or fears because I have learned to balance my books with life through self-discipline and faith.

The Power Of Faith

Our education, background, nationality has nothing what-soever with what we can achieve. It is our state of mind and faith that determine what, where and how we can achieve what we set out to accomplish. The most profound thing that I have discovered is that the change of our mental attitude can change our projection from failure to success almost immediately.

Faith is a mental attitude that the mind is clear of all doubt and fears through inspiration and faith in the Infinite Intelligence. We all undergo test after test as a testament of our faith. There is no such thing as a blanket or vague faith; instead, you must have absolute faith in what you want. We must take action to follow through based on the principles of applied faith.

When we are overtaken by defeat, remember that man is made for the testing. Our personal challenges are the only way one can be tested on his applied faith. We all go through testing times and the ones that come out victorious are those who abide by the law of applied faith.

One must stay humble throughout life so God can open even greater doors and opportunities. I wanted to fulfil that duty to the best of my abilities. I had to use some creativity and devise ways to make such undertaking possible while handling my own responsibilities, limitations, and challenges. I had to go through the test of applied faith to see if I deserved all the blessings that I have in my life.

Faith is nothing but applied guidance, and faith will not do things for you, but the seed of faith will guide you to obtain what you want and pray for.

The Creator has a system where we can get all the good nutritious foods by planting the seed under the right elements and timing it properly by applying the laws of nature. However, you must do all the right things to get what you want. You must go the extra mile, putting in the work, keeping faith, believing that your seeds will multiply. The same laws apply in connection to the subject of faith. You must do your part; you cannot expect faith to do anything for you outside of yourself.

One theory holds that faith works through the subconscious mind, acting like a gateway between the conscious part of the mind and the Infinite Intelligence. I am using this theory. It has produced marvelous results in my recovery, personal growth, and development of my character. When I pray, I am conditioning my mind and giving it a clear picture of what I want and submitting it to the subconscious section of my mind. It is my action that completes my prayers.

Let me give you an example here...

When my daughter was nine years old, she wanted to buy something that cost $50. I asked her, "What are you going to do to earn that money?"

She thought about it and came back to me and said, "Dad, I found a way to make the $50 dollars."

I said, "Okay, what is it?"

She replied, "On Saturday there will be a lot of kids in the park next to us and I am going to have a used book sale of all the books that I have read and don't want anymore. Can you help me do that please?

To which I replied, "What a great idea, absolutely. Let's do it."

The next Saturday we set up a nice table with many of her used books. Lo and behold she sold many of her used books and someone even gave her $10 for one book. By the time it was all said and done, she had much more than $50 to do what she wanted. You just have to act upon your burning desire.

During the final edit of this book while serving my parents, my daughter informed me that she had been accepted by all top three Canadian universities she had applied for so she can pursue her own dreams. She is only seventeen years old, and this is a testament of the application of these philosophies in real life, in my own family first.

Victory starts in the mind and abundance starts in our thinking, that is what faith is all about. When you develop a progressive growth mindset you can take what was meant to break you and turn it into your advantage.

We will investigate how to develop a growth mindset and the benefit of having coaches and mentors in our lives in the next chapter.

Chapter 5

Developing A Growth Mindset – The Coaching Benefit

"A good coach can change the game. A great coach can change a life." (John Wooden)

Bob Proctor, a Canadian hometown mentor of mine, is over eighty-seven years of age at the time of this writing, with a sharp mind, even sharper than a twenty-five-year-old. He says you don't have to stop growing, explaining:

"We are here to do God's work and that is creation, expansion, and greater goodness for all."

If we are going to do that, we have to keep studying and we can never stop learning. And find a mentor. A mentor or coach is someone who sees more talent and ability in you, than you may be able to see in yourself, and helps bring it out of you. Bob continues:

"A mentor is someone who allows you to see hope inside yourself."

Age has no bearing on a growth mindset and one can start at any age. It is dumb to let age control you from growing and expansion of our understanding of life. It is our thinking that controls everything including our health and the way our bodies age. We become what we think about all day long, so if we think health and growth, that is what we will be doing. When you age you get experience so instead of stopping your studies, start to teach from all that wisdom while you are still growing.

You may have heard "You become what you think about all day long."

Science proves that we think about sixty to seventy thousand thoughts in one day. The problem is that ninety percent of those thoughts we think about daily are the same as the day before. If you believe that your thoughts have anything to do with your life or your future and ninety percent of your thoughts are the same, then your life will stay the same. The same thoughts lead to the same choices, the same choices lead to the same behaviours, the same behaviours create the same experiences, the same experiences lead to the same results. Life becomes a loop of the same until we consciously and deliberately break the loop. Our thoughts determine how we feel and act.

How we think, how we feel and how we act is called our personality. Our personality creates our personal reality or our lives. Your decisions and present personality have created the current personal reality, which we call our life. The good news is that we can learn how to make better decisions and we can change our personality.

If our personality creates our personal reality and we want to create a new reality, we need to change who we are. We need to improve our decision-making skills. That is the first step in the process of change, because we must decide to think about and change our thinking habits. We have to be conscious about our habits and behaviours, and modify them based on the decisions we make as we evolve and grow.

One of the biggest problems what we face in the process of personal change and transformation is that most people try to create a new personal reality with the same old personality. In my experience this does not work; moreover, it is like building a new house on an old foundation. To change for the better, we have to become a different person. We don't become different in our body shape or facial features; rather, we become a different person by improvement of our thinking habits. If we think the same thoughts as we did yesterday, we are firing the same connection in our brains.

When you do something so many times, we create the same experience repeatedly. At this point the brain operates like a software program that is on a loop, which becomes second nature. New research shows that most of our mental programing happens between the ages of seven to twelve years old. As we get older, we only operate from our own subjective experiences and patterns that have been created in our brains. By the age of thirty-five we are operating completely from a learnt set of experiences. We lose creativity and put thinking on autopilot.

So where do you start thinking about becoming better at what you do?

Where does the decline of growth start? The better question may be, how do professionals constantly keep get better at what they do? How do they become great and admired by others as they age?

There are two views about this. There is the traditional view that we go to school, study, graduate, and practice what we have learned once we get in the real world and make decisions and grow on our own. That is how average workers, doctors, lawyers, scientists, and other professionals grow.

The contrasting view comes from sports, where we are never done learning. The greatest players in the sports or business field all have coaches where learning never stops. You see many top athletes transition from sports to similarly successful careers in other fields after they retire from athletics.

Coaches and mentors help you transition through periods of life. We have a Persian proverb that says:

"Learn from cradle to the grave," which has been my mantra for life.

The great achievers always have coaches because the traditional way shows that there are numerous problems where mental growth eventually stops. If we are on our own, first we do not recognize the issues that are standing in our way. The characters in a painting don't see the masterpiece or its faults, which are only visible to an outside set of eyes. Secondly, if we do see them, we do not necessarily know how to fix them. The result is that somewhere along the way we stop learning, growing, and improving. We settle in the job or the life we build without trying to outgrow what we have already built.

I thought about this, and realized this does happen to businesspeople as well, so when I arrived in Istanbul during the pandemic, my goal was to find a mentor. Someone I could learn some new skills from, someone who had the capacity to critique my own skills.

Growth Versus Fear Mindset

When I met my new coach, the retired CEO of IHLAS Holdings, one of the biggest corporations in Turkey that employed over eleven thousand people, I was thrilled to continue my personal growth program. My coach, whom I've mentioned, reminded me that fundamentals of business were quite different here. We went on a learning journey about these more traditional ways of negations and skills of being much more effective at resolving conflicts and building collaborations for a ninety-day period. During this time, he reminded me that the way of business negotiations was quite different. He told me that what I had learned in Canada and what he had learned during his MBA studies in the USA was quite different than what was being practiced in Turkey.

He mentioned that in Turkey, oftentimes a star performer becomes a star performer not by their own merits but by nepotism or suppressing other performers and stepping over toes of real competitors. In other words, he mentioned that I was now entering the red zone environment where people might seem to be more hostile, adversarial, more conflicting. This was the opposite of the green zone environment where I came from, where businesspeople are more cooperative, supportive, and functioned in a growth-based environment.

He told me that every time we went into a business negotiation you should attempt to make every person around the table understand how the green zone environment functions but respecting this new environment. He said that this has been his competitive advantage over a lifetime career at the IHLAS Corporation where he started as a salesperson and retired as the CEO of one of the biggest corporations in Turkey. He mentioned that this is what will put you on top if you keep your green zone mindset while staying mindful that now you are operating in a red zone environment.

These conversations were uncomfortable at times. I did not want to sound too naïve or too arrogant but after ninety days of being coached, it made me realize that coaches were onto something profoundly important which is expanding your understanding of your own abilities beyond your current state of mind.

He told me, "You are amazing but it's not how good you are now, it is how good you are going to become that really matters. If you keep developing these new negotiation skills, you can make important things happen."

We know that the starting point of any achievement is always the same, it all starts with a dream. We create a vision and work hard to achieve it. Then we can achieve any realistic goal based on our skill set and disciplines we develop.

One of my other Canadian mentors, Bryan Tracey, talks about clarity as the beginning point of all achievements. He says:

"Clarity is king in all things we do."

When we have clarity, we know exactly who we are, what we want and where we are going in life. Studies show that clarity accounts for more than eighty percent of our happiness and success in life.

Once we know what we want to think about, we reject to think about anything else. Our mind becomes like a magnet. If we can imagine it in our mind and hold it in the screen of our head, we then can attract it into our lives. Often, we live in our outer world as a copy of the inner image we have and hold in our own mind.

Your outer world is merely a reflection and corresponds with your inner world. My mentor Bryan Tracey calls this the law of correspondence.

In computer language there is a concept called GIGO, which means "Garbage in, Garbage Out." For the self-concept it means "Good In, Good Out." The more positive good images you put in your subconscious mind, the better results will show up in your conscious world.

What we think inside our head and what you believe are key factors in how we live our lives. If we are full of fears, doubts and hesitations that is how we live and perform. To believe in fear you believe in something you cannot see, also when you have faith you believe in something you can't see, I choose faith over fear every time. If our head is full of positive goals, dreams, and ambitions, it will also show in our behaviour and reflect in our lives.

Living from a growth mind is positive and filled with continuous learning of new skills. It has a vibration that others tune into very quickly. We must aim to live in this world without allowing this world to live inside us. When a boat sits on water, even in stormy weather, it sails perfectly. When the water enters the boat, it sinks. Similarly, no matter how turbulent our environment may be, if we do not let it affect our inner peace we can float just like a boat.

When I decided to make my journey back to the old country and spend some extended quality time with my elderly parents who were living their golden years, many friends and family warned me that it would be tough to tolerate the environment. It is a tough environment to say the least, worse than three decades ago when I left. Prior to making my way here I had decided that I was not going to let the world that I was re-entering affect my inner peace and growth.

I must be comfortable with myself since I live with myself, I groom myself, I dress myself. No matter what environment I live in, I thrive for a well-balanced life. A positive mental attitude is the determining factor for all the results we get in life. It is also a determining factor whether we find peace of mind or go through life in a state of frustration and misery. Our mental attitude is the total of the thoughts in our minds at any given time. A positive mental attitude has roots deep inside one's soul. It is the median by which adversities may be turned into equal benefits.

Selling Poison Versus Selling Health & Life

Rumi was once asked, "What is poison?"

He replied with a beautiful relevant answer:

"Anything which is more than necessity is poison. It may be power, wealth, hunger, ego, greed, laziness, love, ambition, hate or anything else."

These poisons could indeed be anything that takes humanity out of the human.

There is a famous story of a person who visits hell that makes a good point here. The devil is showing him around and tells him about all the tools and things that he uses to cause people to live in their own hell. Things like lives of gossip, envy, crimes, drugs, and wars and so on. Finally, they come to a closed room. In the middle of the room the light is shining on a glass box, and inside the box there is a wedge.

The man asks, "What is this? It looks like a wedge." he adds.

The devil says, "Yes, this is my joy and pride. I use it to destroy more lives than anything else. This is the wedge of self-doubt. If I can put this wedge between what a person is doing and what they think they can do, then I can create a gap and make them to live in their own little hell for the rest of their lives."

Once you know what you think about is what expands, such as that wedge of self-doubt, you become careful about what you allow yourself to think about. I am not sure this impresses you as it impresses me, but I believe the most outstanding thing in this whole universe is that the Creator gave humankind one absolute gift of power and that is, *control over his own mental attitude*. I am sure that the Creator meant this power to be the most important thing in this universe and that is why He gave us this power to all of us at birth.

We need to develop the ability to control and direct our minds. If we control our mental attitude, we can control everything within the sphere of the life that we occupy. Our mental attitude is the dominating factor in all our behaviours, relationships, and our life outcomes, yet the majority of people never cultivate control over their mental attitude.

Most people get mad at anything and everything that they have no control over at the drop of a hat. It is like a drug. They wake up looking for their fix, for occasions to be offended. This creates a dangerous spiral that we cannot afford to fall into.

I am guilty of this myself from time to time, but I realised that I must have full control and be confident in my own abilities as a human being with the will power to control my own thoughts, feelings, and actions. Action is key. Our mental attitude is reflected in every word we speak or every action we take.

My goal in life is that a day should not pass without personally taking a step towards my major definite purpose, learning something new or taking a step to enhance my physical and mental health. I am sure that if a patient does not have full confidence in his doctor, the patient is not going to benefit from that doctor's advice, no matter who the doctor may be or how specialized he or she may be in her field. Cures take place not because of what doctors do for us, but what the doctors get the patients to do for themselves.

I am utterly amazed that in Istanbul, there are far more pharmacies than there are health food stores, grocery stores and bookstores combined. I know that most drugs damage one part of our body while tempting to fix another. I have tested these ideas on myself during my memory loss and recovery. I never took a manufactured pill after I was released from the hospital. I do not recommend this to everyone, but health comes from the right mindset, wholesome food, fresh air, and enough of the right physical activities.

This principle applies in all areas of life, in financial success as well as physical cures. The thing that will change our lives is not what we read in books or what they teach us in school but what we do after we have read or heard it. The attitude we take towards our lives, and towards other people is what will restore our financial standing without a doubt.

The right mental attitude is also the foundation of all salesmanship, whether we are selling ourselves to gain a favor with someone or selling our services and products. We are all in the sales business of some kind. Even when we talk about religion, politics we are selling the other person on our point of view and our metal attitude determines our success or failure.

I realized the best thing that I can sell you is to sell you on yourself. A better version of you is waiting to evolve. Your better self is waiting to be developed. You and I are always work in progress and most of this work is mental growth.

I believe being in sales is a noble profession and I pride myself in everything I sell, whether I am selling mangos on the street, or my camel wool products like the camel wool blanket I am laying under as I write these words. I always sell with pride because I know the value the products or services that I provide for my customers.

In this writing I want to sell you on the idea that a better version of you is yet to be discovered. A kinder, gentler, better, more prosperous you is available only when you apply these principles. We get to work developing this growth mindset, disciplines and habits that are required to make ourselves better, healthier, and more prosperous.

Unless or until we condition our minds to make a sale, we will never make one. The question is how good we are at selling what we market. So, I am putting me to the test, and you are the judge and the jury. Similarly, unless you make up your mind that you want to grow and get better at who you are and what you do, it will never happen.

When you are selling physical products, someone may buy something that they need, but you had nothing to do with that sale. What I am selling here is not a product and it's certainly not a need, but it is a certain mindset that will make life easier and more enjoyable. I am trying to sell you on the idea that getting better at who you are and what you do by developing a better thinking process. A healthier, happier, and more pros-perous you is not required to complete this journey called life, but it's available for those who strive to obtain it.

Coaching For Your Life's Purpose

If you want to have an impactful life, you must grow your way of thinking. I think you would enjoy knowing that those who have gone down in history books and left an impact on the lives of other had a certain thinking process and a particular mindset.

When we are young, we think that life is endless, and we have until eternity to do things. When we mature, we start to think about why we are here, and what is the result of our lives. What is our purpose?

Imagine knowing what you know now when you were eighteen years old. Would your life be any different? Would it not be wonderful to know that we are here to make sure we are here to provide security for our families and to help improve other lives, give hope, and inspire others to live better?

We all have the capacity to create our own ideal lives and make a difference in the lives of others. We can continue the path we are on, or we can cut out the scenes or scenarios we do not like. You can write a better story because your movie is in production right now. We need to become the critic of our own lives and see what we need to improve or enhance in our life. We can tear up some scenes and rewrite the script of our ideal life and life's purpose.

As a lifelong hobby I like to study great people in history. I want to learn their attributes because I like to adopt the way they think. These figures and the greatest coaches taught me how to prime my mind through the power of repetition of imagination, which we will learn more about in the following chapters.

We can actively visualize our ideal life and equip ourselves with the means to realize that ideal life. The fact is that nothing in life has any meaning except the meaning we give it. We can create meaning by the growth we go through and the possibilities we create for ourselves and others. We are our only limitations and possibilities.

Every time I get stuck in my life, start a new venture or step into an unfamiliar environment where I need to change things around, I tend to go back to the same basics. I take out a piece of paper and ask myself a few simple questions, such as:

❖ What skills, behaviors, or new habit I need to adopt or develop?

❖ What is it that I need to do to get closer to my goals today?

❖ What would a certain person in history that I admire, in my situation be thinking or doing?

Further, I want to build a model in my mind that I can copy and adapt my behaviour. Your self-concept is a set of ideals you have about yourself and your abilities. If you want to lose weight, you must think thin. If you want to learn a new language you must think in that language, similarly, the only way to get rich is to think rich. A growth mindset activates more of your twenty billion brain cells and helps you tap into your own potential. Sometimes, it starts with waking up in the morning.

Morning Habits

For most people it takes from thirty minutes to three hours to come to full capacity in the morning, like an old computer system that loads extremely slow.

Some would say, "I am not a morning person."

Do you know why this is happening? It is because they are not programmed to be a morning person. We can change our programming based on our mental attitude, motives, and the habits that we develop. Similarly, we can change the habit that help us become more successful or stay where we are. Success leaves clues and anyone can follow and copy them.

Through the practice of gratitude and repetition of thought that we can activate the power of our brain. The first things we do right after we open our eyes is to think about all the things, we are grateful for: our family, our children, our spouse, our job, our health, etc.

Mentally go through as many things as you can, and you will be motivated and feel-good right away. It will also get your inner-mind going in the right direction. It's so easy and may sound silly at first but believe me it is a powerful motivator for your day. A morning prayer is also common in most religious ways of living, but if you have a routine for your morning, you will be up-and-going in no time.

In addition to our gratitude ritual, we can write our goals and dreams down on paper and read them every day right after we wake up. This makes our prayer more meaningful and our goals and dreams more real. Through this practice we are painting a picture of what we are grateful for, and then we can submit our new request to our subconscious mind through repeat affirmations all day.

If we make this one single change in our routine, we can change everything. We will be fired up and positive about our day and our brain will get in full capacity function immediately. We are ready to go out there and make things happen, not walk around wasting two or three hours of our time to try to figure the out the rest of our day.

If you get up every morning connected to the feeling of your future, you can maintain that modified state throughout the day. You will no longer be looking for your future, you will be busy creating it. We will be feeling that future all day, the light switch in our mind is fully on and we will illuminate shine with positive energy. This is the moment that new synchronicities, opportunities, and coincidences begin to appear in our lives.

If we can maintain this state throughout the day, unusual new things being to happen in our lives. Opportunities come in ways that we least expect or predict them; furthermore, if we can predict them and expect them, they are nothing new. If they are new, they often catch us of guard and rock our world. They leave no doubt that what is happening inside of us is beginning to produce results outside of us. When we can co-relate the changes that are happening inside of us to what we see outside of us, we begin to believe that we are creators of our lives instead of being the victims of life.

This is exactly what happened to me during my brain injury and memory loss and continues to happen to this day. I started to pay attention to what was happening inside of me to produce new results outside of me, then I started doing more of it. Meditations brought peacefulness, visualizations began to materialize and goal lists started to be checked off.

For example, when I was felt inspired to drag myself through the snowstorms and the pain in my body to go to the gym and I began to regain my memory and felt better day by day. I started to do more of it and the results started to show up to a place where I realized I was recreating my own new reality. I started to think that I am creating these experiences by the feelings and emotions that I was having inside of me and the actions I was taking in the outside world.

Suddenly, the experience was producing an emotion of worthiness and self-control, inspiration, and love for life. As I look back at my entire life, I can see that I have been the creator of my life. I used that emotion to create the next event of my life. There is not one moment I want to change because it brought me to this present moment.

More Than 2% Of Our Full Potential

The average person is born with enormous potential, but the average person only uses a small percentage of their potential throughout the course of their lifetime. Stanford University Brain Science Research shows that the average person only uses about two percent of their full potential. You can be more, have more and do more than you are doing right now because you have room to grow.

We can get more out of ourselves than we have ever done before. Let's say you are a seasoned person in your profession and have a lot of experience. What a great opportunity to teach the younger generations some real-life skills. If you are a younger person, you should consider yourself lucky to come across this wisdom at an early age so you can jump ahead years of life by applying these principles, saving trial and error. Either way there is room to grow, have more and be than you are right now.

The biggest event of our lives starts the day we start to apply ourselves to the business of life. It is like the Olympics start today and you are a main participant. Whatever you have done so far is merely a preamble, a warm-up for what is possible for you. Today is the beginning of the rest of your life because now you have this incredible wisdom that was not known to you yesterday.

As mentioned according to Stanford University Brain Research, the average person uses two percent of their potential so if we could use four percentage of our potential we could double or triple our income. If we could use a full ten percent of our potential, we would become a genius. A person that becomes successful does not change in nature, they only manage to get more out of each day by doing more and increasing productivity and efficiency. If we have one gift to give our children, let it be the power of discipline, which makes them grittier.

In her book Mindset, Ph.D., Carol Dweck has revealed a great deal research done on building a world-class mindset. Dr. Dweck's work has reveals that you can change your mindset. Her research found out that when students had a growth mindset, a mindset which perceives a challenge as an opportunity to learn rather than a problem to solve, they responded with constructive thoughts and their behavior showed persistence rather than accepting defeat.

According to Dr. Dweck's research, the growth mindset regarding tenacity and its effects on achievement, especially in an educational setting has four factors that affect ongoing tenacity or grit:

1. Their beliefs about themselves
2. Their written goals
3. Their feelings about their social connectedness
4. Their self-regulatory skills: the habits we develop

These are all learnable skills that can be developed through self-education and commitment to personal growth I provide you with the formula in the following pages.

Following-on, here are my top five suggestions to increase your grit and resilience through developing a growth mindset learned through years of personal unshakable grit and perseverance. You could say, I am the human camel; that is, once I lock onto a target, I keep going until I reach to my destination. These simple practices have helped me through the tough times; I am sure they will help you as well…

1. Adopt flexible thinking patterns

Being less rigid in your thoughts and actions allows resilience and grit to blossom. Simply because flexible people do not see problems, they see opportunities for growth and learning. Whenever possible, meet challenges with enthusiasm and creative thinking instead of complaints and blame. You will see yourself as a capable person and this confidence breeds resilience.

2. Surround yourself with people who persevere

Whether grit is nature or nurture is irrelevant, but like all things, it is a combination. Surrounding yourself with people who have both passion and perseverance towards their own goals helps us become grittier. It will help to strengthen or grow the mindset required to increase resilience and grit. Be around like-minded people.

3. Focus on your language choice

Praising efforts fosters resilience and reminds people to appreciate their effort. It could be a simple "Thank you." Paint a clear picture of the future, sell them the dream using language that encourages perseverance and praises effort. I have tried this with my own children to build them as realistic resilient individuals.

4. Set tiny goals that align with your overall major purpose

People with a sense of purpose are happier, but purpose is very abstract and often difficult to define. By creating smaller short-term goals which align with the grand ideal outcome for your life, will keep you on-track to find your major purpose. This will keep you motivated and make you grittier.

5. Build time for reflection into your day

When you take a time to reflect you bring awareness to the present. Whether your reflection takes the form of a meditation, a journaling session, a gratitude exercise, or a walk outside while you think things through you will feel better about yourself. Be non-judgmental, just empty your inner-thoughts and submit new images. It takes effort to do trivial things, but it takes inner power to do grandiose things.

Whom Do You See In The Mirror?

When you look at yourself in the mirror, whom do you see? A normal person, a doubter, a determined superhero, a muscle-bound man, or beautiful looking woman? If you do not believe in the person in the mirror, you cannot win in life. If you do not believe you can conquer your world, then there is no way you ever will attempt it. You might not be superhuman or Wonder

Woman, but how about being just a little more effective every day?

Young entrepreneurs ask me, "What is one way someone can build their self-confidence, personally and professionally" here are my answers.

Some Suggestions To Boost Your Self-Confidence:

1. Strengthen your mind

Self-confidence is a state of mind that can be achieved through reprograming of your mental images. Allotting time to nurture your mind, body, and spirit (preferably one hour a day) can be done in a variety of ways. I prefer to read, exercise, walk in nature and run in the morning. If you are not taking time for yourself, particularly to read, then you are allowing someone or something to shape your view of the world. As they say, go within to see without.

2. Discard the negative thoughts!

You simply do not need them. Thinking negatively serves no positive purpose. A whole new branch of psychology is dedicated to mindfulness, but it boils down to this: Negative thoughts and insecurities pop up like pimples, and like pimples, picking at them – even if you mean to discredit and burst that negative bubble – makes it worse. So, mindfulness practice teaches us to treat thoughts as tools. Use and strengthen the ones you need; discard the ones you do not.

3. Live a lifestyle of personal growth!

This one is not for everyone but is my personal favorite because self-education is a lifelong journey. Back in 1994 when I found Tony Robbins' book <u>Unlimited Power</u> at a yard sale and I bought it for $2, it was a hard read, but when, with my dictionary in hand, I read the first hundred pages, a light bulb went on inside my head. I started to buy all the books he mentioned in his book. I looked up all the names he mentioned in the book. Eventually I flew all the way to Dallas, Texas for Jim Rohn's last public appearance. Putting yourself into courses or professional settings that force you to grow ensures your continuous growth.

I have read books like <u>Think and Grow Rich</u> multiple times to clarify some ideas for myself. I recommend you read these concepts as many times as you can or whenever you need a little inspiration to think and act positively.

Remember, repetition is the mother of learning, and we need to learn continuously. Every time you read a delightful book something worthwhile pop up that you never noticed before. You learn something new that sticks to your inner mind like a post it sticky pad. Continuously learning and upgrading your skills is essential parts of all personal development and improved self-concept.

4. Learn about Imposter Syndrome

Many professionals will at some point experience a psychological phenomenon known as imposter syndrome, otherwise known as complete feelings of inadequacy and a fear that everything accomplished to date has been through sheer luck. To overcome this, learn to internalize accomplishments. Peer groups are a wonderful place to talk it out, get feedback and build your confidence. I joined Toastmasters International to learn how to speak in public, improve my language skills and learn storytelling in those early school years.

5. Dress for success

Every day, dress as though you are meeting the most important person in your life because there are no off days for entrepreneurs. If you are going out in public, you better be ready to sell, sell yourself, your ideas, and your concepts.

No matter what level of business you are engaged in, it is important to dress like you are meeting the ideal client or greeting the most valuable clients you have. There is this idea of working from home in pajamas, but most successful people get up early and dress like they are off for a day at the office even working from home. Your dress reflects your personality and attitude. When you look good, you feel good, and when you feel good you do better.

6. Take improvement classes

Improvement classes make you think on your toes in front of an audience. In Toastmasters, you are given a random word or phrase where you have to talk about it for a couple of minutes. This is impromptu speaking, and the aim is to put you on the spot to see what you come up with on any random given topic. Being on stage helps grow your confidence and being in front of crowds teaches you how to think and react quickly in a professional setting or classroom. The bar or the pub is not the classroom. I know people love to talk in such places but that is not where learning takes place; that is for your time off and socializing.

7. Produce a high-quality personal brand

I believe that a key component to building a healthy self-confidence is in publicly building one's own personal brand. Your smile is your logo, your personality is your business card, and the way you make others feel is your trademark. You can have your own style. You can be a student of style and learn what suits your personality. You can learn style by picking up ideas from everywhere, then forging your own personal brand of how you say and do things. Work on your vocabulary so when you present your ideas, it becomes more meaningful, and you communicate in a clear manner to your audience. Only from our present vocabulary can we express what is in our minds.

The dictionary is one of the most important books, especially in the English language. It has been said that how you do anything is how you do everything. You can improve the way you do things through the creation of high-quality standards for yourself. I reflect this through creating content in my writing. "Impact," "sincerity," "extraordinary," and "value" are important words in my world.

8. Recognize your own self-worth

Your self-confidence is rooted in who you are based on your earlier programming. Find ways to get connected with yourself and grow from where you left off. Volunteer, do some *pro bono* work, meditate, work out, read, and hang out with friends who will help you get better. One of the things I did was to join the YMCA right after I settled in Canada. I wanted to improve myself physical wellbeing and connect with other like-minded individuals. Do whatever it takes for you to increase your personal and professional value.

9. Use the ten-minute rule

Mental strength will not magically make you feel motivated all the time. But it can help you be more productive even when you do not feel like it. When you are tempted to put things off, use the ten-minute rule. Take yourself for a ten-minute walk, give yourself permission to rest when you need. Getting started is often the hardest part. Once you are on-track, you can rest when you need to disconnect and reorganize your mind and focus and get right back to where you left off. Once you take the first step, you will realize it is not as bad as you predicted. It's just a matter of changing your mental images.

10. Prove yourself wrong

The next time you think you cannot do something, prove yourself wrong. As a simple practice, start to reverse every negative thought that comes to your mind. Remember, by nature man tends to be negative, so to stay positive all the time will be a challenge for anyone, including myself. When you connect with the people you genuinely love, you feel recharged and positive again.

Constantly recharge yourself and get going again. If you are going to the gym or do workouts, commit to doing one more push up, or if you are in sales, commit to closing one more sale this month. Do what you need to do to push your every limit.

Often when I run, I select a trail that I want to take, but once or twice a week I set a new goal and push further than I have ever gone before. Your mind will want to quit long before your body needs to give up. Prove to yourself that you are more capable than you give yourself credit.

Over time, your brain will adopt this way of thinking and you will be looking for ways to pushing your every limit. Taking the first step creates momentum, the emotional energy, and the inner urge to take another step will keep you moving. Ultimately, you will find joy in what you accomplish.

We need to use our time productively. You divide it into three eight hours; eight hours to sleep, eight hours to work, and the most important eight remaining hours are yours to make miracles happen in your life.

Let's look a deeper look in our own self-concepts and how to build a great self-image in your extra eight hours in the next chapter.

Chapter 6

The Self-Concept – Improving Your Self-Image

"Don't go with the flow, be the flow."
(Shams Tabrizi)

Henry Ford once said, "Thinking is the hardest thing to do."

That is the reason why such a very small percentage of the population engages in it.

Doctor Ken MacFarland, an American educator once said, "Two percent of people think, three percent think they think, and ninety-five percent of people would rather die than think."

If you just stop and listen to what people are saying and watch what they are doing, it is obvious that they are not thinking creatively.

Today most people have their television tuned to the news, just soaking up all the junk that is dominating the media at any given time. They become the playground for what is going on out there, and that is why most live in such fear. Whether or not the information is true, is this how you want to spend your life just listening to that junk all day?

This does not mean you should deny the information, and it does not mean you should say that it's all false. I don't know if what is going on is true or not, I just don't want to be a part of it and spend my time thinking about it. I would rather activate some of my creative faculties and do something that is meaningful and constructive.

We should be thinking about how we are going to adapt to the new way of life when the crisis is over. The world will be quite different in a few years. We should be thinking about what we want to do and where we want to be going and whom we should spend our time with. This time represents great opportunity for those who are equipped and ready for the new wave of opportunities coming.

The goal here is to get you through the tunnel of self-doubt and fear, to help you win the battle between your ears. The beliefs, ideas, and customs we have been programmed to follow limit our creative imagination.

The Six Faculties Of The Ministry Of Miracles

I want to introduce you to the six faculties of the Ministry of Miracles where you can make magic happen in your life.

These are not just words. They are indeed departments of creativity in your mind. We need to work on expanding these faculties whilst we are here on this planet. Everyone reading this has great reservoirs of talents and abilities to use to accomplish anything you want if we cultivate and employ these faculties.

The first faculty is **Perception**. Our perception is how we see they world. I love the way Wayne Dyer put perception in perspective when he said, "When you change the way you look at things, the things you look at change."

You can use your perception to change the way you view the world. Your perception is the way you interpret everything in it around you.

Imagination is the second of these faculties. Imagination is the most marvelous, miraculous, and powerful force the world has ever known. It is the faculty or action of forming new ideas, images or concepts of external objects that are not present to the senses at the current time. It is the greatest creative faculty that we possess. You can use your imagination to go into the future and bring it to the present and anything that you can hold in your mind, you can hold in your hand. The key word being 'holding' the image in your mind. This book is the manifestation of my imagination.

Then comes the faculty of the **Will.** The will is the order to make promises and intention to do something and follow through with it. Will is the ability to hold an idea on the screen of your mind regardless of all outside distractions.

Memory is the next of these faculties. Memory is the faculty by which the mind stores, retains, and remembers information. It is the process of remembering what has been learned in the past. You have a perfect memory and all you need to do is to study how to develop you perfect memory because your spiritual DNA is perfect. Continuous learning improves your memory at will.

Reason is the faculty or process of drawing logical inferences. It is the power of synthesizing into unity by means of comprehensive principles, the concepts that are provided by the intellect. Reason is what gives you the ability to think creatively. It's the ability to create thought. Reason enables you to turn inspiration into thought.

Intuition is that higher faculty that picks up energy and reads it. It's the ability to understand something instinctively without the need for conscious reasoning. We may call it the sixth sense; in essence it is your gut feeling and it never lies. You can develop your faculty of intuition and pick up vibrations. It is where the Creator talks to you.

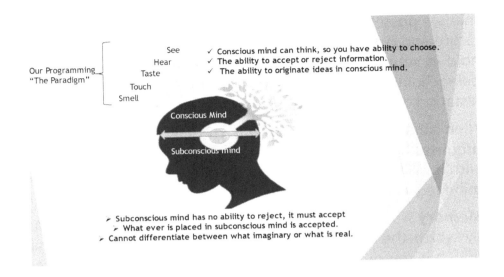

Our Programming "The Paradigm"

See
Hear
Taste
Touch
Smell

✓ Conscious mind can think, so you have ability to choose.
✓ The ability to accept or reject information.
✓ The ability to originate ideas in conscious mind.

Conscious Mind

Subconscious mind

➤ Subconscious mind has no ability to reject, it must accept
➤ What ever is placed in subconscious mind is accepted.
➤ Cannot differentiate between what imaginary or what is real.

Requirements For Miracles

Discipline is a requirement of miracles. There are no miracles in bed, besides getting rest to recharge. Real miracles happen in the classroom, in gyms, on the play fields, in the library, on the stage and in masterminding with other people.

Positive thinking is a requirement. Otherwise, negative thinking will consume your life and waste valuable time. Think about the greatness inside you because that is where miracles happen. To sit in fear and wonder what will happen is a dumb idea where you have a choice be developing your faculties of creativity.

There are no limits to the applications of creative vision. Any man can tune in to the creative vision where he can find the answer to anything that has an answer. We need to use vision if we are going to continue enjoying the benefits of today's modern society. Elon Musk was educated in Toronto and moved on to become the world's richest man by using his creative vision and imagination.

If humans were like animals, we would act instinctively only.

We could not change our responses to the circumstances of our surroundings. We would be hopeless. The good news is that human beings have creative vision by which we can think, design, and create anything in the external world.

Earlier we referred to "Good In, Good Out" as opposed to "Garbage in, Garbage Out." Our new self-concept can replace what we have learned with some new learning. Everything that has been programmed into us can be deprogrammed or over-ridden by new programming.

Your self-concept is like the old MS-DOS software program that runs Windows. Your master programing is the basis of your self-concept. Similarly, your beliefs and behaviours are based on your self-concept. Your self-concept is how you see yourself in every area of your life from parenthood to your work duties.

Your self-concept is your operating system, and your behavior is the windows to your personality. You always perform on the outside, based on how think on the inside. The question is, are you a competent person at what you do? What is your self-con-cept at work? This is an important concept as far as your career is concerned. The good news is you can get better at what you do, no matter what you are doing, there is always room for improvement.

The most important concept that I have found in the examina-tion of human behaviour is a quite simple concept but not easy to practice. It is this: The person that becomes successful does not change in personality but he or she manages to get more out of himself each day. It's possible to be the top ten percent of your company, industry, or career if you develop the skills of the top ten percent.

When I was a financial advisor, I put this concept into practice with great zeal. Starting from the bottom, in two short years we had built one of the top three organizations in Canada within the company. They had an online scoreboard where you could log in and see the results of the work of top ten percent of performers at any given moment. I was committed to get there. When I eventually did get there, I was flown around the country to share my story and these concepts with the rest of the company at meetings, events, and annual kick-offs. It all came down to my expectations.

The Law Of Attraction

The law of attractions says you attract people and circumstances in harmony with the quality of your thoughts. Your thoughts may be positive or negative, uplifting or depressing, but whatever they are that is what you are attracting into your life.

Your expectations tend to become your self-fulfilling prophecies, so if your expectations are based on true information, those thoughts are what you will be attracting into your life. For example, your expectation may be that you are destined to be a remarkable success in your life. Over time you find and apply the principles that will position you to become such a success. If you confidently expect to be a great success, you will eventually be a success story.

Confidence is a product of practice and it's displayed in our behaviours. Millions of people around the world have done this and continue to use these principles revealed first by author Napoleon Hill in his book, Think and Grow Rich, which I highly recommend reading right after this book.

Bryan Tracey says, "You are not what you think you are, but what you think, you are!"

Even the Bible says, "You are as you think in your heart," and your heart is your subconscious mind. You have seen an illustration of the self-concept in my own story.

First, at age thirteen, I thought about living in Canada where I would author books and teach from my own experiences. I wrote it down without knowing how I was going to accomplish this. Later, I wanted to have my own business and something in health and wellness since I was rejected from medical school entry and eventually, I came across the benefits of camel wool products and started my own company.

I always wanted to stay in touch with my parents who lived so far overseas. I wanted to see them grow old and gray together, I was lucky enough to spend a lot of quality time with them where I cared for their needs at old age and personally witnessed the joy in their eyes as their heart glow with happiness. You can manifest your reality based on the thoughts that you constantly think.

When you think about something and decide, you are using your conscious mind. That is when you make a conclusion or judgment using logic based on reason. If your mental set or mindset is a certain way, then you make your judgments based on that mindset. We only understand life based on our own conscious awareness and understanding.

However, ninety-five percent of our behaviours are driven by our subconscious or instinctively driven, which means that less than five percent of all our actions are driven by our conscious mind. Be careful about what you set your heart on, for the subconscious mind does not know the difference between real or imaginary.

Furthermore, research shows that most of our programming is done between the age of five to twelve years old. So, imagine if you never worked on improving your mindset, you could be a forty-year-old person walking around with the belief of a ten-year-old. The beliefs that you are handsome or ugly, smart or dumb, that you are able or unable, rich, or poor all comes down to our early programming. The good news is, we can override this early programming by the practice of these concepts through repetition of thought that I share at the end of the book here.

My Son Gabriel's Example

Let me give you a family secret that I use with my children. Since the day they were born, every time I see them, I say their names and continue, "I love you so much, I am so proud of you, you are becoming great."

Do you think this has an impact on their behavior and performance?

Does it work? You bet it does. Absolutely. Here is an example. Since the day my son Gabriel was born, even before he learned how to walk or talk, every time I have seen him, I have lifted him up or lowered myself down to his eye level and looked him straight in the eyes and I have been telling him, "Gabriel, I love you so much, I am so proud you, and you are becoming great."

In 2019 just before Covid-19 took center stage on a global scale, I had just come back after a long trip in Mongolia. When I saw Gabriel, who was about six years old at the time, I hugged him tight, kissed him and said: "Gabriel," and before I could finish my sentence, Gabriel still holding me tighter blurted out, "Daddy, I love you so much, I am so proud of you, you are becoming great" which brought me tears.

These concepts work. Whatever your beliefs are, you will manifest them in your life. Plant seeds of greatness in your mind and the mind of your children and they will blossom. I have put these principles to the test repeatedly, with my parents, children and throughout my career. All improvement in your personal performance begins with an improvement in your self-concept. Your self-concept is the set of beliefs you have about yourself, your abilities, and your talents.

When Nelson Mandela received the Nobel Prize in his speech to the committee he said, "Our deepest fear is not that we are inadequate, our deepest fear is that we are powerful beyond measure. It is our light, not our darkness, that frightens us."

We mentioned earlier that according to Stanford University research, the average person uses less than ten percent of their potential. Just image learning one single word a day by end of each year we would be 365 words richer in our vocabulary. If you could increase your performance, you could double or triple your income. The real-life example is Elon Musk, an immigrant that started with nothing but a creative vision, and by the time this book is in your hand, he will be the first trillionaire this world has produced and the leading force in space exploration and technology among other industries, including social media.

People think the answer to their problems is money like Elon Musk's. Everyone is looking for the quick fix for lack of money not knowing that more money is not the solution; instead, the answer is to be more human. The answer is more love, compassion, and happiness – and focus.

No Elevator To Success

There is no elevator (or rocket) to success, however; you must take the stairs step-by-step and become a better version of yourself. Your self-concept is the most important ally on your journey of achievement because as within so without. You will also need a goals program that requires commitment to stay focused. It helps you stay the course through all kinds of challenges and difficulties to reach your main objective or major definite purpose in life.

When looking for a suitable residence in Istanbul during the writing of this book, I selectively chose the penthouse of the seventh-floor apartment building without an elevator. Every time somebody came for a visit, they had to put the effort to come up a flight of one hundred steps, and that gave them a good workout.

As soon as the person entered, they had an inbuilt self-concept check. Either they complained or they commanded, based on their level of fitness and self-concept. I personally went down and up at least a couple of times a day just to do my leg work.

When I needed something, I had to walk down and then up one hundred steps which I enjoyed because it's easy to gain weight and be lazy here. The food is very delicious, and the culture is very friendly. Let me assure it has been a remarkably interesting choice. Discipline is a choice so is the lack of it.

Jim Rohn, the great American business philosopher said, "Become a millionaire not for a million dollars but for what you become in the process of achieving a million dollars."

Based on my study of hundreds of millionaires the process is simple yet hard to do. If you have the right business ideas, surround yourself with the right people, and get to work with intent, more abundance will eventually flow into your life. Even most of those who win the lottery lose all their money within a few years because of lack of financial education or the discipline to hold on to the money.

Laziness is the biggest plague that has invaded the human

mind and body. To be successful at anything you must have discipline and laziness is the absolute opposite of self-discipline. Your ideas, products and plans mean nothing if you do not have the discipline to execute them. Discipline is the motherboard for the healthy living and the bases for all personal achievements where outcomes are predictable.

Self-discipline helps you go from positive thinking to positive knowing. You attract the right people to assist you in achieving your personal or financial goals. Developing your self-confidence through a goals program leads to improved self-concept and success in all areas of your life. When you are disciplined, your cup always full of enthusiasm. When you increase your self-concept, your family, your business, and your life will increase.

A part of being born is also dying. Death needs to be understood more than it needs to be feared. Man, like a plant, is born, sprouts and grows. Likewise, both want to grow and aim to reach the sky, then one day they get tired of trying, slow down, eventually stop and lay down and die. It is our self-concept that determines how high we grow and even how long we live.

Purposeful living requires a great self-concept which makes each of us last in the space we occupy in this world. Living without a purpose will eventually end up with a tombstone without a story. You can live purposefully and be remembered for generations in your family, community, or even your country as many before us have done.

Live Purposefully And Be Remembered

I have many personal role models in my family whose name just jumps out as people talk about their legacy, lifestyle, and greatness all of whom had a great self-concept. One such character was called Sayyed Taha Gilany, my great-grandfather, who built a shrine for his disciples in the high mountains of the Kurdish-inhabited area in East Turkey near the city of Van.

His name is spread throughout the Middle East and most parts of the Muslim world. He had ten thousand followers and built an education center with 105 study rooms in the high peaks near Mount Judy, the landing place to Noah's Ark. Nehri, an historic site, southeast of historic city of Van in East Turkey, has recently been restored with the permission of the Turkish interior ministry. His legacy continues in that part of the world.

What happens beyond this life, nobody really knows. The only thing we know for sure is the value that a man leaves behind while here and after he is gone. To leave a legacy, such as the one I mention above, is living a purposeful life. My self-concept drives from such inspiring figures so I am blessed to have that ancestry, but it did not determine my own personal story and development of my mindset.

I could not tell you that I have everything that I need or want to have or wish for at the time of this writing, but I can tell you that I have a balanced mind because of the development of these idea through self-discipline. I may not have everything in life that I desire but I have peace of mind because I have learned to respond to circumstances of life in a positive way instead of a negative way.

I have learned to be at peace with people and the rest of the world but more importantly to be at peace with myself. No matter what kind of material riches you have, if you are not at peace with yourself or your fellow men, then you are no richer than someone who has nothing.

Unless you learn how to be at peace with people of all races, religions, creeds, colors, and backgrounds, you will not have meaningfully rich life. I have risen above these concepts to the idea of letting things like racial, religious, or ethnicity differences distract me or cause me to be out of step with my fellow men. My self-concept includes all these ideals that make up my personality. We are all one brand, the brand of humanity, and everyone is different even identical twins have differences in personality and character.

There was a time when I did not have this mindset, but I have learned that being in harmony with all your fellow men is the only way to complete happiness and peace of mind. We all must learn to live with one another in peace and harmony and when we do, we will have a much better world. As my self-concept improves, the quality of life for everyone around us improves.

I know it's not easy to keep a positive mindset when your balance is close to zero. I know how it is to be hungry, homeless, and lost. I know how it is to be without friends and family. I know how it is to be ignorant, illiterate and poverty stricken. It seems impossible to be able to keep your mind on the opposite, but I did it and if I can do it, anyone can do it.

The first form of self-discipline is the control over one's thinking mind. If you develop a great self-concept and control your own thinking, you will control everything that comes your way. You have to be the person in charge of your thinking before you take control of your life. Taking possession of your thinking is your first duty to yourself and the beginning of building a great self-concept. Protect your peace of mind and inner consciousness so you can direct your thoughts on the outcomes and things you want and off the things and people you do not want.

We often look for all our past shortcoming, judge our present circumstances and under evaluate our futures. Stop comparing yourself to other people, you are the only one on this planet that can be you. You will always have some opposition when you move in a certain unusual direction. You need self-discipline more when the report is unfavorable and when it seems like there is no hope. In those moments your self-concept can be your lighthouse and your self-discipline your vessel in the storms of life. Self-discipline is to keep your mind on your inner desire and off the things that you do not want and desire. Where and when do you need self-discipline mostly? You need self-discipline when the going is hard and when the outlook is grim.

The mind processes thousands of ideas per minute but can only process one idea at a time. It is either negative or positive. Which do you prefer? If you learn to feed your mind the positives and the things that you desire, you will keep your mind of the things that you do not desire. Direct your mind to the positives so it can stay of the negatives because the mind is naturally negative.

Taking Personal Inventory

However, constructive criticism is not negative. I have made a list of traits of personality that I need to improve to raise my self-concept. My personality is always under construction, and I am a work-in-progress. I am a lifelong learner and will not stop this mindset for as long as I live. I work on me constantly because you are not going to do something about your defects unless you make an inventory of them. Developing a great self-concept like anything else requires some evaluation so it is not done out of ego. Our egos often overpower our truths, but ego stands for "Edging God Out" of our lives. That is the God within and when we edge that out, we are left with emptiness in our souls.

Be honest with the man or woman in the mirror and get some

traits that need changing on paper. We easily make a lengthy list of other people's faults but not our own. Write your faults down so you can do something about them. What you do is you start immediately to work on developing the opposites of the traits you want to change.

Look yourself in the mirror and be totally honest with yourself, nobody knows you like yourself. If you are faultless, wonderful, but if you are like the rest of us, we can start the process to improve today.

For instance, you may be a generalist like me and have great visions and ideas, but not be too detail oriented. Then you start paying stick attention to details of things like I started during the composition of this writing. More importantly if you are in the habit of passing down gossip, start sharing compliments. Make up a list of the traits of people around you and do an unbiased inventory list of your team's positive abilities.

There are five mental habits you probably do that you can quit. Here are five things you quit to improve your self-image as of right now:

1. Trying to please everyone: we are here to serve, not to please.
2. Fearing change: it's the only constant in life.
3. Living in the past: it's only a lesson not a life sentence.
4. Putting yourself down: nobody is like you, and that's your superpower.
5. Overthinking: you create problems that do not exist.

Your family can grow and exceed your expectations based on your own personal growth and self-concept. Keep your mind so busy with the things that you do want, so that you have no time to think about the things that you do not want. If you start to work on yourself by improving your self-concept, you can turn a lot of your enemies into friends and unfavorable conditions to opportunities.

You cannot work on the other man before you work on yourself. If a person, does you wrong, you must have the initiative to forgive him because the thoughts of hatred poison your own mind and sicken your soul. When you become forgiving, charitable, and kind towards people, you free yourself and improve your self-concept as a human being. Forgive, forget, and move on.

Building Your Mental Walls

There are three mental walls of protection against outside influences and to immunize yourself against external forces that take away your peace of mind and make you unhappy, resentful, or fearful.

Your first wall is **your sanctuary** where you are one with your creator. I have a morning routine that I have adopted where I program my mind and prepare for a full day of positivity. I recommend one for you too. That is where you ask for guidance through prayer, meditation, and connection to your Creator get instruction through your six faculties of creation.

Another one of these mental walls is **association with like-minded people.** Those are the people you have something in common with where you have a mutually beneficial relationship.

The third wall is **inaccessibility to all people**. You may have to let go of some people who may not favor you in life even if you live under the same roof. Those are the people who have no meaningful relationship where distancing yourself may benefit you and will protect your peace of mind.

You can always informally excuse yourself of such associations as each of us have a different self-concept. Do not to let anyone just walk into your life and on your mind with their dirty shoes and poison your thinking. I refuse to listen to negativity, gossip and oblivion and stop it or excuse myself immediately if someone starts such a conversation where I must be present.

It is the trait of a weak mind to share gossip about others. "Small minds talk about people; average minds discuss events and great minds talk about ideas." said Eleanor Roosevelt absolutely on-point here.

Where do you measure on that scale? The number one positive trait you can start right away is, if you are not sharing yourself with others, if you are greedy about your ideas, knowledge, and opportunities, then start sharing.

Lessons From Gandhi

The most important form of self-discipline for those who want to have an outstanding life is to control our own mind and thinking. You will never be the master of circumstances of life in the space you occupy the world until you first learn to be master your own mind and improve out self-concept.

Mahatma Gandhi, known throughout the world and someone I admire very much for applying this principle, used his time wisely to gain freedom of India and eventually defeated the British empire.

He used the five principles of definiteness of purpose.

1. He knew what he wanted.
2. He used applied faith.
3. He began to do something about it by indoctrinating other fellow men with his vision.

4. He did not do anything vicious; that is, he did not commit any acts of violence.
5. Then he went the extra mile. He personally went beyond what was required of him by any other man.
6. Eventually, he enrolled others in a mastermind alliance the likes of which the world has never seen before. He enlisted at least two hundred million of his compatriots to contribute to his mastermind alliance to gain their freedom without any act of violence. He demonstrated self-discipline unparalleled in modern times, and those were the element that made Gandhi the master of the great British empire.

Gandhi was the total and absolute master of his mind because nowhere in the world you can find a man who can stand all of insults, abuses, incarcerations like he did and not react in kind. He went through all that while standing his ground without striking back. He fought his war with his own weapons of patience and non-violence. If you have to go to battle with somebody, select your own weapons based on the strength of your character and your self-concept.

We all will fight some battles throughout our lives in one way or the other, so we need to remember these principles. To remove your opposition or your enemy you must be smarter than they are. The way to do it is not to strike back on their battleground or engage with the weapon of their choice but to choose your own battleground and weaponry.

This is an important lesson to remember for me as well because when you have a problem to solve and somebody is opposing you, we tend to lose our senses. When you have to face on obstacle, someone or something, you must physically and mentally condition yourself for the battle first.

In fact, the Toronto police and doctors at the Sunny Brooke Hospital had told my family at the time of my hit-and-run accident that if I had not been in great physical shape my chances of surviving the impact of the accident would have been close to zero. The point I am making here is preparation can save your life, as it did mine.

We must create a system whereby we have full control over your own mind and body to improve our self-concept. Keep focusing your mind on the desire of your own choice and take control of your own health by doing all the things that keep the in control and the body healthy and in great shape.

Most people who read this book will have more opportunities and less troubles than Gandhi had in his life, or that I have had in my life. I have been through unbearable challenges by most measures, but here we are. Unstoppable is the word that comes to mind because as long as I live, I will try to top each day more than the one gone. If I can overcome all those challenges, and create my own opportunities, anybody can, so can you.

First you have to take control of your institution, your enterprise: you!

Each one of us as a person is an institution, an enterprise. The mission of this institution is to be on a journey of continuous improvement of our self-concept. Primarily, you have to be in charge of you. You have to be in control of the decisions you make and see them carried out. You must develop the self-discipline to fulfil your potential.

Anything that you acquire by the desire of your heart must be created and acquired by your mind first. You must be sure of it and see yourself in possession of it. It will take mental discipline before it can be acquired in the physical form. The reward for learning this practice is full control of your own earthly destiny through the power of faith.

When I meet with obstacles and come to intersections in life, where I do not know what direction to go, I remind myself that invisible forces are looking over my shoulders. I have faith that this invisible force is guiding me in the right direction. The spirits of my ancestors look over and guide me as a move forward in life. How do I know that this is true? How do I keep the faith?

There have been many desperate moments of in my life that have turned to blessings of equal or more value. The divine intervention has always come to my rescue through faith in the invisible forces of faith in the Creator. I would never write about this unless they happened in my own life and unless I can tell you how to make it happen for yourself.

It is a great comfort and peace of mind for any human being to realize that God has given you a great power to communicate with the Infinite Intelligence. The Creator intended to give you the power of self-discipline which means complete control over your mind and body.

It is nobody's business to tell you what you want or what you should want. Only you know when your head hits the pillow at night, and you wake up in the morning that you realize what your relationship with yourself looks like. If it is missing something, that is a hunch or a call to action that you need to change things up a little bit.

Control Your Thoughts, Control Your Life

If you can copy these principles and develop some disciples to act, you could totally change your outlook and trajectory of your life. I have heard that common sense is no longer common. Of course, most of these principles are common sense, but very few people think common sense in the rush of getting nowhere these days.

The ideas I am presenting here are basic and effective but often overlooked. They are mostly common sense but not commonly practiced. People need more reminders than they need instructions. We tend to complicate life by our own thoughts and the choices that we make along the way.

When we want to make personal growth a lifestyle, we are required to replace some destructive thinking habits that have been instilled in our subconscious mind. If you can control your attitude, you can control every day of your life and move ahead with clear concise steps towards your ideal objectives in life. A great life is different for everyone, but to be able to make an impact in the lives of as many fellow men we must grow through life.

For me, starting an enjoyable day starts in the morning as soon as I have recharged my internal battery with my mental exercises, followed by my physical activity routines. Similarly, if you can control your thought process in the early morning hours and throughout the day, you can control your week, month, and your years to come. Either you control your day, or you allow outside circumstance to control your days.

The penalty for not taking control of your mental attitude is to become the victim of circumstances and all the influences in your life. Along with developing the right mental attitude comes this incredible benefit that you feel content and happy with your own life. What a profound statement that you have been given how you can determine your own earthly destiny at birth, by controlling your thoughts.

Self-discipline means complete control over our own body and mind. It does not mean changing our body or mind, it merely means having full control over your thinking process. The emotion of sexual desire, for instance, gets many people in a lot of trouble but it is not this emotion that gets people trouble, it is the lack of directing it and controlling it that gets people in trouble. You can be the master and not a slave to it. Your self-concept is what determines whether you are the master or the slave of your life.

We need to control our emotions to enjoy sound health and peace of mind. This means developing daily habits by which the mind is in connection with the things and circumstances that one desires to create and off the circumstances that one does not want or desire.

We must prepare and adjust ourselves to deal with any situation that may rise in our lives. You need to understand yourself and other people to adjust yourself to the other people. That said, you do not have to accept or submit to the influence of any outside circumstance that you do not desire. You may have to tolerate it, you may have to endure it, but you do not have to submit to it, accept, or let it conquer you and take control over your mind.

We are stronger than those circumstances because we don't have to submit to them. There is an extensive list of things that you can do so that you do not want to submit to them. It is a personal choice, but you can build a wall of protection around you. Would you want anybody in this world know all about you, or would you want anybody to know all that you think about? Self-concept is not about external validation.

The average person talks too much for his own good but we have been given two ears and one mouth so we must use them in those proportions.

There are a lot of people who make the mistake of letting

anybody know everything that goes on in their mind because they have a low self-concept.

All you have to do is open a conversation and let them rant about everything that is on their mind, and you will find out all about them both the good and the bad. Unfortunately, you can control a man the minute you find out what he fears. I do not want to control anybody based on fear, but if I ever want to control anybody, I want it to be based on the principle of love.

I say out of this principle of love that you need to make a new decision to improve your self-concept. A great self-image and developing your self-concept will lead to fulfilling your potential. You have unlimited potential if you discover and develop your mental faculties that we will talk about next.

Chapter 7

Your Unlimited Potential

"Don't tell of suffering, talk nothing but blessings."
(Rumi)

"Know thyself," the Bible says.

When you come to a point where you cannot learn anything from anybody, which is faraway for most of us, then look inside. Your fountain source is inside that is where all your potential is hidden. The trick is to keep studying yourself and the way will be shown to you as you discover your own gifts, passions, talents, skills, abilities, and your potential.

If you doubt yourself, you have got to know yourself well because the very best is stored inside you, and that is your true potential. External motivation does not last over an extended period. Only when you have internal motives and the discipline to follow through will you be able to accomplish all that you want and discover your true calling in life.

For some strange reason we think that other people can accomplish the things that we cannot. We tend to minimize the things we can do and the goals we can accomplish. You can discover, develop, and utilize your abilities using the six faculties of creativity mentioned in the previous chapter. You are made in the image of the Creator with reserves of gits, talents, and abilities. The following story will illustrate this.

The Spindle Top Story

The purpose of a goal is not to get to the goal, but it is the awareness one develops as you go after the goal.

Around the turn of the nineteen century there was a farmer in South Texas who had a large piece of land. During the American Great Depression, times were so tough, and the farmer was thinking of selling the land to take care of his family. One day an oil company representative came along from one of the few companies that existed at the time.

The oil company representative told the farmer that they believed there was oil on his land and if he allowed them to drill for it, they would pay him royalties on every barrel of oil that is brought to the surface. An agreement was reached, and the construction began. In those days, the oil barracks were made from wood and when they dug for it, they hit oil and one of the world's largest oil reserves, The Spindle Top, was discovered.

Later, three of the biggest companies were born at The Spindle Top and it was the beginning of new fortunes for thousands of people as well as light and service to millions of people around the country.

It was said that the gusher was so big that it blew away the wooden barracks and thousands of barrels of oil spilled before it was controlled. The man became an instant millionaire. Let us think on this for a moment: did he become an instant millionaire or was he already a millionaire when he had acquired the land?

The fact is that the oil was always there but until they drilled for it, discovered it, and brought it to the surface, he did not know of his wealth. He was not aware of his own good fortune until somebody brought it to his attention. He did not know that he was sitting on such a treasure until someone else brought it to his attention.

I find a lot of people are like that piece of land. They will only benefit if someone comes along as a mentor and turns on their inside light so that they see their own potential. Many people go through life never discovering their true talents and abilities. Discover what is within you and bring out the best that is inside you. Don't just stand on the edge of your potential – leap into it.

The Creator has given every one of us some special gifts at birth. You are sitting on reservoirs of talent and ability that can totally make you healthy and wealthy. Study every day to drill for and find your own special talents and abilities. Anyone that discovers their own true potential and cultivate it has the potential to help improve the lives of millions of other people. Many people have incredible fortunes or potential underneath the surface, but they are unaware of it or do not know how to cultivate it, much less present their talents to the marketplace, until a coach, mentor or a teacher helps them discover their own potential.

Coaches, mentors, and leaders have only one job, and that is to help the average person explore, find, and reveal their talents to themselves. We will talk about the benefits of having coaches in our lives in the following chapters.

Consider me the oil company representative and yourself the old farmer. I wrote this simple and easy-to-read book to help you discover and capitalize on your own talents and abilities. Most people can find joy and happiness in life and even make fortunes if they learn these principles and use the wisdom shared here. You get to keep the full price of every barrel of oil you bring to the surface in your life by reading this book and applying the principles discussed here.

If you discover what your unique talents and gifts are you can create the best possible life for yourself and your family by being of great service to others. When you discover and develop yourself and hone your communication skills you will attract the right people, opportunities, and methods by which to fulfil your major definite purpose. As one of my mentors said, "If not you then who, nobody can do this better than you. If not now, then when?"

The Mountains Are Calling

It is time to decide to take the next five years of your life more seriously than the past five. Five years is a long enough period to clarify, develop, articulate the objective of your burning desire. If you are just entering university or college, you could be a specialized graduate in five years. You will be required to push yourself in the process of fulfilling your God -given potential. It is time to stop thinking "meanwhile" and to start thinking "lifetime."

Friends and family often ask me how I managed to travel the world, pursue different businesses, and arrange family reunions and team meetings where my family, friends and colleagues gather from all over the world. Well, my ambitions and enthusiasm have something to do with it, but most of the things I do are parts of my written goals.

I am flexible enough to change direction if my direction needs changing but determined enough to pursue any objective when I put my mind into. I intentionally pursue my accomplishments through honing some simple habits and practices. You can design, build, and live your desired life once realize you can connect with the higher power where you attract the means of achieving your goals.

With these incredibly simplified techniques and practices you can cultivate and capitalize on your own talents and abilities. Take your best self to the marketplace where people will be happy to pay or partner up with you for the value you bring to them.

We can all grow where we are right now, and I am personally just beginning to start to dream about the future that I am about to create. None of this happens by chance, but it is a direct result of the choices I have made and continue to make daily.

My first book <u>The Mountains Are Calling</u> was a personal development adventure and an attempt to restore my lost memory. I researched and documented my recovery from a total memory loss and a blank past, and my journey to remembering who I really was and what had happened to me. It was just an attempt to reintroduce myself and regain my memory and discover why I am here after a near death experience.

I can imagine that you may not be able to fully comprehend what would it be like to wake up from a coma on a hospital bed not knowing who you are, where you came from and why you are here. I had to rediscover myself, relearn how to eat, walk, and talk from a blank memory.

I had the help of some of the most dedicated professionals and love of some wonderful friends and family whose assistance and commitment has not gone unnoticed. My recovery was also a deep discovery and an awakening inside of me to the power of my deepest passion, the art of communication through creative writing and teaching.

Prior to the accident I loved to share my message in business meetings, seminars, and workshops but during my recovery I discovered my own penmanship and my passion for the art of inspirational creative writing.

Over the years, I have had my team members, students, friends, and family talking to me about their ambitions, goals, and dreams. They ask about how they can start new businesses, further their careers, and move to another country or build their own businesses. Many have tremendous desire, incredible talents, and unique skill sets but they do not know how to turn them into furthering their careers, getting better jobs, or creating profitable business. They do not have a systematic formula to follow so I authored this book to reveal some secrets that I have learned and used in my personal and professional lives.

A burning desire is the yearning to have, be and do more than you do right now. It is a great starting point, but it's not enough by any means. There is no simple, real, and viable formula for success and overcoming the odds, but luckily, through research and study and practice, I have coined my own formula that I am sharing with you through this writing. I have had a few people test read the first draft of this book and they gave the green light to my simple, easy, and comprehensive way of communicating this message.

Some friends and family that hear my story or read my books and are in awe, like standing on the rim of the Grand Canyon. They wonder how I was able to overcome all these challenges, unfortunate events and persevered to regain my mental and physical health and create opportunities to help others. I am here to share some ideas to help you turn your dreams into reality.

We all have different paths and challenges to deal with and overcome, but the formula is the same. You can build stronger connections, and a beautiful life around their own story, unique skill sets and strengths that they can take to the marketplace and capitalize on.

Another one of my mentors the American business philosopher

Zig Ziglar days, "If you help enough people get what they want, you can have everything you want."

I am here to help you get what you really want because in one way or another it all works out perfectly in end. Every vibe, good deed, or service that you give comes back to you multiplied. We are all connected, and that connection is through the source of creative vision, synthetic imagination, and the power of faith in the Creator.

I want to make a real impact on the health of those who suffer from physical pains, mental inabilities and improve the quality of their lives. There are millions of people around the world who could use a simple book like this and totally change their lives. It could start with yours.

I am here to guide the readers to find their own unique talents and create their own personal brand. I am highlighting some habits, traits, and daily practices that have been honed, polishing, and tested in the real world. These techniques, learned, practiced, and put into use will be helpful in getting anyone started on their journey of creating a better life beyond the shadow of a doubt. This is my favorite way of fulfilling my potential.

No Laziness, Alibis, Or Excuses

Allow me to caution you that good habits will be hard to master and bad ones even harder to quit. Laziness, alibis, and excuses are the biggest pandemic of all times that society is facing collectively.

Many young people waste a lot of time using their cellphone playing games or surfing the Net for entertainment instead of making self-education their new pastime. You are not like most because you are reading this book and for those who do not know me, I am here to burst your invisible bubble. You need to wake up to your own potential to create your own legacy, rather than wasting any time on things that don't benefit you in fulfilling your potential.

It's easier to jump from one app to next or from one Internet page to next all day long but there is very little real learning happening if any at all. The Internet is full of distracting news, entertaining content, funny videos, quick fixes or quick get-rich schemes and irrelevant information that does not translate into any real value but a waste of your time. Most people waste a lot of their time, instead of using the Internet for research and development purposes. Some wisecracker told me once, "I don't need to learn anything because I have Google." I replied, "Does Google teach you manners, how to behave, how to be kind and how to control your inner peace?"

Be conscious of how you spend your time because there are too many distractions and vultures are around every corner to attack.

Professional guidance is provided in a professional concise manner, online, in a manual or a book so focus and have a single-minded approach in your search. One of my favorite online resources is TED talks, not only for its educational content but also the new research being presented. And there is YouTube, a great resource to learn the answer to many of your other questions.

I am drafting this book as a reference that you can keep in your library or on your mobile devices. You can read and refer to the wisdom here repeatedly when you need it. I have read many terrific books multiple times and each time I have learned something new.

Most people have never taken the time to devise a plan or have had the guidance of any strong caring mentors who would be honest, truthful, and brutally direct to coach them through these processes. The most disappointing part about having the access to this kind of wisdom or personal development philosophies would be not having the will power to follow through and develop these disciplines on your own.

Everything that you may resent, or reject is telling you that you are entering a new opportunity for learning that is unknown to you. Continuous learning is the only pathway to progress. I am impressing upon you the fact that there is a chance anyone can live a life on his own terms and do what you love.

In my journey, I sought out mentors and asked to learn from them and copied their methods. I always ask for their constructive feedback on my progress. Remember that most of this knowledge is not discussed in family settings, parents do not know about it, and it's not part of our formal education systems so it's up to everyone to seek, adopt, and apply it.

Turning dreams into reality will require thought leadership, a plan of action, unmatched discipline, and unparalleled work ethic. If anyone tells you it's easy, they are not being sincere. In fact, it is the opposite, and it's quite a challenge to follow the path I am suggesting here. If your back is against the wall or your thinking unclear, I am lending you my ladder to get out of your fight feeling fabulous about yourself. I promise with every step that you take; you will feel better and better while your view keeps improving.

Sometimes at the end of a long disappointing day, you just need to tie up a knot at the end of your rope, take a break from your work, go for a walk, and know that everything will be okay. I have survived the worst and it made me wiser, stronger, and more focused. I relate to all your pains or shortcomings because there are not too many I have not experienced.

Challenging Times Need Good Thoughts

We all feel pain, stress, and anxiety in some way, so be kind to others like a true Canadian, but do not let nobody take you for granted or takes advantage of you. Ignorance is not bliss, ignorance is poison to your mental wellbeing, and it leads to a life of poor health, pain, and misery. Everybody hurts the same way.

Through my challenging times, multiple injuries, and devastating psychological trauma, I have learned how one overcomes deeply stressful emotional, physical, and psychologically challenging times. When I could not comprehend what was happening to me, I left it in the hands of the Creator. I have developed a simple belief system for my own life adopted from the ancient Persian religion of Zoroastrianism: "Good thoughts, good words and good deeds."

All religions promote goodness of humankind, equality of people and prosperity amongst nations. All I can say is that I believe because my belief is that I was saved from certain death a second time to serve my fellow man and bring some clarity to some critical issues.

I have endured some dark moments and in such times all I did was to focus on what was going right in my life instead of what was wrong at that moment. Your mind is like a magnet. If you focus it on blessings, you will attract more blessings. If you focus on problems, you will attract more problems, so always count your blessings, cultivate positive thoughts, focus on the good and be optimistic.

I never complained about things, I am not a complainer, I just know there is no use, so I am always grateful. My mother still tells me:

"My boy, you never complain and always say everything is great!"

I tell her that I learned that from her. No matter how hard a day may be, if I am alive and breathing, I am blessed because I stared death square in the eye. I have also witnessed the devastation of war first-hand.

I chose to enjoy the blessings in my life instead of focusing on the tragedies even when the burdens of life weighed heavily on my shoulders. When I did not even have bus fare, I walked miles and miles just to see a loved one or a friend to talk to and to listen to their challenges.

You can be future-focused even when odds are against you. No matter how tough your life may be, no matter how unbearable your conditions, there are certain habits that can help you overcome your situations. Developing these habits will help you navigate the turbulent times without crippling fears. This is your action guide. The aim is to lead you to action by having set an example under my own the worst imaginable conditions.

If you love and enjoy your work, you will be successful regardless of your education level or position. There is a magic in loving what you do. You can always learn new talents and skills required to be more successful but not without hard work. Your race, religion, creed, or background do not matter but working hard does make the difference.

Your desire and willingness to learn and apply the disciplines in this book is all that matters. Your attitude matters, your faith, character, desire, and persistence in the direction of your goals and major definite purpose matter. This writing was put together to push you to act in the direction of your dreams even if it's only one tiny single step.

You cannot put your life on hold and wait for everything to be perfect to be happy. I decided that I was going to be happy and grateful under any given circumstances or situation. The ultimate freedom of man, as you learned from Dr. Viktor Frankl, is the freedom to choose his own thoughts and behaviours under any conditions. To reach inner peace and equilibrium you must choose positive thoughts and maintain that feeling by the images your feed and keep in your mind. Remember, wherever your attention goes, your energy flows, so to keep your energy in the direction of your goals and dreams. Yes, you can grab the wheel of your own thinking like grabbing the steering wheel of your car and drive it any direction you choose.

During difficulty, when the medical report was not good or when I was treated unfairly, when I was rejected, that is when I chose to stay positive. Positivity is a choice. You choose positivity by controlling the images you allow in your mind. I did not panic, and I did not give up. Instead, I took a deep breath and took just another step forward with the power of the faith that was instilled in my heart.

To stay positive and optimistic in a negative situation is the mark of true leadership. Unbreakable faith in yourself and your abilities is another attribute of great leaders. A bird does not sit on a branch because it believes in the strength of the branch. It sits on the tiniest branch because it believes in its own ability to fly away in the case of the unthinkable. People may think you are arrogant and of full of yourself at first, but you can be humble and voice the facts gently in a way that it does not hurt people's feelings where it awakens them to their own consciousness.

Editing My Life Movie After Tehran

Your life is the result of the decisions you make based on what you think about all day long. You are the only person in charge of your own thinking. Many of us store so much general unnecessary information in our brains that does not translate into any real value. Just like the library is full of books that nobody reads. Reading self-help books and not putting the ideas to practice is like building a lottery machine just to feel good about the jingle. It is a waste of your time if you do not act on what is being presented here.

I love writing, I have many ideas for fiction, novels, movie scripts and other types of writing, but I choose to write non-fiction self-help books. These are instructional books, but nobody can do the work for you. Together we can work on getting you on-track because all you need as a seeker, is a hint in the right direction and to be clear about what you want. Clarity is the starting point of all achievement. Every book I have read has talked about getting clear about what you want. This book will help you get total clarity on what want and how to get it because there is a formula you can apply to your life.

I remember when I became a Canadian citizen, I stood in front of the citizenship judge and swore to remain true to Canada and its values. He was a tall man with a long clean white beard. When he swore in our group, we took The Oath of Citizenship and became Canadians.

After the ceremony, I went up to him as a young man and introduced myself by saying, "Sir, my name is Arif Gilany, I am a new Canadian citizen as of today. I promise you if Canada is ever attacked by any country and needs me, I will be ready to serve and defend it."

I will never forget his answer as he padded me on the back as he looked down on me gently with wide open smile, he said, "Son, no country will attack Canada, we are a peace-loving nation. Congratulations on becoming a Canadian citizen. Now it's your responsibility to get out there and become an outstanding Canadian citizen."

With great zeal and enthusiasm, I answered, "Sir, yes, sir. Thank you, sir."

I shook his hand firmly, with tears running down my cheeks. My long-term dream of becoming a Canadian Citizen had finally materialized.

I remember walking out of that courthouse with my citizenship document in my hand like I had just won the grand lottery jackpot. I was ready to write the next chapter of my life and I had been given an order to fulfill. I am still in pursuit of becoming an outstanding citizen of the country I love and admire.

When a director makes a movie in Hollywood, often the director will shoot and reshoot the critical scenes. Prior to making it ready for public viewing, the filmmakers show it to the critics and test audiences. If the critics and test audiences do not approve some parts of the movie, the director will reshoot those parts that need changing.

You need to be a critic of your own life story, see what needs changing as you go along, and make the necessary changes. Canada was very much like Hollywood for me. My citizenship was my permanent ticket to freedom. It has allowed me the freedom to change anything that needed changing.

What is so great about Canada is that if you do not like any parts of your life you can tear up the chapter, rewrite it and move on, unlike Tehran. Now I had the chance to rewrite the story of the Kurdish refugee who was rejected as a medical school nominee at Tehran University.

Today I get the chance to rewrite that story and make a difference in other people's lives. If you have been a victim of bullying, ridicule, and discrimination, do not feel sorry for yourself. I have experienced all those first-hand and survived them. It is only a chance to prove them wrong and make you strong.

After the Iranian revolution, my father was exiled to Tehran for fifteen years, and he took me with him so I can spend some time healing from my war injuries and first coma while I studied. My jaw was crushed and was reassembled by a platinum bar in my jaw for two years. I was injured in the mayhem of war, but I refused to become its victim. I was the joke of my school and the source of ridicule and belittlement of my classmates and strangers the first two years of my life in Tehran.

I did not look feel like I belonged to the place, but I do not blame those kids for making fun of me, I looked like a character from the "Addams Family" series. Those two years were miserable, I felt very out of place. I missed my family and my comfortable village in the Kurdish-inhabited area in the North-west of Iran. By the third year I ranked the top three in all my academic classes and won several awards. In fact, they awarded me with a basketball and some academic recognition that I took back to my village that summer with immense pride.

I was raised with a magnificent work ethic, and I knew kindness firsthand. My grandmother was a wonderful, kind, and caring woman. She taught us the value of demanding work, kindness of the heart and the value of sharing.

My sister always jokes around. "Grandma even worries if our neighbor's sheep were fed at night." She was the most caring woman character in my life. She used to wake me up at the crack of dawn to water the gardens or help the workers get the livestock out to the pastures.

We had a great, yet simple life. I remember it being much the like the American television series "The Little House on the

Prairie". Life was simple and beautiful, and then came the war.

War is the biggest and most devastating waste of human potential. There are no winning sides in any war, everyone is a loser, but even in war you have the choice to be a part of the solution or the problem. With the encouragement of my family, I decided that I was going to become a doctor when I grew up.

At the end of high school, I took a general test with over two million participants and ranked amongst the top five thousand, but I was denied the right and forced to join the army. I decided that I was not going to a part of the nonsense of war. I decided to leave the land of the familiar and go abroad to pursue the dream of becoming a doctor, so at eighteen years of age I began my long journey to Canada.

It took me five years and being a refugee in four countries before reaching Canada. I had a burning desire to do some-thing special with my life even in my early years. Eventually, I made it to Canada and became Canadian.

Desire is the starting point of all achievements and I believe you can overcome any challenge with a bit of luck, hard work, and some direction.

Seven Days, Twenty-One Days & Ninety Days

I drafted this writing to share the true and important message of hope. Your story may not be as eventful or painful as mine, so let me be the change agent in your life and the catalyst of your dreams. If you have not heard some of the unique inno-vative ideas presented in this writing, you will be challenged to change your thinking. Do not let the truth offend you, let it change you.

Today's access and especially addictive need to stay connected to the Internet has changed how we behave and learn. We have taller buildings and shorter tolerance, bigger houses but empty homes, more opportunities, but less ambition. Let us investigate changing some of your self-destructive habits. I firmly believe that you learn more from books than any other mode of communication because books can help us make fundamental changes in your belief system like having a eureka moment of your own.

One of my mentors said, "The educated people of tomorrow are those who learn, unlearn, and relearn new skills fastest."

When I read a book or watch a movie, I have my highlighter or a pen and paper ready to take some notes. I am always looking for ideas that stand out. I highlight or write them down the innovative ideas that I notice or those I have not heard before. You cannot remember all that you watch, so you need to write down what is important to you. Whatever can make a difference in your belief system and your life, writing them down makes them real and understandable.

In today's world you can learn any skill or develop any habit in less than ninety days. You can use my seven, twenty-one, and ninety-day principles to build any habit that you desire.

You do anything for **seven days** and you will prime your mind with the activity, you repeat it for **twenty-one days** and you are creating a habit, and finally, when you continue for **ninety days** you build a new lifestyle. You can be a more effective individual, leader, manager, entrepreneur, and parent by incorporating this simple formula in your life. You can start a new seven-day priming period any time you choose or when you for some reason slow down or get distracted for a few days. If you can push yourself into a new practice or habit for seven days, then hold yourself accountable for twenty-one days, and practice a new procedure for ninety days, you have a solid foundation for a lifelong change.

Today is the best day of your life, for the rest of your life. You can rebuild, reset, or reorganize and refocus your life as many times as possible. You will never be younger, stronger or have more energy and opportunities than you have right now. I am not just here to author a book; I am here to open-up and offer new and exciting opportunities. When there is hope in the future, there is power in the now. Use the power of now to your advantage. You were born a miracle, so let's find out what is inside that bundle of joy you call 'self'. Let us direct that self in the direction of your burning desire.

An Introverted Adventurer

Most people will live the same year fifty, sixty or seventy times repeatedly and call it a life. I never intended to do that with my life. I was born an introverted adventurer. After a quarter century of world travel, when visiting unfamiliar places, I follow an incredibly simple unique ritual to familiarize myself with the area.

Usually, on my first day visiting anywhere in the world, I *intentionally explore and usually get lost* in the streets or terrains of my new habitat. I usually make this my first morning, since it helps me keep my running routine, plus I can find new future trails. I become a modern-day scout on the first day. It also helps me explore the area to find places that I would like to revisit and things that I need to purchase, as well as resources and places that I may need during my stay.

I will say that navigating your way somewhere you do not speak the native language could get complicated. After many such experiences, I have acquired enough interpersonal skills to navigate my way anywhere without any challenges. This is my own coined practice to make it a fun event even if it is not so pleasant getting lost.

I have done this practice in Ulaanbaatar, the capital of Mongolia, the streets of Casablanca in Morocco, in Sydney, Australia, and many other major cities around the world. There is so much to be learnt from people and history.

You must be your own journey's scout in this adventure called life. In the old days, they had rider scouts to go ahead of camel caravans and new frontiers to find the pathway forward or bring back the news of an enemy ambush or attack. You need to push forward to unknown frontiers of your mind. Today, do something you have never done before. You are your own life's scout, so explore the possibilities laid out in front of you.

I am here to hold the torchlight for you for a little while, so you can see your way through the future. Today the use of technology and navigation systems has made things easier to get around, but even as an introvert I know there is no substitute for human interaction. I love people and have made some incredible memories from around the world that has brought me here.

You need to take some calculated risks to explore life. Remember, if you only follow the footsteps of tradition, you will be looking backwards more than you are looking forward. This is a quite widespread practice in the Middle East. Everyone has a glorified history, yet we learn very little from that glorious past to build a better future. Most of these fantasy stories comes from over five thousand years of the history of the region. Our ancestors lived there for a long time, but what you do today is far more important than what has gone in the past. A good question to ask yourself is:

"What are you doing today to build a better tomorrow?"

You must own up to your responsibilities, make decisions and see them through. You need to be more daring and curious about your future. Times have changed, and your thinking needs to be updated with added information around the latest version of yourself.

In the end we are the choices we make, and when we are faced with a choice, that choice requires us to decide. When you decide, it means you cut off other options. We will talk about decision-making next because it affects every minute of our lives.

Our decisions impact our health, family life and success in life.

Chapter 8

Decision-Making

"You cannot make progress without making decisions."
(Jim Rohn)

Your mind has to be stronger than your feelings. Every poor decision you and I have made in our lives has been a consequence of there being more emotion that was involved in it, than mind. Your emotions tell you to stay in bed in the morning, but your mind tells you to get up. Making the right decisions requires a strong mind and not over-thinking. Decisions also relate to morals and ethics. Your moral and ethical conduct reflects your self-image.

At the beginning of the 20th century, Napoleon Hill, the author of <u>Think and Grow Rich</u>, was a young struggling journalist with absolutely no money when he was invited to meet Andrew Carnegie the first billionaire in American history. Mr. Carnegie was the most successful man of his time. He offered to give Napoleon Hill a letter of introduction to 500 of the most outstanding and successful people in the United States of America, in return for his work to gather and organize the first handbook on the study of success philosophy. That book is the most read book globally and has changed the lives of millions of people around the world.

After a weekend of brainstorming and explaining his philosophy to young Napoleon Hill for three days and nights, came to the moment of truth. Mr. Carnegie told him that I will ask you a question, to which you must give a yes or no answer as soon as you have made your decision.

He said, "If I commission you to become the author of this

philosophy and give you letters of introduction to all the men you need to meet to interview, are you willing to devote twenty years of your life to research and organize such a philosophy, earning your own way along without any subsidy from me? Give me a simple yes or no."

Meanwhile Mr. Carnegie was sitting behind his desk with a stop-watch in his hand and had given Napoleon 60 seconds to make up his mind without Napoleon's prior knowledge. Napoleon said "yes" in twenty-nine seconds.

What would you have done if you were a young man with empty pockets sitting in front of the richest man in the world that would give you no money to devote twenty years of your life to such a project?

It is strange that when you put an opportunity in front of a man his mind will jump to the "no" part and find the reasons why he cannot do it. Napoleon had hundreds of reasons why he could not do it, but his answer change the course of history for millions. If you cannot make a prompt decision when given all the facts, you cannot make anything happen.

We know now that when you make a real decision, you put your brain on higher frequency. You begin to attract every-thing on that frequency and that is when your situation starts to change. Luckily as human beings we have been given all the equipment, the machinery, the mechanisms to put ourselves on the new frequency based on the decision we make and the commitment to keep it.

We have been given the ability to make accurate decisions. There is something ever-present in falsehood which notifies the listener of it. It is there, you can tell it, you can feel it, and similarly you can feel when someone is telling the truth. The most talented actor could not deceive you if you tuned into your innate intelligence in reference to their performance.

If you want the accurate facts, you need to study the remarks made by others closely to make your life and business decisions. Every result that you get in life is based on the decisions that you make along the way.

When you search for the facts, they may not be what you are looking for, but they will be there plainly so you can make better decisions regarding the people you associate with and the businesses that you may start. I am not trying to make a Doubting Thomas or cynic out of you, but I am trying to bring to your attention that you need to be alert to the truth in making your decision.

A lot of people tend to fool themselves with misinformation and lack of the right guidance in making decisions. People fool themselves better than anyone can. It is important to do some accurate thinking to make the right decisions in life and business. When you make decisions, you make a judgment and calculate all options, because a decision means cutting out all other options from your mind and not acting solely on wishes.

Wishes are often the fathers of so-called facts, and most people have a bad habit of assuming facts to harmonize with their inner wishes and desires. Instead, you and I should look through a magnifying glass when searching the facts upon which we make our decisions. Having a growth mindset, as discussed, helps you reach a firm accurate decision.

If you wish a thing to be true, oftentimes you will assume that it is true, therefore you act as if it is true. If you love a person, you will overlook his or her faults. We do not need to overlook people's faults until they have proven themselves entirely. We should never overlook the facts.

History proves that we have admired many people who turned out to be very dangerous for all of us. In fact, most of my personal troubles in life and business have come about based on trusting the wrong people who took advantage of my good nature. I have made the wrong decisions based on emotions instead of the facts and mere truth.

In the same vein, do not be too harsh on the person that steps on your toes and irritates you when it causes you to examine yourself, your unpleasant habits, and your bad behaviours. Take the truth with a grain of salt because it could be very constructive for your future.

The person that criticizes your behavior may be the most important friend you have in your entire life. We all like to meet and associate with people who agree with us, that is just human nature, but often people who we associate with, who agree with everything we say and do, may lead us to making the wrong decisions based on wrong information.

The capacity to stand constructive criticism without resistance is a quality that helps develop a personal initiative. One of the finest sources of improvement in your personality is to have friendly constructive criticism of your personality. We continue to do the things we do – thinking everything is alright – until someone maybe brings it to our attention that those things are not alright. Fortunately, I did not lack the ability to receive constructive criticism because I have seven sisters and plenty of female figures in my life, so you can just imagine the scrutiny that I had to endure while growing up, and even today!

We keep repeating our behavioural misconduct unless somebody brings them to our attention. We need a source of constructive criticism to measure our performance and behavioural conduct with others. Mentors are the great people in our lives who care about our progress and performance. I am not talking about the people who do not like you and are there to bring you down, but about the people who love you and genuinely want you to do better.

We all need the privilege of looking at ourselves through the eyes of the other person. We need constructive criticism and analysis of our behaviour to find how to improve our performance and our results. When change takes place, it is your personality being polished and your performance start to change accordingly.

Did you know that majority of people resent any kind of criticism and anything that would require them to change the way they do things? I believe you do yourself a great damage by resenting constructive criticism. I believe constructive criticism is a wonderful way to help fine-tune your personality traits and develop your character.

Just remember no matter who you are, what you do and how well you do it, you will never get the approval from everyone. I don't expect the approval of all others for what I do. I value the opinion of those mentors who are ahead of me and genuinely care for my health and wellbeing and overall progress in life.

The habit of learning from our mistakes and the mistakes of others are the greatest teachers of all because we figure out what works and what does not work. This helps us make better decisions.

All this will require working on your mindset, but not doing anything about it is also a decision. It is a decision not to take any action, to stay the same, which often can result in loss of time and lead to failure and regrets down the road.

Failure is not an option when you decide to base your future on facts. Only an educated decision can be worthy of all your effort and energy. Decide to be get better at making decisions. Our brain starts to look for solutions when you make good decisions. Decide to practice these techniques and to follow through based on logical facts.

How Do You Know?

Today we have the Internet, Google, and other search engines so information is abundantly available and most of it is free. Facts can be illusory habit and there is a price attached to them. The price is the painstaking labour in examining them for their accuracy and doing the due diligence to find the facts and separate them from fabrication on which we base our decisions. The favorite question of all the great thinkers and decision makers I have met and read about is to ask:

"How do you know?" or "What is your source of information?"

The business of asking people for their source of knowledge is very important in decision-making. If you ask them that question, you will put the person out on a limb, where he or she will not be able to give you an accurate answer. When I ask that question, which I do often, people say, "I believe so." My answer is how can you believe anything if it's not based on the accurate information, facts, or some solid background for your statement?

For instance, there is God, and there are a lot of people that say they believe in God as well, but I bet if you asked them *how they know* they could not give you the slightest evidence of the existence of such power. I can give you all the evidence when I say I believe in God if you ask me, "*How do you know?*"

My answer would be that the information and the background that I have is through logic as well as my personal experience.

Anything that exists, including God, is capable of proof and where there is no proof available it is safe to assume that nothing exists. When there are no facts available for the bases of an opinion, a judgement, or a decision, you can turn to logic for guidance.

I do not have as much evidence in connection with anything in this world as I do in connection with the existence of the Creator. The order of this universe that is going on infinitely since the beginning of time and to eternity could not exist without a cause, plus I have personally witnessed the presence of God in my own life through two near-death experiences and my miraculous recovery. There have been moments in my life where I would not have been able to do what I did except without someone looking over my shoulder and guiding me through those moments and those decisions.

According to Google, a decision is:

"A conclusion or resolution reached after consideration." It is "A verdict, finding, ruling, recommendation, judgment, pronouncements, adjudgment reached after a conclusion."

To decide means to cut off, to sever, to separate or isolate one course of action from the rest. When you base your decisions on solid facts, then you can cut all other options because if you are still thinking about them, you are wasting your time and energy when the decision has clearly been made.

If someone tells me that their major goal is to make a million-dollar next year, my first question is, "How will you do that?" I want to hear your plan, and when I hear the plan, I am going to weigh-up the person's ability. Then I ask what you are willing to give in return for it.

After a careful consideration of all the facts, my logic will tell me whether your plan is probable, workable, and practical. I would read the plan if it were a written plan, which it rarely is, and I would analyse it. I would analyse the person, their capabilities, their past experiences, their track-record and their people abilities.

I would also ask about the people who would help the person in making the million dollars. When I completed the analysing, I would be able to tell the person if it was possible to do it. I would tell the person it will take longer, maybe three years, five years, or even longer or I might conclude that they would not be able to do it at all. If my reasoning and conclusions tell me that it was the right answer, that is what I would tell them.

You may have heard the motto:

"Whatever your mind can conceive and believe, your mind can achieve."

I do not want anybody, especially my students, to misread that to say:

"Whatever your mind can conceive and believe your mind *will* achieve."

It is '*can*' and not '*will*' and oftentimes people do mix the two without paying attention to the difference. It *can*, but I do not know if it *will*, and that is up to the person. Only they know that. The extent to which you use your mind, the principle of faith, the soundness of your judgment and your plans will all be factors on how well you carry out that epigram.

The way that an accurate thinker proceeds is that she does not allow his emotions to get on the way of weighing the facts properly. She makes decisions based on logic not emotions. I have learned not to let my emotions do the thinking for me, but to base my decisions on facts. This way I reduce my chances of making mistakes.

When the pandemic hit Canada in 2019, I sat down and had a meeting with my mastermind group and another one with my family. In both meetings we concluded that it would be better for me to move overseas to Istanbul to work on my business and spend some time with my aging parents.

I had a lot of work planned prior to the pandemic and now I was stuck with no way of making any progress, but this decision allowed me to pursue other goals. I made my move, and this book is the result of that very move and other wonderful things that have happened to me since. I made the right decision because many of my friends in Canada wasted their two years worrying and discussing what was happening. I was busy taking care of my parents, drafting my book, and organizing my next business plans.

Through my thinking and analysis, I realised that most people are trying to prove themselves to others. You cannot separate your way out of your childhood wounds and dramas. You can use your story to help others get a better grasp how deal with such experiences. After the recovery from my coma and the subsequent memory loss, I concluded that my sustainable mission throughout my whole existence would be through helping improve the lives of other people.

Considering an increasing global health crisis, the most important relationship that you need to pay attention to improve and maintain the one you have with yourself. If you are not loving you, if you are not taking care of you, you cannot help anyone.

Your friends, family, clients, and potential customers depend on you, so that makes you the most important person in the equation. It is less about your constant joy and more about constant expanding of your personality and how you can help others find comfort and joy. My family, my community, my country, and the world depend on me being my best, because that is how I feel my best. You cannot get advice on what you should do, nobody knows what makes you the happiest but yourself, so you be your own advisor in this matter. Once you have a hunch, you should take your shot.

Separating The Facts From Illusions

It is a massive undertaking to be able to separate the facts from illusion that is why most people avoid making important decisions. First, scrutinize with unusual care every bit of information that you read, watch, or hear. Get into the habit of never accepting any statement merely because you read or heard it on the news or expressed by someone. Statements bearing some proportions of fact are often intentionally or carelessly colored giving them an erroneous meaning. We all have heard or read that "a half truth is more dangerous than an outright lie."

If you can understand a man's motive, you can tell how truthful he is in what he is saying. If you can locate a man's motive for doing what he is doing or saying, you will be able to separate the truth from falsehood. You should judge a person only based on how much influence of good or bad he or she has on other people, and that is the way you should judge me or anyone else too.

Before accepting any statement as fact, explore the motive that prompted the statement and do not condemn anyone if they do more good than harm. You may not like a man's brand of religion or politics but if he is doing a decent job in his field and helping a lot of people and doing no damage to anyone, never mind about his brand.

When making your decision, learn to be cautious, and if someone is trying to influence you in any way, use your own judgement in final analysis. If you cannot use your own judgment because you do not have all the facts or enough information or you do not understand the circumstances, you can always turn to people who have a broader experience, different education, or keener mind for analysis for advice.

In seeking facts from others do not disclose to them what facts you expect to find. For example, if I call you up to make a reference check on someone that I am thinking of hiring and call you and say to you, "You used to employ John Brown, he has applied to me for a position with my company, I think he is a wonderful man, what do you think?"

Now if John has any faults, I am not getting the facts with that kind of a question. If you ask a man a question and give them the slightest idea of what kind of answer you expect to hear just because most people are lazy, they do not want to go through too much trouble explaining. They will give you the answer they think you want to hear. You cannot make a proper decision based on tainted answers, you can only make a sound judgment based on pure facts.

I do not know of any virtue or quality in this world that would help a person have better relationship with others more than being an effective, enthusiastic speaker but being a good analytical listener even tops that one.

When considering facts to make major decision in your life, your mind should be an eternal question mark. It's wise to question everything and everyone until you are satisfied that you are only dealing with facts.

Avoid questioning people verbally as much as possible. You can question people silently; in other words, be curious to find things out on your own. If you are too outspoken, you will put people on alert and oftentimes they will attempt to cover up and you cannot get the information you are looking for. Quietly go about seeking information. You can do that by being a good listener because if you just let people talk, they will tell you everything. People like to talk more than they like to listen so be a good listener and an analytical thinker to reach the accurate conclusions.

Science is the art of organizing and classifying facts. When you want to make sure you are dealing with facts, seek scientific sources for testing of those alleged facts whenever possible. True men of science do not have any reason or inclination to modify or change facts, otherwise they would not be real scientists.

I have been seeking facts about my health, happiness, ability to make decisions about my own health, and the growth of my company over the past few years. I have no evidence of any professional giving me any false information. You can use logic in determining the truth of facts because the head is more reliable than the heart, but a good combination would be to seek a balanced approach.

There are a few enemies of your thinking that need to address within yourself. This is where you stand in front of the mirror and face yourself and resolve some of these deep feelings and emotions within yourself. For instance, the emotion of love stands on the head of the list of the enemies of sound thinking and right judgment.

If you have had any love experiences, and I hope you do, you will know exactly what I am trying to convey here. The emotion of love is one of the most powerful influencers that can sway our judgment and lead us to the wrong decisions. In fact, it is like playing around with TNT in one hand and a box of matches in the other hand. When it starts to explode it does not give any notice.

If you question how could love ever to be so explosive in decision-making, you may have not had too much love experiences in your life. It is a fact that the emotion of love can blindside you to the facts and overshadow decisions. Other emotions like hatred, jealousy, revenge, anger, and procrastination are amongst other destructive enemies of sound thinking. Your whole future depends on you thinking accurately and making the right decisions, so you need to have all these emotions under control to be accurate.

A real decision will require the effort of fact finding, discipline, persistence, and the patience to weigh the facts before you decide. Temporary distractions will tempt you and hold you back every day from your main course of action. Distractions are those trivial things your heart wants to do to stay comfortable, and feel momentary pleasures, but discipline is what your brain does to stay in control of your thought processes.

Write Your Goals Down

The willpower to make and stick with a decision can be developed through consistent practice of making decisions. Distractions could be a good starting point to discover the degree of your decision-making willpower. Developing a strong willpower is also a skill that can be developed through a goals program, which we will talk about in the next chapter.

These goals and all other goals require discipline and clear consistent thinking patterns, including the decision to:

- ❖ Live a healthier lifestyle
- ❖ Move and live in another country
- ❖ Start a new business

- ❖ Get married
- ❖ Have or not have children
- ❖ Make an impact with your life.

When you write your goals down, read them to see if it is really what you want, check to see if it resonates with your inner-self. To put a check mark or cross out and replace it with something more suitable is the process of decision-making. This works in your family life, personal life, and professional endeavours as well. You can be more of an asset to your community and a credit to your profession, your company, community, or your industry if you decide to do it.

Goals must have deadlines, or they are just wishes inside our head. It has been my long-term dream to author inspiring educational books but when I decided to write, I wrote the exact date to finish my book. When you put dates on your goals and dreams, you are reverse-engineering your plans. When you have a clear goal on paper, then you work backward to do the work required to get to that ideal outcome in the future.

Once you set your clear written smart goals and visualize them daily, first your brain will reject them like a transplant organ. The brain has not been trained with this kind of thinking, so it rejects the idea at first. Your body is trying to get adjusted to this unfamiliar self-talk. When you submit your goals to your subconscious mind, your brain will reject them until you practice enough so they become part of your thought process.

If you are a lazy person or comfortable where you are, you tend to stay the same. Staying the same is really going backwards because we never stay the same. We are either green and growing or rotting and dying. You are a reader, you are a doer, you are a dreamer, you are an achiever, and that is why you are reading this book.

It becomes easier for your subconscious mind to accept the orders when you think and talk about them on daily bases. This is also the processes of making them real because you are most likely to take steps in the direction of what you think and talk about all day long.

The discipline to educate yourself beyond scope of formal education is an awareness and a decision because this material is not taught through our educational system. You have to be proactive in seeking this essential science.

Jim Rohn said:

"Formal education will make you a living, but self-education will build you a life."

"Know thyself," says the Bible with many verses on the topic, so knowing yourself could be a wise starting point. Make a list of all your strengths, talents, and abilities so you have a clear idea of what is in your toolbox.

Jamaluddin Rumi wisely said, "Let yourself be silently drawn by the strange pull of what you really love. It will not lead you astray." In other words, knowing your inner desires will lead you to the better future.

You may be a good listener, you may be a hard-working person, or a detailed-oriented self-starter, and all these intangible qualities can help you in your advancement.

Educating yourself about yourself helps your brain to find further solutions. Your most critical areas of talent and abilities can be developed. The goal is not to focus on improving only your weaknesses but getting strong at your strengths.

Reading the right books plays an important part in building you self-image and it is such a blessing to learn the discipline of reading books that not only entertain you, but help you rediscover yourself. I have given away hundreds of such books from different mentors and coaches to my own students and family members over the years, whether they read or not is their own decision.

In fact, I love books (worth reading), and if you ever wanted to buy me a gift that I would love for certain, give me an informative book I have not read yet.

J.K. Rowling, the author of the Harry Potter books, once said:

"I do believe something magical happens when you read an informative book."

Great books give us a new perspective on life. You can lead a horse to water, but you cannot make it drink; similarly, the role of mentor is to lead his students to the right books, and whether they read it or not is their own responsibility.

A person that does not read is no better than a person that cannot read. It is time to decide to be the source of good things like good health, harmony in our relationships, good books, and growth-minded amongst friends and family, because you will never be younger, stronger, and more energetic than you are right now. You are smarter because you are reading, and you will be stronger tomorrow because you work out today. Realisation could be as simple as looking around and seeing all failures and simply thinking, "I don't want to end up like that." We can learn as much from failures as we can from successes.

Lack of commitment to reading can have many devastating consequences, like poor health, poverty, and result in many regrets down the road. Making a permanent decision can be based on a revelation, realisation, education, calculation, or simply because of an impactful event in your life.

Data shows that the average forty-year-old American has less than thirteen hundred dollars in the most powerful country in the history of man. Meanwhile there are thousands of books in libraries and bookstores with clear instructions on how to make and save money.

It is no secret that your mindset will eventually determine your future. The missing ingredient in all this talk is discipline. A nation of readers is a nation of leaders, and that is why I am so proud of being a Canadian. I have seen scores of people in libraries and bookstores, the likes of which I have not seen anywhere in the world. A well-educated person makes the right decisions.

At The Homeless Shelter

Back when my daughter was going to grade school one, on Thanksgiving Day we were going to feed the homeless people at a shelter where I stayed the first week I arrived in Canada. A bunch of homeless people were out on Jarvis Street in Toronto. The weather was cold that day. I took my daughter and a bunch of other kids for a ride before heading out to the Red Cross Salvation Army Shelter to distribute the food.

I had a quick conversation with a car full of kids. I told them we are to feed these people but do not be afraid, do not belittle or be ignorant to these people. Most of them are people just like us, but for some reason or another they have made the wrong decisions in their lives. I told them to treat everyone with respect.

I asked them, "Do you have any idea why they ended up here?" Then I continued, "It is mainly their thinking that has conditioned them to make the wrong choices in life." I continued, "Now you see why I expect you to focus on your schoolwork and carefully choose friends that you want to keep for life."

Many of those people were there because they had no means, did not know, or never made the decision to educate themselves, so they got lost in their journey and ended up homeless.

I talked to a few of them the couple of nights when we shared a space when I arrived in Canada back in 1993. I did not know anybody and had no other resources, so I stayed till I could find my way around the city. Some of these people just live like this most of their lives. Your mind is you most important ally, so use it well or it could be your worse enemy if you neglect its development.

I told the kids, "Anyone could end up here."

I continued, "You must focus on your schoolwork and make a decision to develop your talents, abilities, and fulfil your duty to yourself."

To this day my daughter still remembers that conversation because I wanted to make a point out of what we were doing. You do not have to be that dramatic as I was, but that was my story and I wanted to drive a point home and make sure it stuck.

I wanted them to realize the consequences of not making the right decisions. I knew that at that age, focusing on their school education could be the key to shaping their lives in the future. I was making sure that they understood that their destiny was in their own hands not even in their parents, the government, or the school system. An educated decision has many attributes, but self-education is the foundation of all sound decision-making.

The Franklin Method

Big events also have a significant impact on decision-making. Many big companies use events to bring people together and to the point of decision-making to get involved in their cause or business. They create a full agenda for the event to educate the audience by bringing in powerful speakers to give a crash course on any topic related to the business, all just to make a decision.

The ultimate goal is to help the audience in deciding about what they offer. They say big decisions are made in big events. Now that COVID-19 has paralyzed the events business, it is even more important that we have the will power to decide for ourselves.

Sometimes the excitement of a moment in such an event can be electrifying. While in financial services, I was regularly flown to different cities all over North America to give such speeches. I would tell them my story and how I started from the bottom and built the third biggest organization within my company in less than three years, thereby inspiring the audience to decide to join or get involved in the cause.

I told them what to do every day and how to communicate their message to new clients or prospects as clear as possible. I was usually the speaker that lit the fuse and set the room on fire. I was full of enthusiasm, but as I matured as I grew as a speaker. I would have standing ovations that I would bring me to tears, I loved the crowd and they loved me back.

Apart from the stimulation of big events, many big decisions are usually a result of personal awakening or a deep realization. There are simple methods you can use to make small or big decisions.

The Franklin method is the one I use when I am undecided about a particular decision. Benjamin Franklin was one of the founding fathers of the United State of America and America's first millionaire also known to be one of the wisest men in history. He developed and used this method to make important decisions.

He would take a blank sheet of paper and draw a vertical line right in the middle of it. On one side he would list all the pros (positive outcomes) and on the other side he would list all the cons (negative outcomes) of his decision. Then he would add up each side and came to a simple, easy and logical written decision. You may have heard of a pro and con list, but you may not have heard Benjamin Franklin invented it.

You can use the Franklin Method to make some of your important decisions. It is an easy mechanical way that takes emotions out of decision-making. I hope you have already realized how important decision-making could be in building your character and your future.

Finally, it's worthy of note that today there are great opportunities available on a grand scale like never before, but opportunity waits for no man. The person with vision who recognizes opportunity and has the promptness of decision to embrace it will get ahead of the crowd. This is directly related to each person's mental attitude and the ability to identify such opportunities.

A written goals program is the topic of our next chapter. This has had more to do with my quest in the journey of my life than any other idea we have discussed so far. You will need a pen and paper or a highlighter for this chapter. Let us dive into a goals program that has shaped my enter life and change the course of lives of millions of other people.

Chapter 9

The Personal Goals Program

"A goal is a dream with a deadline." (Napoleon Hill)

Only five percent of the of the world's achievers have a written goals program, which is why they know where they are going and how to get there. No matter what they are doing now, they have forward direction for their overall life. A goals program is a step-by-step process of setting, acting upon and accomplishing predetermined worthwhile written goal statements. Many people have the wrong idea about success, thinking it happens to lucky people. It happens to focused people.

All world-class people have a written goals program for their lives.

A goal should be simple and within grasp but big enough to give us a sense of accomplishment and the urgency to take personal initiative.

Winston Churchill said:

"Success consists of going from one failure to another without loss of enthusiasm."

So, aim to make simple, basic incremental improvements to your current situation.

It is a challenge to find a mission, purpose, and goals when you are twelve years old. Your only concern is to go out and hang out with your friends, so you have to find some activity that inspires you, such as music, dance or anything that makes you feel good, and throw yourself into it and start creating goals around what you love.

Consider a wooden pencil. We know that it for it to be a useful pencil, it must go through sharpening repeatedly. If pencils had feelings, you could imagine how difficult it would be, but that is what it takes to be useful. Life is the same. Painful experiences and challenges come along to create the opportunities to help us fine-tune and build our characters and grow.

Bryan Tracey says, "You cannot hit a target you can't see."

Setting goals is the starting point, and it begins with contemplation. Do you have an unclouded vision of what you would like your life to look in three, five or ten years where you would feel, "Wow, this is going great!" We talked about clarity as the starting point of all achievements.

When you sit down and brainstorm your goals and clearly write down your big and small goals, you will start contemplating about achieving them. Consider this chapter your homework, like the type you had in school. You can write down the type of person you want to be, the type of life you want to live, and every other thing that you desire.

Goals are like frequencies. If I dial your phone number, I will be on your frequency. I will not get anyone else on the phone. If I take a picture and send it to your phone somewhere around the world, you will get that picture simultaneously. Thought works the same way. I could be thinking about you, and I can trigger your brain cells and you will start to think of me. This must have happened to you before where you would say," I was just thinking of you." We think in frequencies, and that is how a goals program works.

When you set a goal, you switch your mind to the outcome that you desire. Most people don't decide about goals because they don't know how to get it. You don't have to know how to get it. You decide before you have something or the resources to get it. You make the decision first, and the results follow next. When you make the decision, you flip your brain into higher frequency. Once you are on the new frequency you begin to attract all the resources you need to complete the goal or complete the picture. That is the basis for the law of attraction.

Oddly, if you set a goal that you know how to get done, it's probably not going to work, because if you know how to accomplish it, you are going sideways. You have to go after something when you have absolutely no idea how to do it.

The purpose of a goals program is to grow as a human being while trying to make the goals a reality. There will be a big learning curve there and that is where miracles happen. When setting goals, pick a goal that you really want but have no idea how to do it.

You can only attract based on the frequency that you are operating on. The primary law of the universe is the **law of vibration,** and the secondary law of the universe is the **law of attraction.** When your thinking gets on a certain frequency, you start to attract people and circumstances into your life that are on that frequency. When you think about a person often, sometimes you just bump into them on the street. Or when you think about the kind of people you need to achieve your goals, you get referred to people you never knew to help you get to the object of your desire or your goal.

You can attract what you are in harmony with, but when you set goals, you must see yourself already there. That is called your mindset. You set your mind on the frequency that you have to be in to attract what you desire to bring about. That is how goals get into form. You get emotionally and intellectually involved first before you have it in physical form.

The Personal Goals Program

Setting A Goal To Be Happy

The more focused you are on your goals using your six faculties of creativity, the sooner you will get to the object of your desire. You can put everything that you can think about your future life down on paper in an organized manner and that is the essence of your goals program. Then you can arrange them in the order of importance and priority.

Once you have everything written down, it will be easier to identify the limitations that are standing in your way. Once you are clear about your possibilities and limitations you can move forward to make plans for achieving your SMART Goals. Without written goals, you cannot measure the consequences of your daily actions.

Do you have a vision of the kind of lifestyle you want to live within the next five years? Do you have a vision of how much money you want to earn? Do you have a vision for where you are travelling or your home, your car, for your clothes and for your family, your ideal spouse, or charities that you want to help?

If you do not, do not feel bad. Most people do not have written goals or goals program. In this part we are going to create that vision because when you start to clarify your deepest desires on paper they tend to materialize. Only after you write them down you start to think and talk about those things all the time. A goals program will show you how to get everything that money cannot buy, like your relationships, healthy habits, and mental and physical wellbeing, but also all the things money can buy.

It is now time to put all the principles shared to the test and make them real for yourself. It is time to keep the main thing – to have a balanced life. A goals program will move you from survival to stability, then it will move you from stability to success, and eventually from success to significance. It is a continuous progress program for your life.

When you set goals, a light goes on in your future, and the future always happens to be in front of you. With a clear game plan for your life, you become more confident and focused. The fact is that you cannot be everything to everybody, but a goals program will give you clear path to walk towards what you really want.

A goals program will help you focus on what you want and how to get it. I have researched the answer to this question, "What is it that we all want?"

I have concluded and believe that what everybody wants is to be happy and healthy, have peace of mind, great family relationships, and better hopes for the future. Most people want to love and want to be loved. We all have to deal with the physical, the mental, the financial, the relationships and the spiritual aspects of our lives, so a goals program dissects each of those parts.

The most important question is: can you set a goal to be happy?

The answer is, yes you can. Let me explain by asking you some question and see if you agree with my answers:

- ❖ Do you believe that your health has any bearing at all on your happiness?
- ❖ Are there specific things you can do to improve or destroy your health?

Yes. Your prosperity has to do with your happiness as well, and you can set clear goals about your prosperity and the amount of money you want to make and save.

Sometimes life does get out of balance, like it did during the COVID-19 pandemic, or my brain injury and memory loss. A natural disaster may take life out of balance. It could be that your company downsizes or goes out of business, and that eliminates your job. We have to deal with the reality of life and should be prepared for all those things that could happen to any of us at any time.

If you had a complete goals program, it would take about an hour of your time to develop but could help you prepare for all you want to accomplish in the future. Those unforeseen circumstances of life could be met with a peace of mind and clarity. That is less than the time than you would go for a coffee with a friend or to get a haircut.

The good news is if you have never had a goals program, I will give you the formula and the steps that you can take which will allow you to free up some time. You will find at least ten to twenty-five to hours of extra time each week as a direct result of having a goals program.

So much time slips through your fingers because generally "people that have no goals, or nothing to do, want to do it with you."

Life is tough but when you have a goals program you do not get bogged down with the daily struggles or get tired by the hustle.

Goals Versus Goals Program

You do not just need goals; you need a goals program because everybody has goals. Even a thief has a goal: the goal is to steal without getting caught. The inner-city janitor has a goal: the goal is to work hard to pay the bills and survive.

Since a goals program is not taught in schools, colleges, or universities and our parents do not know about it, most of us don't know about it. If you do not take the steps to learn it independently, your children will not know about it and that is the reason most people do not have a goals program.

When you learn to set one goal, you can set any goal because the formula is the same regardless of the goal. You can plan every event of your life in advance just like you would plan a vacation. You can take a piece of paper or your notebook and follow the formula I am sharing here and check your progress.

You should ask yourself, "Why do I want to be, do, and have these things?"

Your "why" is the engine of your goals program. And if you cannot answer these questions in one sentence, it is not a legitimate goal at that point. Then you need to ask yourself these five questions that are very important:

1. *Is this really my goal?* Is it my goal or did my parents, teachers or other influences of my life tell me what I should do with my life? The goal you set should be yours and based on your inner desires.
2. *Is my goal morally right and fair to everyone involved?* You cannot take advantage of others and climb to the top ladder of success. Your goals have to be morally right.
3. *Is my goal aligned with my other goals?* Can I emotionally commit myself to this goal? Every goal should align and in direction with your other goals.
4. *If I reach all these objectives, will my life be in balance*? The ultimate goal is to have a balanced life and that is the ultimate goal that directs all other goals.
5. *Are my goals categorized properly*? This is to line up your goals based on timelines that you create to hit each goal.

There are short and long-term goals. Short goals are one to three months, intermediate goals are year or less and long-term goals are five years or longer. Some goals much be big and long range, other goals must be small and daily. In time it will manifest in your life. You just don't know what the timeline is, and when you are setting the goal, you guess at the timeline.

Some goals must be ongoing and other goals must be because of consultation, but all goals need to very specific. We must remind ourselves of those things; otherwise, we may have everything happening in five years from now and have nothing going on today. We may have a busy day planned and be so busy in the daily grind that we forget what is going to happen in five years.

Let me give you an example, while in recovery in 2015, I set a goal to run at least twenty-five kilometres every week for the rest of my life and as long as my physical body allows me. I made a commitment, created a daily schedule to do this and have kept up.

This goal is consistent with my health goals and the idea of not seeing a doctor beside my yearly physical check-up. Whether your goal is to raising positive kids, getting a better education, becoming the number one salesperson, losing twenty-five pounds, buying a new home, getting a significant raise or being a better parent, the formula is the same.

A Formula For Goals

If I asked you what three times three was, you would say nine and may think it's a childish question and may even be offended. If I asked you what is 1,971 multiplied by 1,350 you would not be able to give me the answer right away. However, if you get a pen and paper, you can figure out the answer in no time because you know the formula for the multiplication to solve such a problem.

Goal-setting has a formula that you can apply to any goal,

similar to a mathematics problem that you are able to solve with the formula you already know. When you know the formula for setting one goal, you will know the formula to set and accomplish any realistic goal. I will be giving you that formula right in the chapter but before I do that, let me caution you about something that is very important. The question is:

"Who do you share your goals with?"

If it is a *'give up'* goal, you share it with everybody. For example, If I want going to give up smoking or going to give up drinking, or lose twenty-five pounds, I am going to give up these things and you get encouragement from others. You share you *give up* goals with everybody who encourages and helps you to firm up your commitment, but your *'go up'* goals you want to share very specifically and carefully.

If your goal is a *go up* goal, you would only share it with the people who support you and have your absolute best interests at heart. For instance, you share an educational goal with your teachers and mentors, you share a sales goal with your directors, and you share a professional goal with your master mind group.

Let me clarify it with an example here. If you are going to set a goal to be the number one in sales in your company and share this goal with your colleagues who are also doing the same work, obviously you will not get support and may even have people sabotage your goals.

SMART Goals

Write your goals carefully based on the formula I will reveal here and list all the obstacles that you must overcome to reach those goals. Your brain looks for ideas and creates patterns that are consistent with the achievement of your written goals.

This helps you identify people, resources, and organizations to work with in achievement of your written goals, create a plan of action and set a date for their accomplishment. Follow the specific steps I am sharing with you here and you will be able to save months and even years of frustrating effort and move with confidence in the directions of your goals.

Data shows that over eighty percent of college graduates are earning their living in a field completely unrelated to what they studied while in college ten years after graduation. Think about what it would have meant if, as youngsters, a parent or school councillor learned and thought this formula on how to set small daily goals and gradually extended them for to longer-term goals. It would have saved years of trial and error and help them move faster in the direction of where they would eventually be headed and find out where their true passions lay.

The best acronym I found for GOALS that I have found is that Godly Objectives Assure Lasting Success. Here is the formula on how to set these objectives. When you set those goals, you are taking a big step in getting there. Let us talk about those goals and how to set, hit, and enjoy them.

As far as creation of any sort is concerned, I always work in **90-day periods** for my short-term goals. I call them **seasonal goals** like the changing seasons. **long-term** goals could be yearly goals, three, five years and there are **lifetime goals**. This is how I set my SMART goals. I will give you clear examples of how you write them down.

A goal is a predetermined worthwhile objective we are trying to achieve, and a goals program has a formula just like in mathematics. Let me break down SMART goals for you like this. Each symbol stands for a specific purpose that will help your memories and clarify each of your goals.

S = **Specific**. The more details you write down, the better and clearer your goals become. You should write down every detail you can think of in your brainstorming session.

M = **Measurable**. You need to be able to measure on your progress on 7, 21 and 90 days. This will help you measure your progress along the way.

A = **Attainable**. You are physically and financially able to use enough skills and abilities to achieve the goal. Your goals should be within your realm of your abilities and talents.

R = **Relevant** and Realistic. They must be your goals, not your parents' goals, and aligned with your purpose in life. Your goals should be yours and yours only, not what others have told you that you should do.

T = **Timely**. You need dates, times and other specific for each goal. Your subconscious mind loves deadlines. Timelines give you a specific time in the future to complete each goal like and exam date that you prepare for in school.

The Blue-Sky Method

So, you want to set these SMART goals, but you do not know how to get started. You may have the desire but do not know where to start. There is a part of your brain called the left prefrontal cortex that is the GPS of your brain. That is the part that helps you load and lock onto goals like an archer with a bow and arrow looking at the bullseye. Your major definite purpose in life should be that bullseye and your goals are all the circles around it. By activating the visual frontal cortex of your brain with your vision, you activate the motivational part of your brain and its motor engine. Doing this is relatively easy.

Let me give you a simple method I have employed for my kids and that is what I practice my seven-year-old son. We called it

The Blue-Sky Method, also conceived by Bryan Tracey.

We have a big grass field and playground close by in Toronto. Gabriel and I go there often, and sometimes on nice sunny afternoons we lay down on the grass on our back, look up the sky and see if we can find shapes in the clouds and close our eyes and dream up things and talk about it.

Most of us have tried this as children. When we get older this visualization method is forgotten. It is the simplest way I know to dream up what is it that you mostly desire and want to happen in your life. In the New Testament it is said:

"If you want to enter the kingdom of heaven, you must become like a child."

By using the Blue-Sky Method, you can awaken your inner-child to reactivate your imagination.

I used this method when I was thirteen to dream up living in Canada. I did not set a date as I was not aware of this wisdom, but it was just a simple natural way to think ahead. I had a burning desire for what I wanted and years later I did achieve that goal as a testament of the power of the subconscious mind.

When using my creative mind, I personally prefer nature. You can choose anywhere you feel comfortable, close your eyes, and try to imagine your ideal life with every detail. This is the simplest method I have found that you can use to get your mental engine started on figuring out what you really want in life. Ask yourself if you were happy in your life, you would want to have happened the most. Start from that first image when you close your eyes.

Take ten to fifteen minutes to really think things through, then take a pen and paper start your new life story as you want it to unfold. Then write your ideas down. When writing down your smart goals the must follow the 3P formula.

1. **Positive:** Your subconscious mind only accepts positive commands. I have gone through detail in the previous chapters on how to keep your mind positive.
2. **Present:** Your goals must be written in the present tense. This helps you make it as real as possible and pay attention to the feeling of having accomplished it.
3. **Personal:** Your goals must be yours personally not your spouse's, parents' goals, or anyone else's. Often, we think our goals are what others want from us, but goals are very personal and must be yours only.

Your subconscious mind is like a command center that *only accepts a written goal* in the format explained above. Your mind only accepts positive, present, and personal goals. This is so simple and easy, but what is simple and easy to do is also easy not to do, and that is why 97% of people choose the latter, and never create their goals.

Your goals must be as clear as possible because clarity is the key in goal-setting. The more the details, the better chances of achieving them because you are breaking it down to every detail. The clearer the goal, the easier it becomes for the subconscious mind to accept and start working on them.

Furthermore, all your goals start with the word "I" because you are the only person in the world that can use the word "I" in relationship to yourself. Nobody can call you "I," only you can do that. Let me give you a few examples so you can follow while writing your own goals. This is how you would write your goals as follows:

❖ I am so happy and grateful that I am earning $100,000.00 a year by December 30, 2022.

Or

❖ I am happy and grateful live in Istanbul Turkey by Jan.01.2021 and spending valuable time with my parents.

Or

❖ I am happy and grateful to run twenty-five kilometres a week starting Jan 01, 2016.

Or

❖ I am so happy and grateful to interview 25 top achievers on my YouTube channel by December 25, 2022.

These are some simple go-up goals and the most relevant goals that I have had and that I pursue using this formula. Your subconscious mind loves deadlines and works best when you tie up all lose ends by giving them the deadlines.

If you are wondering if my goals program works, all you need to do is to test it out for yourself. When you do the right programming of your subconscious mind, the mind will work on it while you sleep as you practice these methods before you fall asleep every night. You will realize that it may not be easy but if you follow the instructions given here you will have a clear direction for your future.

You can measure to see how far you have come from this starting point. When you use my seven, twenty-one and ninety-day habit-building formula explained earlier, you have a measurement formula to use to access your progress. You have nothing to lose and everything to gain by putting these simple instructions to use.

The vibration of your thoughts and your mental attitude will start to change if you use the visualization techniques explained and practice it for seven consistent days. It is miraculous when

I look back at some of the things that I wrote down in my notebooks.

I write down and read my top seven goals and meditate on them every night before I fall asleep and think of solutions and obstacles, I may come up against a counter-force on the way to realizing the goal. I may encounter unforeseen obstacles on the way to achieving my goals, but when you consider all your obstacles, you discover the solutions to around those obstacles. The subconscious mind never sleeps while the conscious mind is asleep, and the subconscious will work on creating thought patterns and finding solutions for the achievement of your programmed desires and goals.

One Brick At A Time

My actions each day are consistent with the achievement of my goals and finding solutions to the obstacles that I need to overcome. I think about how to get them most of the day. I build my life one goal and one action at a time. When you set goals, you are building your life one brick at a time. I am not saying that it will be easy for you or anyone to do this, but I am saying that if I can do it, I believe anyone can do it. Realizing your dreams is a marathon, not a sprint, so be patient with your results but impatient with your daily activity.

You have already the will to overcome many obstacles in your life and quitting on your goals and dreams will never make your life any easier, significant, or impactful. Start setting some bigger goals because there is magic in that.

Start using these laws to draw people and circumstances you are seeking by means of goals setting and visualization. You must be the scout of your own life, find out what is possible for you, and find some new things to get excited about. Go after what you really want because we only live this life once. It is not easy, but it is beautiful to find purpose in this lifetime. No challenge is too big when you work from purpose, and often you go right from purpose to profits in no time.

I want to caution you here because the conscious mind is naturally negative and if you have not trained your mind to be receptive to such ideas, it may reject some or all the ideas share here because the mind is primarily a survival mechanism. It will reject these ideas and give you all kinds of reasons and excuses why it's not possible for you to achieve them.

I know most people have no written goals or goals program and there are certain reasons for it. These are four basics reason people do not have a solid goals program:

1. **Fear:** Fear is only False Evidence Appearing Real, but if it appears real to you, then it's real for you.
2. **Poor self-image:** Lack of confidence and growth mindset about achieving goals so we overlook its importance.
3. **Never been told about a goals program:** Ignorance is a curse, as my grandmother said so wisely, so learn and practice.
4. **Do Not Know How:** A goals program is only offered through the care and passion of coaches and mentors in higher levels of performance, so most people have no access to such information or support.

We are not taught this incredibly impactful skill and information anywhere. I was lucky to learn this life-changing program from some of the world-renowned thinkers, philosophers, and mentors of the past and present. I am not doing my work to get your attention but gain your respect and make an impact in the lives of those who are willing and have the desire to make changes in their own lives.

One day, if I am lucky, my name may appear in your testimonials as someone who provided you with the guidance in the direction of your goals and aspirations. That would be the biggest achievement of my life.

When you have a goals program you become optimistic and confident, as my example in the previous paragraph shows. Confidence is a good thing; however, let us not allow people (even ourselves) to delude themselves into thinking they can do things they cannot. Confidence is based on reality, not delusion.

Most people live all their lives the way they never want to live or always are looking for something out of reach. This is because they do not know how to design and develop their own lives through a goals program, so they are satisfied living in the mundane or confusion. I am offering you the chance to learn this simple yet powerful process by adopting this goals program.

Start by picturing your ideal life in five years. Five years is long enough to see it coming and make real progress, but also the event and progress of the last five years close by so you can look back and see how it has gone.

Those who have a goals program are futuristic, versus the rest who think and talk about the good old days. The past is only your experience to use as a torchlight, not a gateway in communication. Your knowledge and connections are dead if you do not use them to improve your tomorrow. Nothing but good lessons can come from the past so focus on the future through a goals program and you will have a much better chance of achieving them.

Start by thinking if your life were perfect in every aspect, what would it look like in five years in these areas:

- ❖ Where would you be living?
- ❖ What would you be doing?
- ❖ Who would you be associating with?
- ❖ What would your health be like?
- ❖ How much money would be making, or would you have saved?

You can follow this formula for your goals program to create a blueprint for your future so you can design it exactly the way you would like it to be. It is like going on a vacation, you must decide where you are going before you pack your bags. Visualize your ideal life and write it down in as much detail as possible as a starting point.

Reprogram yourself in a ninety-day visualization program. The process of mentally rewiring yourself is a lifelong process, but a seven, twenty-one and ninety-day practice will transform your life. If you think ninety days is too long to commit to your improvement, consider a lifetime of lack, scarcity, and struggles, and it will become really easy. Take it one step at a time. The first and easiest step is to visualize that ideal life every night before you fall asleep for the next seven days straight.

Seven days practice will turn it into a daily habit. Close your eyes and focus on the image of your perfect life in your mind and bring it to the movie screen of your mind like a camera lens by focusing those ideal life images. Once you fall asleep your subconscious mind will work on the actions you need to take to make it real when you awake each day. It feels like magic as I experience these kinds of hunches every single day.

See, feel, and smell every detail of that ideal life by holding the images in your mind as long as you can. The more you think about it, the more pieces of the puzzle will fall into place. Every night you will be able to see new images and more details of your ideal life will emerge. As more ideas and images emerge you can revise and prioritize your goals as you go along.

When you do this, your subconscious mind works on those images overnight. The next day you will start getting ideas, phone calls and clues on what to do next. In fact, that is what I am doing for the next ninety days for the written goals I have created for the next season of my own life.

It works in small incremental steps, but it works like magic. It has worked for millions of people around the world as mentioned before, so do not be lazy here. It's your whole life you are trying to change. One such small step is to look into the mirror and greet yourself with a "Good morning."

Then you should write down your top seven goals every morning on a piece of paper just to remember what you are going after this day. Throughout the day, whenever you get a chance, read, and review them or when you are feeling low energy review them. Then get to work on taking steps towards achieving the goals you have written and just read. Be open to divine intervention and expect miracles in your life. Always be open to guidance and be alert to all clues and hunches that come your way.

Act Like The Person You Want To Become

When you set out and start your day, begin acting as the person you want to become, not the person you were yesterday. If you want to be that person, then act like him or her right now. Do you want to be the CEO of your own company? Then act like one right now. This is your training and a check to see how badly you really want that life.

Start going to places you want to be and more importantly associate and collaborate with the people who will support you in your ideal life. People who want to see you successful and prosperous are your best ally, and if you think you have nobody like that, let me tell you that you do.

Your mother, if she is alive, will always support you in your dreams. Your mother always has believed in you. Talk to your mother whether she has passed away or is alive, and let her remind you how smart, talented, and beautiful you are. We all love our mothers and that is the greatest support system nature has given us.

A goals program gives you the power to carry out your decisions. Most people carry their cage wherever they go by associating with people who do not support them. Break free from other people's ways and judgments. If a person does not support you, appreciate your effort and value your presence, I would not even think about or associate with them. If they do not impact your bottom line, I would not even consider thinking about their opinion. Let things and people who weigh you down go so you can move around with ease and comfortable in your own skin.

Most people say, "I will do all that as soon as I have the support, the money, the job, or the opportunity." You don't need any of those things until after you have made the decision that you want those things. We have talked about decision-making in previous chapters to help you increase and solidify your decision-making skills.

You do not need the job until you make the decision that you want that job. When you deeply decide, everything changes. We are talking about a part of your brain that is still unexplored, the part of us we do not understand and that most do not feel comfortable talking about. Stop making excuses and take a serious look at your life, read this book or other books on the subject repeatedly to really grasp the ideas presented.

No matter how big or small your aspirations, unless you make a clear decision nothing major will happen. The most important thing you can do is to decide to change!

President John F. Kennedy asked Dr. Werner Von Braun, the man who engineered the first NASA space program:

"What will it take for us to send a man to the moon and bring him back safely?"

The short answer was: "The decision to do it, Mr. President."

Let us say your goal is to double your income. If it is, I have good news for you. If you earn a 3% or 4% raise each year at your current job, which is about the average rate of inflation in North America, it will take you 20 years to double your income. But who has 20 years to wait? So, the real question you should be thinking about is: "How fast can I double my income?"

There are many ways to double and quadruple your income but the most practical way to double your income is through a goals program. It is simple, fast, effective, and takes the guess-work out of the equation. It is guaranteed to work if you put it to practice and have the discipline to follow through with commitment to the work required to complete the job. This works in all areas of your life. Once you make the commitment to your goals, you will need the discipline and challenging work required to get you there. This reprogramming of your subconscious mind is not an easy task, especially if it goes against your existing beliefs and values. It requires discipline, a plan of action and the will to follow through on your decisions.

This chapter particularly is of essential importance because of the instructions you have about your goals program. If you do not get anything else out of this book, take away the principles of goal setting and follow them for 7, 21 and 90 days and assess your progress. You will see the difference in your areas of concern.

Like all our products that we offer at our company, the value of the information you get here is also guaranteed. Quality is a lifestyle, not just a product. Continuous change can be overwhelming in a rapidly changing world; therefore, if you want to change your life you must set SMART goals.

We can no longer afford to walk around as generalities. Have I said it enough times yet? You know that I have put enough reliable content and research in this book to be honest and blunt with you.

Goals & Principles

Here is another blunt assessment. A man enters the world and leaves traces behind everywhere he goes so be memorable, make sure you are leaving a good trace behind wherever you go. Have the courage to live according to your ideals and principles. Principle-based conduct makes you more trustworthy, reliable, and committed to your word. Your principles are the set of ideals that never change.

Do not worry about the opinion of others except those of your mentors and coaches. Be real with yourself. You should be the same person with your parents, children, and everyone else as well as the man in the mirror. Most people are so many different people based on what they are trying to accomplish. In front of their children, they may be a loving father or parent, and in the workplace, they may be a gangster. This example may be far too extreme, but I'm sure you get the point.

When people talk to you, they should know exactly who they are talking to. Nobody should be guessing who you might be based on your mood or temperament. They should not be thinking, "Oh boy, let's see what mood he is in today." Be consistent in your conduct so people know how to approach you.

Answer these kinds of questions for yourself:

❖ Are you known as a cheerful or grumpy person?
❖ Are you timely or always late?
❖ Are you known to be a committed person?
❖ Are you iffy or reliable?

All these traits are describing our code of conduct. I know people who take hours before you can have a meaningful conversation with them each morning. Their brain just is asleep while they walk around like zombies. Discipline will help you iron out all these character deficiencies. What you have is a result of your past residue, and what you want could be is the result of your discipline.

You are the master of your destiny. Do not let others sway you from what you really want. Most importantly do not allow yourself to sway yourself from what you want. Millions of people like you and I have used these principles and have changed their lives, and there is always room for one more. That person could be you.

Be clear about your goals and get serious about your goals program. Learn how to use the power of your subconscious mind. Cleanse your mind of anxiety, worry and stress, and you can do it all through this goals program.

Think and talk about your written goals all day long, in your conversations and phone calls and see how you feel. Be future-focused while living your current life. You can double your income in one year, you can move to a different country in the same period. You can start a new business and move in a different direction with your goals program.

You need to clarify, what, where, who, and when, then you will get to work on the *how*. All you require is the decision to make it happen like the answer to President Kennedy about going to the moon.

Your True Heart's Desire

So many times, we have these so-called goals that are not so smart. They are not aligned with your real desire or not even a possibility for you to achieve them. I do not want you to be disappointed, or sound negative, but you need to know the difference between illusion and reality.

Let me give you a clear example, no matter how often you go on hiking trips, you will find it hard to enjoy them if what you are really interested in is swimming. Likewise, if you are strongly drawn to learning Spanish but are forcing yourself to study architectural design instead, you are not likely to drive a deep sense of fulfilment from your studies.

Our true talents are hidden within the areas of our interest. Those are the things our hearts are most strongly drawn to. For instance, I work really hard at my business and focused on my writing. In fact, my partners tell me numerous times; "You are the hardest-working man we know." Indeed, I do work hard, but I am on a mission. I love to teach and guide, and I want to make an impact on the lives of other people.

It is in my nature to work hard, I like to focus on things that make me happy, which is serving others, but I do enjoy variety in my personal life and professional work. I am also very naturally drawn to writing and teaching. I love the English language because it's simple, and highly effective in driving the exact point home.

You are naturally drawn to your areas of interest, so use that as a leverage to move things along on the right direction where you will find your true purpose. Begin by choosing an area of interest that you absolutely love and want to spend time developing. It is something you love to do when you are alone in your spare time. It is playing a sport or learning a new language, playing a specific video game.

Yes, even a video game. A young friend of mine, someone I have known since he was a small boy, loved video games from the time he was a child. While other kids were chasing the ball at the park, this kid was mesmerized by video games. He played them for entertainment after school after doing his homework. He did not enjoy academics as much as I did, but he had his own potential he was able to tap into early in life.

When he was a teenager, he got involved in hosting online gaming and before he was twenty, he got involved in hosting a network that facilitated tens of thousands of players from around the world. Now still in his early twenties, he travels the world with his gaming friends while hosting one of the biggest networks in the gaming industry. He really enjoys his work and make a handsome income from doing what he loves. He works hard and enjoys the rewards of his challenging work loving what he likes to do.

So, no matter what you do, begin by choosing an area of interest that you absolutely love, where you spend ample time submerged in the creative activity. According to Zig Ziglar, there are fifty thousand ways of making an income in North America.

There are so many ways to make money and be successful, yet

most will stick with one or two choices in their entire career and most fail at it. It can be anything if you love spending time doing it. If you are fascinated by your work where you dive-in headfirst then there is an opportunity arising.

They say if a business stays alive for more than three years straight you can turn it into a solid career or thriving business. Why three years? Because that is long enough to see if you stick with it or lose interest along the way. If you just started something to make money, it was not really a passion, but a survival means.

When I worked for one the world's largest transportation companies in Toronto, by the fourth year in the hub where I was finally stationed, I was getting bored. Eventually I resigned from that job and pursued something different.

Three years is ample time to develop your true talents in any area. You will be able to reach a level that is close to that of a professional or at least a semi-professional in any field. The top ten percent of any field make ninety percent of the money in that field. If you really want to make a lot of much money in a profession you have to be top ten in your category or career.

So, choose a career that you have a chance or the perseverance to be the best at what you do. I have many friends in the real estate industry, some live off their income comfortably, many more are struggling agents, but a very few make tons of money in real estate. Guess why it is, that so few make the most money?

- ❖ They are really good at what they do.
- ❖ They listen to audio programs about sales and marketing from experts.
- ❖ They improve their communication skills.
- ❖ They are usually active in their communities.

❖ They are usually multilingual (learning) and very personable.

These are all the qualities that I have highlighted as leading to success. Other agents just run around keeping busy trying to drum up some business while no one hears their drums. Those that hear them have no money to do business with them. And furthermore, the Internet has changed the game, if you are genuine, you will find the right people, or they will find you. Especially if you are an expert and have followed a goals program to become one.

Be The Expert

The human mind is naturally inclined to seek a wide range of interests, which makes it difficult to limit ourselves to just one area. To be successful in any field, we must widen our horizons but focus like a laser in that one area and become the authority in that field.

Be the expert at anything because money is the reward for expertise. The question is:

"How long will you be able to patiently maintain focus in your area of interest?"

Do you have the discipline to stay focused or while change course when challenges arise?

When we started The Camel Company of Canada, it was only an idea. I started to become interested in the animal itself, then I found out about the benefits of camel wool and milk, then I read about the characteristics of the animal. It fascinated me tremendously. I did so much reading on the animal that I saw camels everywhere.

Then we started to chase camels up and down the deserts in

Africa, the Middle East, and eventually Mongolia, and finally by this time the research came out that the camel was indeed originally Canadian. Yes, you read it right! Camels originated from the Canadian Arctic.

I am considered, if not the number one expert in camel research, the top ten globally. When building our clientele, we took an educational approach in building a customer base. The animal was unknown in so many ways, so new to many that they had only seen it in the movies or in a zoo, so it took us seven years to step into the next stage of our business.

COVID-19 brought things to a halt where it provided me with the opportunity to put this writing together, but I am still pursuing my business and I have another book written.

What will you do when challenges arise? How will you handle them?

A good question to think about because eventually most business and individuals will hit a bump or plateau. A goal program definitely helps you stay focused, but you will need more than that. You will need to develop leadership skills and leadership is all about personal initiative.

Let us look at how taking personal initiative means to be a leader of your life and business.

Chapter 10

Personal Initiative

**"Initiative is doing the right thing, without being told."
(Elbert Hubbard)**

What is going to bring more health, joy, gratitude, and effectiveness in this world is taking personal initiative and the study of the topic of your interest.

We cannot leave life to the element of chance. We need to train ourselves to act upon the knowledge we learn. A great purposeful life requires continuous directed action. Whatever the circumstances may be, personal initiative is the starting point of all accomplishment in life.

Taking personal initiative is to apply and use the principle of applied faith. We know that there are two ways to use "applied faith." The first is what most people do which is to put their mind in the reverse gear. We use it in a negative way by allowing your mind to dwell upon the circumstances and the things you do not want such as poverty, poor health, failure, and defeat. This phenomenon leads to procrastination, which is the killer of dreams and the opposite of taking personal initiative. That is why most people go through life with misery and want.

The second way of using applied faith is when you take personal initiative and take possession of our minds and direct it to the circumstances we want to create or the things we want to have. Allow me to remind you that every man comes with the ability to direct his own minds in any direction he desires. If you have been neglecting this principle, it is time to learn how to do it and apply this habit daily so it can serve you all the days of your life.

History is filled with those who almost did it. Those who almost adventured, those who almost invested, those who almost achieved. For them, it proved to be too much to handle, too hard to overcome, or too impossible to learn. Then there are others, the ones who embrace the moment, commit, and take personal initiative. Those who begin without being asked. The main difference between successes and failure in any endeavour is our capacity for the belief to see new opportunities in every challenge in life.

In that decisive moment, these men, and women who, like you and I, are mere mortals but peer over the edge of fear, laziness, and incompetence, steel their nerves with four simple words that have been whispered by the intrepid since the time of the Romans:

"Fortune favors the brave."

This short section is the action producing part of the philosophies and the most important goal of this writing because nothing happens until something moves. It is the action we take to start using all the values and philosophies that will make a change in our lives. This book would not have any value to anyone if you did not take any action after reading it. What you want to accomplish is only possible by you personally taking some sort of action.

The action you take is the starting point of materializing all these instructions, otherwise nothing that is said here will do much good for you. I try to educate, enlighten, and entertain in my writing, but its main aim is getting my reader to take some action through their own personal initiative.

I do not need to remind you of the importance of your major definite purpose, which I have done, because obviously if you did not have an overall objective in life, you would not have too much personal initiative. One of the most important goals of having a major definite purpose is to explore what we can accomplish or what impact we can make over a lifetime but let us start by finding out what you can accomplish for the remainder of this year.

Let us not set your goal too high and too far in the distance. However, if you have some highlights for this year, you could review them at the end of this year and measure your progress, then check to see how far you have come and to set another one-year, three-year or a five-year goal that you can follow and track.

Your first step is to find out where you are going and how you are going to get there. Most importantly why you are going in a certain direction and what you want to get out of it financially and in other terms. Most people could be successful if they just find out how much success they want and in what terms they want to evaluate success.

Success is the progressive realization of a worthwhile ideal. If a man works toward a predetermined goal and knows where he is going, that man is a success. If not, he is a failure. Failure is conformity, which is people acting like everyone else. The schoolteacher who truly wanted to become a teacher is a success, because that is what she wanted to do. A success is a mother who takes care of her children and is doing a good job at it. A success is someone who becomes a storekeeper because that is what he wanted to do. A success is a top salesman that wants to record all the sales records in his company. A success is anyone who is doing a predetermined job because that is what he wants to do.

I am a success in my own right in many fronts because I have long been doing what I want to do. I make conscious decisions to follow certain outcomes in my life. I'm most proud because I decided to spend valuable time with my parents when I realized this may be the last chance to do it

Think about what you want to do to create success in your life.

There are a lot of people in the world who want to have a respectable position and a lot of money, but they do not know what kind of position, how much money they want and how to get it?

An adequate motive to act continuously in pursuit of your major definite purpose is necessary. You need to evaluate yourself carefully to see if you have an adequate motive to do what you are doing.

You need a motive or multiple motives, and I believe the more motives you have, the easier it will be to take personal initiative. Your motives will not let you quit or give up on your dreams. Normal people move only on motives and the stronger the motive, the more active they become on their own personal initiative.

The Workshop Of Miracles

You do not have to have a lot of brains in this world to succeed or be financially well-off. You do not even have to be so brilliant or have a wonderful education. We all know the stories of college dropout millionaires, but you do need to take whatever little you know and apply it. Application is the workshop of the ministry of miracles. Use your wisdom in operation, do something about it. All this calls for a personal initiative.

From those early years under the watchful eye of my mother and grandmother, I learned principles of discipline and motive. My father, like his father, was either away fighting in some cause, exiled, or running away from the troubles that Kurds were facing in the sixties, seventies, and eighties in the Middle East.

I love my father, but he was not around too much until he was exiled to Tehran, the capital of Iran, where we really bonded when I was a teenager. We had lots of fun, going to film festivals and events together, and meeting some incredible people. I was learning from all his experiences as the two of us lived together alone for several years.

I learned that it is the quality of time you spend with your children that matters, not just the amount of time you spend together. Most average families may spend time in the same house watching a lot of TV together but there is truly little learning or teaching going on under those circumstances.

I was a shy introverted boy, but I observed everything that was going around me. Later, I had to learn to be more enthusiastic. The first step in creating enthusiasm is having a burning desire to do something. When you want something really bad, you make up your mind to get it. You step up your enthusiasm to do what you mostly want to make it happen. A burning desire backed by a motive makes people persistent and enthusiastic. It forces one to develop the discipline to develop the persistence that requires personal initiative.

I have always had a vividly controlled and directed imagination for what I wanted to happen. That is a quality that still drives me to go further than I have ever been as I take a new direction in the middle of the pandemic.

Imagination is a marvelous thing, but if you do not have it under control and direct it, it may be dangerous to you. Uncontrolled imagination for the wrong things may be extremely dangerous, as we see people with uncontrolled wild imagination fill the penitentiaries all over the world. Most of them are sitting in the prison cells because they had too much of an uncontrolled imagination not directed at the right things.

One of the tenets of personal initiatives is to direct your energy and make firm definite decisions. When you have all the facts and can clearly analyse them you can make firm decisions promptly. If you do not have the habit of making decisions promptly and definitely, I doubt you could go too far in life. If you are unable to make firm decisions and stick with them, you are destroying chances and opportunities that come your way. Decisions come from discipline.

Discipline Is Initiative

You must protect your character. That is who you are and what makes you unique. Some people see how hard I work, and when I run most morning, they think that it is strange to have this solid discipline. Make no mistake, I would never run those miles to impress anyone but myself. That is how I keep my personal initiative in check.

My morning routine is part of my character and the healthy habits I have developed, based on taking personal initiative. Your discipline could be your creativity time. I love to listen to uplifting music when I am running. It's like my brain spins wheels as my legs start to move. I enjoy walking or running because it's one of the simplest, cheapest, and most effective ways to stay healthy if you develop the discipline and the personal initiative to do it. It has everything to do with pure unadulterated discipline that will save you thousands of dollars in doctor visits and medication. Discipline can save you from the fires of your own personal hell and the walls you build around your abilities. All these disciplines require personal initiative.

The COVID-19 pandemic was a perfect example of why it is so

important to always be training to stay healthy. A well-disciplined mindset allows you to handle every punch life throws at you. None of us are exempt from life's unexpected screw-ups and misfortunes. You might get that call in the middle of the night with unexpected news that says a loved one has just passed away, or hear one day that you are being let go from your job, etc. What discipline can do for you in those disappointing moments of life, nothing else can. Emotional discipline can help you stay composed and have control over your emotions in moments of distress. You do not have time to sit on your couch and wallow in self-pity. You must be able to go back to your corner and regroup for your next move and develop the discipline to handle those tougher moments of life.

It's not always easy to stay focused. Sometimes you work so hard and get no results to show for, no recruits, no sales, no followers, and no clients. In these times the tendency of human nature would be to feel self-pity and low energy and eventually quit. It's chaos inside your head, you doubt if you were made for this, and you think of quitting. All of that is a test of nature to see the strength of your character and development of your personality. Doubts start to creep into your mind and the devil starts to use his shiny little wedge, widening the gap between your abilities and possibilities. When you are prepared to handle all circumstances of life, nothing will derail you.

The average person gives up and make excuses and creates alibis about why they could not do it while a disciplined person takes a break, recharges, and prepares for the next round, with humor. When people express negativity about what you are doing, give them a silly answer and move on. Use humor to your advantage and everything sounds even more fun until results show up to prove them wrong.

If you do what is required to generate results, they will show up. To be in a constant state of joy you will need to train your mind by practicing some simple disciplines that develop personal initiative. My body does not tell me what to do, I tell my mind and body what we are doing. I am in control of my thinking and the activities of my body.

Those who find purpose in life live happier, longer lives; thus, happiness is an inside job. We always need something to live for, even more so as we get older. Age in my mind is truly a number and it's your thinking habits that determine your health and wellbeing. You cannot shirk from this personal self-care responsibility, and when you find purpose in your work, your profession, or your company, you don't want to shirk. You act every day through personal initiative, and you become an unstoppable force of nature; without enthusiasm, there is no initiative.

Lack Of Enthusiasm Is Lack Of Initiative

Many lose enthusiasm in life because they lack a sense of direction, drifting aimlessly through life, hoping, wishing, and sitting down praying for things to happen. Lack of enthusiasm can be caused by a wide range of things. It may vary from person to person, but no matter what the cause is, I have a great suggestion for you. Firstly, think about what is causing your lack of enthusiasm. Think about the person, the feeling or thought process that gives you that sagging feeling. Second, do something about it. Once you find out what is causing your lack of motivation which is draining your enthusiasm, do something to change it.

Take a nap, go for a walk, meditate, or simply call up someone you love and tell them how much you love and appreciate them. This will often change that sagging feeling inside your heart and reenergize you. One very tangible way to change your lack of enthusiasm overall is to set goals and enroll in a goals program. Big or small goals give you direction and purpose. Having direction in life is very motivational; moreover, it helps you develop the mindset to take personal initiative in everything you do. Anything that has direction has motion and directed motion restores enthusiasm. With some direction, you will find the steps in your feet again. You simply walk faster, talk louder, and smile more often. Those are the three visible signs of an enthusiastic person.

If you want to improve your health, for instance, taking personal initiative is a major step. I suggest starting with small achievable goals. As small as walking for 15-30 minutes a day all by yourself. Sometimes we set such huge goals that the mere fact of impossibility if achieving them make us immobile and depressed. Even such a small act as getting a haircut can give you a feeling of happiness which can be used to increase your enthusiasm.

Remember, Rome was not built in one day, but they did lay bricks every day. When you lack enthusiasm, remember the feeling of accomplishment and the taste of success. I am sure you know how that feels, because everyone experiences these moments at some point in their lives. If you take the next step through personal initiative, make one more phone call or do something physical for someone else, I am certain your enthusiasm will be restored. You can get your feeling of excitement back again.

Enthusiasm can be shared to communicate ideas using proper language that can move people. It does not matter where you are in life because your next move is what counts the most. Personal initiative requires consistency and when you act consistently, you develop the quality of resilience or grit. We will see how to develop more grit in the next chapter.

Chapter 11

Resilience – Develop Grit

**"Grit is living life like it's a marathon not a sprint."
(Angela Lee Duckworth)**

Guess how many times the average person fails before they are crowned with success? Many. Failures are usually the lack of capacity for belief. How many times can you try before you see the ghost and quit? Why do not you start by developing a mastermind around you that believes in you even more than you do in yourself.

You should recognize that you can take full control of your mind and you must have the perseverance to go through the test of applied faith before you achieve anything substantial in life. You can do anything within reason if you develop the quality of grit and apply the principle of applied faith and keep your mind directed at certain objective.

I do not believe achievement only means financial gain. A successful person is a wholesome being, a human being in control of the faculty of his mind and heart. He is an empathetic thinker. His health is intact, and his mind lives inside a healthy body.

A healthy body can be trained through the power of habit. Habits are those powerful forces that shapes one's destiny. Grit combined with discipline builds the habit of becoming unstoppable in whatever you do. In your health, like your wealth building effort, you need to develop discipline and resilience.

All my life I have been an enthusiastic fan of studying stories of successful men and women of all backgrounds and settings.

I found out that most successful people are hero-worshippers of some sort. They are also the ones that broke the norm and got away from the masses and creating something unique that most often outlasts their own existence.

My questions always were:

"Who are these people?"

"How did they think?"

"What were their habits, routines, and procedures?"

Nido Cuban, the Lebanese American businessman and life coach, says:

"Success leaves tracks."

I followed their tracks to learn their behaviors and mindset, and eventually I set out to acquire the skills required to create my own pathway in life. I explored if it was possible for people like me to adopt, learn and adapt some of those traits and create my own everlasting story.

The more I researched, the more I learned about the process they followed. It became evident that one characteristic emerged as a significant indicator of their success. It was not their education level, social intelligence, their family status, connections, good looks, or their IQ. It was their grit that helped them become local or global successes.

Grit is commitment, passion, and perseverance in achieving long-term worthwhile goals. Grit is having stamina beyond your current abilities.

Grit is sticking with the future day in and day out long after the excitement of the moment has gone. When I realized the value of camel wool products in health and therapy, I figured everybody would love these products like our existing clients and my family members. I quickly learned it was not the case. Most people are ignorant of the benefits of camel wool. The only way forward was through re-educating ourselves and our clients and developing our own mental abilities.

I tested all the products we had developed on my own body to understand real effect on the body first-hand. In fact, anyone that has tried any Camel Heal products have loved them. As a sales trainer, I cannot sell anything that I personally do not test, use, or love. I needed to confirm all the facts based on research and personal experience.

Those who had travelled and knew camels were familiar with the dromedary camels of middle east and North Africa. Very few people know about the Bactrian camels of the Gobi Desert. We had to persevere through by re-educating the public on the wonderful benefits of these products, and soon the word spread. Existing clients started to refer friends and family.

Grit is working hard not for a week, a month, or a year but sometimes for years to turn an idea into a profitable business. In short, "Grit is living life like it's a marathon, not a sprint."

I knew building a natural health brand and making it a global company would be a challenge. I love solving problems. I was drawn to tackle this challenge, but in the middle of my hustle, I was knocked out in the accident that wiped out my memory.

Have you ever heard of the expression, "Mr. Magoo Syndrome?" Well, this is another learning moment; I was partly to be blamed because I was not wearing a safety helmet, so the severity of my injuries was partially my own fault. I was blind like the character Mr. Magoo and not looking for this accident in the middle of my greatest business endeavour. However, there was a divine intervention to keep me alive to persevere through all of that to bring you this particular message.

I have always been different in my approach to life and have mostly often taken the road less travelled because exploring new ways always appeals to me. I had to persevere and wanted to become my own icon for grit.

War, homelessness, hunger, disappointments of all kinds, and physical and mental pressures and pains and eventually the hit-and-run accident that totally wipe out of my past memory, are only a few experiences I have persevered through. All I needed was to develop some more grit and go head on against all that was coming at me. It has been truly a blessed life, but all these challenges have made me stronger and grittier.

I have learned that talent does not make your grittier. In fact, data shows the opposite. Smart, talented people are always trying to find an easier way around obstacles, steal ideas and become copycats to get ahead. It becomes even harder for them to succeed in business because they forget the principles of authenticity and grit.

So far, the best idea I have discovered about developing grit is through personal growth and understanding the psychology of achievement. Written goals make you gritter and empower you to peruse your passions despite difficulties and hardship. Realistic dreams are the key to happy, purposeful, and energetic life.

The ability to pursue all we can become in this lifetime requires outstanding work ethic and grit. You can always become more than you are right now. Even if you lived ten lifetimes you would not be able to use up all your current potential and God-given gifts and talents, yet grit is required to use up all of them.

The most shocking fact about grit is how little we know about building grit in ourselves and our children. Parenthood is an art, not a burden or an accident of nature. Parents often enter their role unprepared but are expected to have acquired the fundamental skills and be familiar with the hierarchy of human needs to raise other people.

According to Dr. Carol S. Dweck Ph.D. at the Stanford University grit is developed based on the understanding that "The ability to learn is not fixed and it could be changed based on your effort." She has shown that when kids learn about the brain, its functions and how it grows and changes in response to challenges we face, kids are much more likely to persevere when they fail when they understand these functions. They learn that failure is an event, not a permanent condition.

In times of disruption, trauma, and tragedy you either dig in your heels and give you energy to the things that you have lost, or you let the pain and disruption break you right open and shine a light on the seed of imagination to create new beginnings. Growth and personal development are the key components of building grit. Through personal experience, experiments, and observations I have noticed that we need more than just grit. We need to develop the ability to act in the face of fear and mental distress.

Grit requires us to take our best ideas and intuitions and test them out in the real world. We need to take time and assess whether we are making any progress. We need to be willing to fail, to be wrong and ridiculed to restart over with the lessons learned.

In other words, we need to be grittier about teaching our kids to be grittier and more persistent in their lives, but that is only possible if you set the example of such traits first. When you become grittier, the universe conspires to turn your dreams a reality. Here is the proof of one of the grittier creatures I have come to know and love.

All I Need To Know About Grit I Learned From Camels

As I read about this quality of grit, the more I learned about grit, the more I was reminded of camels, the grittiest of all animals in the animal kingdom. As you may know camels are also known to be the wisest. I have personally a great amount of respect for camels and admire all their attributes.

A camel can walk about one hundred kilometers without a drink of water where a horse would drop down in exhaustion. Camel milk can kill cancerous cells and improve Alzheimer, Hepatitis-C, diabetes, tuberculosis, and ulcers conditions. It is the closest to mother's milk loaded with incredible nutrients that heal the body naturally. A camel can also get through any sandstorm with a set of special double layer see through eyelids. A camel can carry loads twice as heavy as a horse can and it never stops until it arrives at the destination.

Camel wool products, of course, help relieve pains of arthritis and improve circulatory problems and much more. That is why it is called "nature's magic fabric" where camels are known. Camels, not horses or dogs, have been man's most loyal, best, and most useful friend. That is one very gritty friend we can learn so much from.

When I realized this quality of grit and applied the principles explained here, I realized that you could carve out your own piece of the world and live there happily ever after. That piece of the world is inside your own head in your thinking mind. When I am laser-focused my blinders are on, and I do not see or hear anyone or anything, I do not watch anything; instead, I turn into my intuition.

Family and friends often ask me how I am always able to keep a smile on my face through all the challenges I faced. I am always happy and energetic, that is most of the time of course. I tell them I am happy by nature, but in my secret mind, I think and talk about my written goals and dreams and how to get them most of the time. I follow that with action through development of the quality of grit. This is not just what I have read, it is a life I have lived, I walk my talk.

In other words, I am gritty in the pursuit of my goals and dreams and the impact I want to make in the lives of other people. The possibilities, the opportunities, the willpower, and grit that I have developed are no less than a human camel. That is why I smile most of the time. I believe in myself, and you will believe in yourself when you develop the quality of girt.

The beautiful ancient city of Istanbul is magnificent treasure chest of culture and history. It's locally also called the seven-hill city because it's all built on beautiful hills that overlook the seas. I love spending time here. My beloved sister and her family live here. Also, it is the bridge that connect the East to the West (Middle East that is). It is a spiritual place of the past sages and mystics and many of my own ancestors lived, studied, and were eventually buried here.

On the New Year's Eve of 2021, I was on the fourth floor of my sister's home overlooking the Marmara Mah Bay resting under my Camel Heal Therapeutic Comfort Blanket. After a long deep sleep, I was reflecting on the last seven years of my journey. A soft rain that was hitting the window, was making a mystic music with to my ears. Istanbul weather is a very dump and high in humidity most of the fall, winter, and spring seasons. Some days it gets really windy and temperatures hover below zero degrees.

Our research shows that when moisture fills the air at night and temperatures drop around zero degrees, arthritic pains, and other joint and circulatory problems worsen. I was cozied up in my Camel Heal blanket and I was feeling the dry heat around my body as I did some reading with a cup of warm coffee.

Usually when I travel for an extended period of time, I carry three suitcases with me. One suitcase of my clothes and other necessities, the second one is a handbag with my electronics, laptop, chargers etc. but the third suitcase is what I call "Just in Case."

My "Just in Case" has all my healthy aging products and apparels mostly Camel Heal and Camel Heal Bamboo shapewear and other gifts and products that our team has researched and developed over the last few years.

Besides a few gifts for my family, most of them are my personal care apparels and under layers and a one hundred percent camel wool blanket for the cold nights just in case I spend the night on the road or if it gets really cold on the plane. It is the ultimate comfort sleepwear. The dry heat makes anyone fall asleep in no times.

My "Just in Case" usually has a couple of pairs of Camel Heal socks, my favorite pair of leather Camel Heal gloves, a waist support to keep my kidneys warm and of course my favorite camel heal blanket and few other items. I have learned how to keep my visits to a hospital or doctor's office to an absolute minimum especially during pandemic crisis like the outbreak of COVID-19.

On this trip, I was fully prepared and equipped with all kinds of camel heal therapeutic apparels for the unpredictable as vaccination was not as widely accepted and available as later in the year. In fact, one of my business associates told me, "Do not get sick while you are away." I wanted to make sure that I would not need doctor visits except usual checkups for as long as possible.

When the air is heavier on rainy days, arthritic joints start to be painful immobilizing the elderly. Part of avoiding these pains during the aging process is prevention, and what better protection than Camel Heal, *nature's magic fabric*. Most people eventually learn how to live with these pains and aches since there is no pharmaceutical drugs, cure, or remedy for arthritic pains or lack of sleep.

The only natural comfort from these pains and aches that slow most people down to a painful halt is the therapeutic wool of the two-hump Bactrian camel. Camel Wool blankets and comforters are the magical sleep comfort wear that protect the body from the cold during the cold season. Sleep comfort wear is important in any weather.

According to my personal research the decimation of sleep throughout industrialized nations is having a catastrophic impact of our health and wellness even the safety of our children. Lack of sleep is fast becoming one of the greatest public health hazards. The addictive behaviour to technology and phone connectedness that we face in the 21st Century does not help solve the problem either.

The disruption of deep sleep is an underappreciated factor that is contributing to cognitive decline or memory decline in the aging process as well. There is a structure that sits on the left and the right side of the brain called the hippocampus. It's really good at receiving new memory files and holding on to them. Without proper sleep the memory circuits of the brain eventually become waterlogged, and you cannot absorb new memories. If you are overtired, there is no developing grit!

Lack of good sleep will even erode the very fabric of biological life itself, the DNA genetic code. How do you get a good night sleep then? The first thing I have experienced through my own recovery is regularity which is a requirement for developing grit in our sleep patterns. Go to bed at the same time and wake up at the same time every night no matter weekday or weekend. Regularity is king and it will anchor your sleep patterns. The second is factors like light, sound, and other distractions.

Sleep wear like Camel Wool comforters and blankets also help increase the quality and quantity of your sleep. Better sleep at least for me is unfortunately not an optional lifestyle luxury. A good night's sleep is a nonnegotiable biological necessity. It is my life-support system, and Camel Heal comfort wear supports a great night's sleep in my experience. I made sure I was comfortable and in my happy zone, so Camel Heal products provided me with dry heat of the desert and made me comfort-able, where my creativity flows naturally. My great night's sleep every night helped me have grit the next morning every day in Istanbul.

Preparation Fuels Grit

I had planned for a longer stay, so I had prepared like I preach because I had a lot of work planned ahead. I had my elderly parents to care for and spend time with, so I needed to prepare before embarking on this new journey.

My early morning and evenings were flexible, so I decided to write and edit this book for our mutual benefit while working on my other plans. I have two passions, one is my immediate family, especially my children, and the other is my work.

The kids being in Canada, here the main focus was two-fold: care for my parents and the work at-hand. I get a burst of inspi-ration right after the call and morning prayer that is heard all over Istanbul every day, which is my daily meditation time when the body is still asleep, but the brain is awake.

Most of this book was written in that spirit of connectivity with the Infinite Intelligence as the words just flow through me during such early morning hours.

I am the CEO, the Chief Encouraging Officer, for my family, my students, my team and my clients. I want to inspire you and prepare you for the future "Just in Case."

We all need some uplifting and direction when we feel a bit low or life weighs heavy on our shoulders, as it sometimes does.

When I was leaving on this trip my daughter told me, "Dad, please come back alive."

We all fear the unknown, so I wrote this as a guiding handbook not only for my own children but also as a modern manual for manifestation of our desires. I aim to help guide the reader and those who are seeking some real answer to life's most pressing questions.

Nobody knows what happens next, but you always have to be prepared and ready for the unpredictable "Just in Case."

I wanted to make the best use of my time and be as productive as possible, as which is one of the requirements of being an entrepreneur and CEO of your own life and business. The universe is in perfect order and all you have to do is just to tune into that order, pick up the cues, get to work, and prepare the meal you want to be served.

Self-Rediscovery & Grit

I tell you parts of my story to show you the reality of application of this wisdom as a proof in real life. My aim is to help you build enough skills, confidence, and the required instructions to in the construction of your own dream life.

Last time I was Istanbul, I wrote my first book to tell my story,

<u>The Mountains Are Calling</u>, while going through the notes from hundreds of doctors' visits and interviews and talking with my family members about my past life.

The details of my medical record and what had happened to me was a 187 pages long report that I read on the plane flight over here to refresh my findings in preparation for the writing of this book. All the results of treatments, brain scans and research of my doctors at the Toronto Rehab Clinic, an affiliate of the Toronto Medical University, was in the report, so I had a refresher course before embarking on this writing. I started to focus on brain research and read many books and listened to audios on brain development and thought leadership.

My family here in Middle East had no idea that I had sustained such traumatic injury and incurred a total memory loss. I did not tell anyone until there was a need to explain my absence. I never told them because I did not see the need to have them worry about me while they could do nothing about it. I like to avoid unnecessary drama as much as possible. I started to write my findings quietly and organized them in my first book and that is how I started to tell them about what had happened.

In that time, I was just trying to rediscover who I really was; I had no memory of my past. I did not know who I was until my therapy was completed, which took me two long years, and my family thought I was just being my old smiling, quiet, active self. After the two years, I was prepared and even healthier than before the accident, in other words I had changed, physically, mentally, and psychologically.

Now, I am truly blessed to have this opportunity to connect with you and I do not take this opportunity for granted. I am here to bring you great value and a unique educational perspective.

The applied wisdom in this book alone could totally change

anyone's life. I wanted to give back in an authentic way of encouragement, inspiration, and provide direction so you can live every day of your life like there are miracles happening.

Dr. Wayne Dyer said:

"When you change the way you look at things, the things you look at change."

Life itself is a miracle and every day that we open our eyes to a new day is a new miracle in my mind.

The Dalai Lama once said:

"Man sacrifices his health to make money. Then he sacrifices his money to recuperate his health. And then is so anxious about the future that he does not enjoy the present. The result is that he does not live in the present or the future. He lives as if he is never going to die, then he dies having never really lived."

Since my brain injury and memory loss, I have realized the value of every moment of time and the true value of my personal relationships.

I have fully recovered since, and an incredible thing has happened to my brain. I am able to process information much faster and with greater clarity. I have discovered the power of grit in building new habits. I am able to analyze and expand on innovative ideas and complicated issues much better than prior to the accident.

Research shows a brain injury can paralyse your body or it can trigger awakening of dormant cells in the brain resulting in an increased functionality of the brain. I was lucky that the latter has happened to me as I feel like more dormant brain cells got activated as a result of the internal shake-up.

I was able to tap into the knowledge of experts to properly reprogram my mind and create new thought patterns. I did also read over one hundred books on business, health, and entrepreneurship during my recovery which all helped in this incredible reconstruction of my mind and body.

I am sharing these experiences to understand the process of healthy aging and its relation to brain function as a guide for myself, individuals, and entrepreneurs. I witnessed this phenomenon by going through this process with my parents until their mid-eighties and through my own personal health challenges.

Gratefully, today I am in the best shape of my life, I eat healthier, and I run at least twenty-five kilometers per week. I use some simple routines in the morning to grow and enhance my mind and personal health. It is the repetition of new habits rather than the intensity of those habits that count in building grit.

When COVID-19 brought business as usual to a slow halt, it gave us chance to revaluate our progresses and plot a new direction. We were organically forced to grow out of this uncomfortable situation because of the requests of our loyal customers who appreciated and demanded a wider variety of products to take care of their own health and wellbeing.

They asked us to keep bringing them this beautiful natural comfortable gift of nature to deal with their aches and pains in various parts of the body for comfort or better sleep. We put in the work to bring them our best products and keep adding new ones, but now business is in a new phase and our vision has expanded beyond what it used to be. I have learned about the quality of grit, and we keep on moving forward in faith by being totally proactive about our future.

Learning From Sheep, Camels & People

When I was only a boy, I though the world was big beautiful open fields of green grass and lush mountain hills. Our lives were not easy, but it seemed like a perfectly comfortable world as I was tucked in under my natural sheep wool comforters handmade by my grandmother.

As a child I wore sheep wool socks in the colder days of winter while listening to grandma's stories. I never imagined one day I would find the gold of the desert, camel wool, and relive my childhood dreams as a middle-aged entrepreneur. The seeds of your future life are planted in your early childhood programming as we discussed in earlier chapters.

My love for natural foods, fibers, and other natural derivative products, like my love for Canada, has been a lifetime love affair and a true passion. Since those early days, I have learned that doing well in school, life and business depends on much more that the ability to learn quickly and easily. In other words, it's not your smarts that make you successful, it's your grit.

When we grow up, we learn about all the traditions, customs, systems, and rules that we have to follow and all the boxes we have to fit in to have a secure common place in society. Then we learned about all these different boxes to fit in just to belong to be like all the other normal people. That is the paradigm of our lives. When I learned these principles, my rebellious instinct took over and lead me to places that I only dreamt of as a child.

No person or thing makes you happier than to think independently and talk about what you really want in your life. It lights me up to live up to my name (Aref – The wise one) and be able to guide others or organizations on how to manage through tough times and challenges. Man is programmed for success and happiness but conditioned for failure by a paradigm of his own. Having written goals is a great starting point to break this conditioning plague that has spread out throughout the world. So is the company you keep.

I was blessed to have been surrounded by many wonderful people in my life who held my hand, guided me, and pushed me through painful moment and celebrated the breathtaking moments with me. You need to surround yourself with good-hearted, smart, gritty people. Birds of a feather do flock together, but thankfully we are not birds, we are humans being driven by choice more than instinct. We can choose your own tribe of like-minded intellectual people that we want to associate with.

Someone also said, "If you are the smartest person in the room, you are most likely in the wrong room."

I usually do not want to be in that room, but as I mature, it is becoming more and more challenging to find rooms to fit in. Perhaps this is a call for leadership.

I want to learn from other people's experiences, knowledge, and wisdom. I want to learn and to grow throughout my life. I have realized that I am just starting to begin to dream. I am just beginning to start on my journey of learning from some of the greatest people on the planet, many in my own family.

You can find good-hearted, smart, and successful people and befriend them. First you have to personally grow, become grittier in your pursuit of a well-lived life, and develop better communication skills to be able to connect with such people.

It is said that in North America ninety-five percent of all failures are the result of lack of social skills not technical skills. In the Middle East and some other parts of the world, social interaction on a broad base is the fabric of family and society. However, developing social skills is totally a different ball game. It is about becoming a better thinker, and a seamless communicator.

In the Grand Bazaar in Istanbul, it's not uncommon that the vendors invite you into their store or restaurant right off the street. They love to talk about anything and everything that really does not matter just to get your attention. No matter where you are, social skills and proper communication are where every conversation has a revelation on both sides. An enjoyable conversation is like a tennis match, it flows back and forth effortlessly.

However, some socializing takes away from your goals. Have you noticed that the people who have nothing to do usually want to do it with you? It is okay to spend some time alone to evaluate and refocus on what is import to each of us. Most people have nothing to do with their time, so they just want talk about anything and everything. If no exchange of valuable knowledge or business ideas have been made, social interaction is a waste of time. People will waste time and drain your energy if you do not learn to say NO. There is no gain in such a conversation except the exchange of useless information.

For the longest time I isolated myself from my ethnic community in Canada because I wanted to become a true Canadian. I wanted to learn a new way of communicating and connecting with mentors and businesspeople of higher caliber so I can learn from them. I did not want to be around my circle of friends from home or the time-wasters that crossed my path.

I wanted to meet people who were smarter than I and make new friends that I can learn new skills from. I hungered and still do, to grow as a human being because I did not come to Canada just for the sake of living here. I want to make an impact on the social and economic growth of my country in return for all the freedom that Canada has given me.

Grit & Thinking

One day one of my relatives here in Istanbul told me:

"Arif, I think you are going to grow to be an old man like the European old men."

I did not know what he meant exactly but I could guess the image he had of such men.

I said, "Thank you sir, I take that as a compliment, but I do not have to like anybody. I just want to be myself; this is me, Arif. I learn, grow, observe, associate, and learn from people from all over the world. Canada is the young child of the old world. We have people from all over the world in Canada. I have learned from all of them. Canada is a global mosaic of people and cultures."

Yes, you can learn, grow, and choose to have a different path in life. I am excited to continue to learn, create, build, and teach some of these valuable new qualities that are required to survive and thrive in our new reality. However, you must break the habit of being your old usual self because we are creatures of habit. We seek the comfort zone by nature, yet no growth happens there.

The quality of our thoughts determines our personal realities. One could feel cold, sad, and miserable, shrinking into a corner and let all kinds of fears roam into our heads. Or we could get busy feeling good by knowing we are getting better day-by-day in every way.

Remember Bryan Tracy's saying:

"You become what you think about all day long."

We can think thousands of thoughts per minute, but only one at a time. My question is, are those thought positive or negative, constructive, or destructive? Sadly, most of these conscious thoughts are negative repetitive thought of scarcity, lack and inability. It is like going to our own pity party in our own head every single day, then waiting for someone else to make us happy. You are the only source of your own happiness, or the lack of it.

Oftentimes we think the same thoughts, which leads us to the same emotions, driving us to make the wrong choices resulting in dismal outcomes. Making the same choices leads to the same limiting behaviours that keep our results small and unnoticeable. Do you see the patterns?

This is a dangerous loop that could lead to depression, anxiety, even suicidal thoughts. It is a destructive mental loop we can and must break. We need to break this loop so happy thoughts, new experiences and exciting opportunities find their way into our minds and settle in.

Negative repetitive thoughts are usually formed in our childhood programming based on your upbringing and environmental influences. Imagine if you often heard in your childhood:

"No! Don't do that. You cannot do it. You are too small. You are too clumsy. You are too rude. You are too loud. You are too quiet. You are too dumb. You are too poor, etc."

Guess what happens by age twelve?

These ideas become crystallized in our minds and become permanent part of our thought process and self-talk pattens. The answer to most of life's endeavours is "No" in our minds before we ask ourselves the real question. We refrain from asking ourselves and others for better quality questions. Asking takes grit.

We know that asking is the key to the future, but most do not even ask. We can ask politely, we can ask humbly, we can ask kindly, but we can ask for what we want knowing that the answer may be no. If the answer is yes, it's a new beginning and if the answer is no, we have not lost anything. Even the Bible says:

"Ask and it shall be given to you."

We also need to ask for happiness…

International Day Of Happiness

Happiness plays a significant role in your overall progress and success of an individual and an entrepreneur. Grit and perseverance play and equally important role in finding our own personal happiness. Albert Schweitzer, the French-German theologian, philosopher, and physician wisely said:

"Happiness is nothing more than good health and a bad memory." I am blessed to have symptoms of both. You need to forget the bad and focus on what is good and inspiring to stay in your happy place.

The German Philosopher Arthur Schopenhauer said, "The two enemies of human happiness are pain and boredom." I attempt to tackle both enemies of your happiness in this writing. We develop comfortable natural products to address the aches and pain of getting old and I author books so to help fill boredom, with wisdom.

The highest form of charity is spreading love and happiness, so I wanted to spread health, love, and happiness.

The International Day of Happiness came into being in 2013 when the United Nations recognised the global mental health crisis was on the rise. Since then, 20 March has been celebrated as the International Day of Happiness, which corresponds with

Nowruz, the Kurdish-Iranian New Year, a time of happiness, gratitude, and celebration of all the people and all the blessings in our lives.

It is time to commit to finding your own personal happiness by tapping into your God-given potential. With all the wars, violence and tragedies around the world, happiness is now more in demand than ever before. The recent pandemic will play an even bigger role in the mental health of millions of people around the world during and after the COVID-19 crisis.

Let us see how we can tap into our own potential to find inner-peace, comfort, and happiness by going the extra mile. It is the sole formula to creating miracles in our own lives.

Chapter 12

The Miraculous Formula – Going The Extra Mile

"The way to get anybody to do anything for you, is to do something for them first." (Napoleon Hill)

I do not know any one quality or trait that can get a person an opportunity quicker than going out of their way in doing somebody a favor without any expectations in return. It is the one thing that anyone can do in life without asking for permission because everybody loves a free hand.

In fact, if we are going to be free, independent, and self-determining individuals, we have to go the extra mile. If you make sure that all the philosophies discussed here work for you as well as they do for millions of other people, going the extra mile with cheerful attitude and a genuinely pleasing personality is the key.

The only success principle that marks the tuning point of every person who has achieved higher grounds in life is the habit of going the extra mile. Doing so is the habit of rendering more service and better-quality service than expected and doing it in a positive mental attitude.

I do not know of any other way for someone to make themselves indispensable in any company other than by going the extra mile and doing it with the right mental attitude. I am going the extra mile by adding this one very important chapter here to give you a last formula for rendering more value, better service and doing in a pleasing manner, and pleasant mental attitude to get everything you want.

Napoleon Hill calls this the QQMA formula: "The quality and quantity of the service you render with the mental attitude that you render the service will determine the space you occupy in this life and the value of compensation you receive from your services."

One of the reasons that there are so many failures in the world today is because majority of people will not even go the first mile, let alone the second one. Most people like to do the minimum just to get paid, and they often do get paid the minimum.

Oftentimes if they do something that is not expected of them, they gripe as they go along and they make sure they are noticed for doing the organization or a person a favor. I suppose you know that type, but you are not one of them because you are reading this book. If you are one of them, before you finish reading this chapter, you will get out of this habit fast as we come to a great conclusion. While rendering more service or going the extra mile, keeping a pleasing mental attitude is important because if you gripe about the extra you do, chances are it's not going to bring you many great returns.

Laws Of Nature

You can guess why I emphasis the fact of going the extra mile, and what makes me the authority to ask you to do so. I am doing it because I came from farming community where I spend most of my teenage years. I watch and love the way nature does things. Anytime you can notice the habits of nature and follow them you are not going to go wrong.

There are a set of natural laws that this universe operates on and by noticing these laws and adjusting yourself to them sooner rather than later you will gain the favor of these laws. One of these vital laws is the law of going the extra mile, which is that nature demands every living creature to go the extra mile for them to eat and survive. Man would not survive for a season if it were not for the law of going the extra mile. We need and should eat food that grow out of the ground. A farmer follows the principle of going the extra mile by way of observing the way nature performs its miracles.

Nature goes the extra mile by producing everything in excess its needs even for emergencies. The blooms on the trees, fishes in the seas and everything else that we see around us all follow this principle.

Nature is bountiful in going the extra mile but in return it demands that every living thing also go the extra mile. Bees are rewarded with honey for the services of pollinating the flowers, but they have to perform the service before they are rewarded. If you watch wildlife documentaries as I like to do, you will notice that no beast will eat without going the extra mile. Canadian geese are known to fly south in winter to reach places to reproduce to continue to survive the harsh climate and continue the journey of life.

Most of my family back in the Middle East have beautiful farms and love nature, live and work on it. A farmer knows and under-stands this principle very well. He has to clear the ground first, he has to plow it, then he has to plant the seeds in the ground. He has to fence it, weed it, and protect it against animals and so forth. All those cost money and a lot of arduous work and labour before he can enjoy the harvest and the fruits of his labour in the next season. Notice all of this has to be done in advance and it costs time, labour, and money, or he will have nothing to eat.

You do have to go the extra mile for a while before someone

takes notice, just like when you plant a seed in the ground, and it does not get noticed until it grows out of the ground. Do not expect to go the extra mile, render service, and expect to receive a check for a million dollars tomorrow.

That said, if you happen to go the extra mile and no one takes notice, look around and find the right person who will. This is the same as saying if your present employer does not take notice of your effort of going the extra mile, go ahead and find some other employer who will take notice, appreciate, and compensate you for it.

There are many great reasons to get into the habit of going the extra mile. I am going to mention some compelling reasons why you as the entrepreneur, a new graduate, or an individual with a growth mindset should get into the magical habit of going the extra mile starting today.

The first reason is the law of increasing returns, which says that what you give comes back to you multiplied, whether good or bad, positive, or negative. It works all the time. You go into any organization, and you will know who are the ones that go the extra mile. Employers are always looking around for people who do go the extra mile, and surprise, surprise, those are the ones that get the opportunities and promotions when they do come up. It is those people that become part of the company history and often make themselves indispensable to the organization.

You will notice that if you do the extra, some people will be surprised because most people just do the minimum, just enough to get paid. Have you ever been to a restaurant that the waiters have been so gentle and nice that you felt obliged to leave a big tip? Well, that is going the extra mile at work.

The only way that you can fully occupy your space in the world and in business will be determined by the quality and the quantity of service you render with the right mental attitude. Make it your business to render extra service in everything that you do because everything that you do in your life and business will come back multiplied.

There are a lot of things in life that cause us to have unpleasant feelings but going the extra mile is one thing you can do that always gives you a pleasant feeling. Going the extra mile not only gives you a pleasant feeling to render more service than is expected but also helps one feel better in your soul. It gives you greater courage, and it helps you constantly challenge to yourself to do your best to top all previous efforts. I have never done anything in my life that I did not intend to do better than what I have done previously.

My first book was a great practice and attempt to restore my lost memory, but this book is the true labour of love. I did go the extra mile to put it together in an easy to read and simple to follow instructional book for our mutual benefit. I wanted to exceed what I have done previously by far. I hope you endorse that effort. I have read thousands of books that start with a great chapter or preface, but then somewhere in the middle they start to get dull, I wanted to make this a great educational tool from the beginning to the end.

My goal is always to do better than before as I walk the talk because I want to grow, and I want to learn. I feel like I am just getting started here. You do not have to advertise going the extra mile in the workplace too much as I am doing here because going the extra mile advertises itself. Eventually people will start to talk about your commitment to your work and refer friends and family like they did in the beginning of The Camel Company of Canada products marketing.

Every organization that I have ever worked for or joined since the early start of my career, I have had a promotion within my first ninety days of service because of the application of the principle of going the extra mile and it has been a trend throughout my life. Ninety day is suitable time and a season to make a real impression, or get any project completed so you are noticed for your efforts, like nature gets noticed for doing its work.

I believe if everyone went the extra mile, we would live in a greater world, but I assure you very few people ever do it. So, you do not have a whole lot of competition. Additionally, the people who do the bare minimum may not even like you. Remember that the important people will notice your effort, will love you for it, and promote you accordingly.

Going the extra mile will help you in the development of positive mental attitude and it is amongst the first traits of developing a pleasing personality. It is a marvelous thing to know that you can change the chemistry of your brain so you are positive instead of negative and you can do that so easily.

All this starts with a special frame of mind that you can do some-thing useful for someone else just because of the goodness you feel inside yourself. If you render more and better service than you are paid for, sooner or later you will be paid for more than you do. That is the law of increasing returns we mentioned before.

You can be sure that when you do this you are piling up credit that will come back to you in multiples. It also helps you develop a keen, alert imagination helping your personal development. In finding out means and ways of helping someone else, you are eventually helping yourself.

You Were Born A Miracle

It is your individual responsibility in this world to succeed. I believe everyone can be best at something. You were born a miracle, so do not underestimate yourself and your individual potential. You cannot afford to let anybody's ideas or notions of you to get the way of your success.

You should be fair and just with other people all the time, but you are under no obligation to let other people's ideas and behavior to stop you from going out and becoming anything, you want to be. I would like you to put these laws into action if they make sense to you. Do not let anybody to distract or stop you from doing what is right for you – including helping others.

When you are stuck and cannot find solutions to your own problems, forget them for a while and look around and find someone who needs a helping hand and help them. You will unlock the solution to your own problems in the process. We are social creatures, and we love to help one another.

I have tried these principles hundreds of times myself and they work as sure as I know that tomorrow the sun will rise again. I do not know why it works but I do know that if I follow these laws, I always finds solutions to my challenges. It also builds your personal initiative and makes it a part of your personality trait. The habit of doing something useful for someone always opens up opportunities that help one get ahead. Just try not to put off doing it.

Don't Put Off The Extra Mile

It all comes down to action, which has one major enemy called procrastination and its best friend, laziness. Procrastination is a plague in which most people who put off things until tomorrow that they should have done yesterday. We are all guilty of procrastinating.

The most important asset we all have is the time we have on this planet. I believe it will do absolute wonders in your life if you commit to putting this simple principle-based advice to action. You could save valuable time and create miracles in your life.

Just do something, even a small act of kindness, because when you act your brain releases endorphins (the happy drugs) which in turn creates new thought patterns in your mind. Going the extra mile creates that pattern which helps the brain release more endorphins.

We are all guilty of procrastinating but let me give you my quick fixes for overcoming procrastination in this closing chapter. Firstly, procrastination is a protective mechanism that causes a lot of trouble in our individual lives. I want to share some ideas on how you can overcome procrastination.

There is something called the law of secondary gains that says when you procrastinate it is because you are getting another gain from procrastinating. For example, when you do not act on your improving your health you get some temporary relief, feel safe, sleep in or whatever excuse you give yourself not to act.

Another example is you may fear public speaking, this is because you want to avoid making a mistake, look silly or be embarrassed, etc. The law of secondary gain says that I will be safe from those things if I avoid speaking in public. You have to see what side of the scale benefits you most then act on the side that is more important to you overall.

There is a mental technique you can use when you do not want to act or are aware that you are procrastinating called the law of little actions. It is the reverse of the law of secondary gains. When you become aware of your own procrastinating, take one small little action any way, do something no matter how small.

For example, if I feel really tired one day and do not want to go on my morning run, I go for a walk along the beach, in the hills or I do some physical work at home. This way I am interrupting the pattern of procrastination and creating new patterns regardless of how small the activity may be.

When we replace procrastination with a little act of micro-positivity, there is a slight detour from our usual brain function patterns. If we do this continuously, start with 7 days only, we are priming our subconscious mind. Extend it to 21 days and we are building a new habit and extending it to 90 days, we have created a new lifestyle mastering the skills of creating any habit, as explained earlier.

It will start to increase our self-worth, self-trust, and self-confidence over time. Start with a plan for the next seven days and no matter what happens do not break your promise to yourself, to do something you have never done before, for the next seven days, then see how you feel about yourself. Why seven days and why do I repeat it so many times? In most religious beliefs God created heaven and earth in six days and on the seventh day He rested. It is the creativity timeline and reasonable enough to give it try.

No matter how small your actions are, you will think of yourself as an action taker not a procrastinator. One small act based on awareness in the inner-mind changes the entire spectrum in your subconscious mind. This way we are changing our inner-mind thought patterns and processes. Procrastination is a devastating behavior that we need to interrupt by taking very small action thereby creating new patterns.

How do you feel when you act? Do you think you are reinforcing a negative thought, or reinforcing a positive thought? Well, one releases stress hormone, the other one releases dopamine.

Dopamine is the happiness hormone, and when you act you start to get addicted to acting. If you need to take the slightest action to change the pattern, it will still have the same effect in your brain. You are activating your reward center in your brain which releases dopamine as a reward for acting making you feel happy instantly.

You can also use the law of bigger fears, which states that there is way to frame things in your mind to say that not acting will be more painful than acting. Let say you are procrastinating on something right now. Ask yourself, what am I gaining by procrastination? The answer may be, "Oh, I am feeling safe, I feel secure, I enjoy my time, I can sleep in, I am safe around my friends, etc."

Now write down what is the cost of procrastinating. Write down what will happen if you do not work out. For instance, my health will deteriorate, my finances will suffer, my personal relationships worsen, and my self-image will be damaged. Your self-trust will lower thereby clarifying the cost of procrastinating such as illness, pain, loss of self-respect, and so forth.

If you make the cost of not acting greater than the reward you are getting from acting, you will create a new pattern based on the fear of inaction, which will force you to act. We have to clarify that not doing anything will cost you far more than the pain of acting. Fear of losing is sometimes a bigger motivator that the excitement of winning.

If you stay the same, there is a huge cost to be paid in the future. Whatever behaviours need changing, we must reinforce and change. We need to get to the state of auto-plasticity where the brain does not require any conscious thinking for a new pattern to be established. One often moves automatically based on the subconscious mind programing.

There is no active thinking involved and it becomes part of your subconscious functioning. The logical brain will go from avoiding the bigger pain to its new protective mechanism of acting automatically. My morning run has become automatic, whereas if do not run for three days, consequently my entire body start to feel painful.

Every time you go the extra mile you get joy out of doing it and you eliminate procrastination. Going the extra mile is my happiness drug. It also builds definiteness of purpose without which one can and does not hope to find lasting success.

Labours Of Love

If you are not engaged in a labour of love, you are wasting your time. When you go the extra mile, you are engaged in the labour of love because you do not have to do it. No employer asks you to do it, they may ask you to do something extra occasionally, but not as a regular thing. That is something you do based on your own personal initiative.

Going the extra mile in your personal relationships builds trust and makes the quality of your life more joyful by the feeling of personal satisfaction. It raises your standard of living and makes your work and life much more enjoyable and harmonious. Try it and see how it works like a charm.

I have turned foes into friends just by going the extra mile. There is nothing that does more damage to human relation-ships than pride and ego. Do not be afraid to humble yourself if it is going to make your life easier with the people that you have to associate with all the time.

Going the extra mile in your career is the only way to ask someone for extra pay or promotions without saying a word. You cannot ask any employer to give you a promotion or extra pay unless you have been going the extra mile previously for some time and doing more than that for which you are paid.

First you must go the extra mile and put the other person under moral obligation before you ask the other person for a favor or a promotion. If you have enough people that you put under your moral obligation by going the extra mile when you need some favour, you can always find someone that will do it for you. It is a great feeling to know that you have that kind of credit hanging around with the people in your circle.

That is why I have no trouble in making the point that everyone must go the extra mile before he can enjoy the benefit of his own labour beyond a question of doubt. If you want to lose weight, for example, you have to put in thousands of hours of work and discipline before you enjoy the ideal weight and subsequent health benefits.

A new employee for example going into a new job cannot expect to have promotions, top wages, and benefits before he can establish a record, a reputation and get recognized for his exceptional extra work. In fact, if you go the extra mile in the right mental attitude, chances are that you never have to ask for a promotion or a raise because it is tendered to you in a way of promotions, increased salary, and benefits automatically.

The whole universe is arranged in such a way that nature's budget is balanced through the law of compensation. Which is that you get paid for your extra efforts. Everything has its equivalent in nature: positive and negative, day and night, success and failure, happiness, and misery.

We see the law of action and reaction in operation everywhere and in everything. Everything you do and everything you think causes a reaction on the person that releases the thought. Every thought that you release creates a pattern on your subconscious mind and if you store enough positive thoughts in your subconscious mind, you will become a positive person who wants to go the extra mile.

If you are positive, you will attract all the things that you want and if you are negative, you will attract also only the things that you do not want. I have had the great privilege of observing thousands of achievers and CEOs, and every one of them has adopted the trait of going the extra mile. If you neglect to apply the principle of going the extra mile, you will have very little chance of becoming financially independent.

The habit of going the extra mile is one of the finest ways of educating your mind to attract the things that you want and repel the things that you do not want. Developing a pleasing personality along with going the extra mile will create magical moments in your life. We will go through some details on how to create a pleasing personality so that you can accelerate your outcomes along the extra mile.

"To succeed in the twenty-first century we need business skills, and we need life skills," as Jim Rohn mentioned.

Here is a very important lesson on creating life skills.

Developing A Pleasing Personality "Along The Extra Mile"

Now I want to introduce you to the most wonderful person in the world. That is the person sitting in your seat right now. Your personality is what determines whether people are attracted to you, like you and collaborate with you or shy away and turn their back on you.

Your personality is the window through which you display your character to the world. Your smile is your logo, your personality is your business card, and how you make others feel is your trademark. It is your trademark by which people recognize you. You should know your personality and how other people see it so you can improve your personality where it needs improvement.

Nothing pays off better interest than being pleasing in the eyes of the other person. When you break down your personality point by point, you will find out where you are so wonderful and why. As you read along grade yourself against these factors. Be honest with yourself and grade yourself from zero to one hundred against each of the traits explained here. You will know exactly where you stand and what areas you need to pay attention to improve in terms of having a pleasing personality.

Developing a pleasing personality and going the extra mile are part of a lifestyle and attitude that anyone can adopt and develop. All of these are traits can be adopted and learnt because it is the sure way to open great doors to anyone.

According to my studies these are the twenty-five traits make a person a pleasing personality. I have accepted these wonderful "Canadian" traits in good faith, adopted them and have witnessed miracles unfold in my life as a result. I have also added tips of how to cultivate them experimented in my own personal way.

Keeping an open mind is the first trait of a pleasing personality. That is when you have the mindset to have no prejudices against anyone or about anything. You would be surprised at how many people do not have an open mind. In fact, some of them are so closed-minded and tightly sealed, that you could not crack open their mind even if you tried to break it open with a curl-bar. You could not put a new idea in there even if you tried.

You and I need to have an open mind because the minute people find out that you have prejudices against them, their race, religion, or political views and so on, they are going to back away from you. We all need each other's cooperation to live in peace and harmony so always keep an open mind.

While in financial services in Toronto Canada, I had people from all races, religions, genders, and backgrounds working out of my office. You know how I was able to assemble such variety of people to work together in harmony and in the spirit of cooperation? It was because I love them all, to me people are all one brand, they are my fellow sisters and brothers. I never think of anybody in terms of their, race, color, creed, political beliefs, religion, or financial abilities.

I think of people only in terms of what each person is doing to better himself or help better another person. We are all human becoming's that is why I get along so well with everyone. That is also the reason I was able to build teams of cohesive well-functioning people stretching from Mongolia to Canada.

What a marvellous thing it is to keep an open mind because if you do not know what it means to have an open mind, let me explain a closed mind.

A closed mind means you cease to grow, develop, or associate with others as a person. It means you will miss a lot of opportunities for learning and growth along the journey of life. When you have a closed mind toward other people, it does something to you on the inside that puts you under constant personal pressure or guilt.

The second trait of the of a pleasing personality is **a positive mental attitude** because nobody wants to be around a negative complainer, no matter what other qualities he may possess. Without a positive mental attitude, you are not going to be considered having a pleasing personality. Other people tune in and pick up your mental attitude by telepathy without you saying a word or making a move.

The next trait of a pleasing personality is having flexibility of personality. This is the ability to bend, to adjust yourself to varying circumstances of life without breaking down or going down with them. There are so many people who are stale in their habits and their mental attitudes because they cannot adjust to anything that is unpleasant to them. They do not like anything with which they do not agree. If you want to get mad at anyone, do it when the other person is in a good humour so you will have a much better chance of not getting hurt by them.

Positioning yourself for greatness requires the flexibility of personality. I have seen what how it can help navigate others through challenges and creating more opportunities for oneself.

There are so many circumstances that we must adjust ourselves to, so why not prepare by developing a pleasing personality to get the cooperation of others? It can have a wonderful impact on your health and wellbeing and create peace of mind. If you are not flexible, you can become flexible.

Number four of these traits is having a pleasing tone of voice. You need to learn and experiment with it because so many people have a harsh tone of voice and do not even notice it. It is that little something in their tone of voice that irritates the other person.

Over the last two decades I have met hundreds of speakers, salespeople, and successful entrepreneurs, every one of them uses some pleasing pitch and pleasant tone of voice to get the attention of others. In lectures, public speaking, conversation, or a sales presentation, a pleasant tone of voice is a real bounce.

If you are unable to do it, you can develop this with a little practice. Oftentimes it is simply by lowering your voice and keeping a smile on your face while you speak. Nobody can teach another person how to make their tone of voice pleasing. You have to do that by experimenting yourself.

Before you have a pleasing tone of voice, you must feel pleasing. You can feel pleasing when you like the people you work or live with.

Tolerance, the fifth aspect, is also a wonderful trait of a pleasing personality. It is to keep an open mind about all subjects, towards all people, always. In other words, your mind is not closed to anything and with anyone at any given times. That is the quality where you are always willing to hear the last word from anyone. It is a tough one to develop but it pays off marvellously.

The sixth trait of a pleasing personality is a keen sense of humour. You have to adjust and to disposition yourself to all the unpleasant circumstances of life without taking them too seriously. You cannot take yourself too seriously because if you do, you are doomed to live a life of constant stress. Incidentally one of the tonics that you could take is to have a good-hearted laugh at least several times a day.

If you have nothing to laugh about, just cook up something to laugh at yourself. Look yourself up in the mirror and crack a joke with yourself. You will be surprised at how it changes the chemistry of your brain and the expression on your face.

A keen sense of humour is a marvellous thing. I do not know if I have a keen sense of humour, but I do know my sense of humour is always alert. I can have genuine fun in any circum-stances of life because I have seen all the worst already. Nothing really bothers my soul because I know that laughter is one of the best medicines for your health.

Frankness of manner in speech, with a controlled tone of voice based on the habit of thinking before speaking, is the seventh trait. Most people do not do that, they speak first and think afterwards. Frankness of manner is a wonderful trait in your conversation to find out whether your speech is going to benefit the other person or damage them or your own peace of mind. If you follow these simple rules, I think that you would reduce your retraction and the things you wish you did not say, at least by half.

There are a lot of people that get their mouths going before they think, and they forget what they said. Frankness of speech does not mean you have to tell everybody what you think of them because if you do you are not going to have any friends left. Frankness means being honest and frank in making your point in a pleasing manner.

The eighth trait you need to adopt is a pleasing facial expression. Check your own facial expressions in the mirror several times a day and that is the first person you will greet in the morning. So, smile and tell yourself "Good morning." It is a marvellous thing to see that you can make your facial expressions more pleasing at will. Smile a little more because it is an important trait of a pleasing personality to smile when you talk to people.

You will be surprised at how much more effective your speech is when you smile than when you frown or are too serious. A smile is a beautiful thing but be cautious not to grin at people when you do not mean it because even a monkey can grin.

A genuine smile does not start in your face, but it starts in your heart where you feel joy. You do not have to be pretty or handsome, in fact you do not have to be anything special, but a smile embellishes you no matter who you are, and it makes you much more beautiful.

The ninth trait is a keen sense of justice toward all people even if it is to your disadvantage. What a wonderful thing it does to people when they know you are being just to them. There is no virtue in being just to the other person when you are bene-fiting by it. Most people are only honest when they know it is going to benefit them in one way or another. They quickly turn dishonest when they know they cannot profit from it. A keen sense of justice makes a pleasing personality where people go out of their way to cooperate with you.

The tenth trait is sincerity of purpose. Nobody likes the person who is insincere in what he says or does. The person who says something that he does not mean or does something that he really does not want to do. You know and feel when somebody says and does something that is not reflective of their inner thoughts. It is not as bad as outright lying, but it is a first cousin to it.

The eleventh trait you need is versatility, which is a wide range of the knowledge and experiences of the world events outside of one's immediate personal interests. It is another great trait of pleasing personality. We all know people who have their nose so into the grindstone that someone thinks that he or she does not know anything outside of that limited awareness.

He will not be interesting as a conversationalist because a versatile person should have a wide range of knowledge to talk to anyone about and the things that interest the other person. You know that the best way to make yourself to be liked by other people is to talk to them about the things that interest them.

The twelfth trait is to have tactfulness in speech and manner toward other people. You would be surprised how much you can do with people if you are just tactful with them. Even if you are an authority, it is still better if you ask them if they mind do not doing certain things.

You could always ask, "would it be convenient," "would it be suitable" or "do you mind…?"

In Canada people are so polite and tactful that when they come to a four-way stop sign at the same time, they often get stuck because they want the other person to proceed first. "Sorry" and "thank you" are the most spoken words in Canada.

Promptness of decision is the thirteenth trait we all need to master because nobody is well-liked if they put off decisions when they have all the facts and figures to make one. I do not mean for you to make snap judgments but when you have all the facts, and the time has arrived, you should decide.

Making a prompt and accurate decisions is one of the most powerful traits of great entrepreneurs. In case you make a decision that is wrong, you can always reverse it. Do not be too big or too little when you are wrong to reverse your decision.

The fourteenth trait is true faith or a belief in the Creator, God, Allah, Infinite Intelligence or whatever you may call the Higher Power that has created this beautiful world we live in. Faith is a very personal relationship, but only you know your faith based on your religion. If you follow your religion, you should rate yourself exceedingly high on this one. I have met people from all faiths and all backgrounds, and you would be surprised how many people only give lip-service when it comes to the question of faith, and do not do much to treat people according to their faith.

Many claim to believe but do not indulge in any outstanding acts outside their alleged faith. I do not know how the Creator feels about it, but I believe one act of kindness towards someone in no position of power is worth of thousands of tons of good intentions, prayers, or belief.

Appropriateness of words is the fifteenth important trait of a pleasing personality, which is to be free from slang, sarcasm, wisecracks, and double-talk. I have never read or learned about a time where people indulge in such behaviours and got the ideal results. The smart cracks may seem smart to the person who saying it, but I guarantee that it will not sound so smart to the person who is listening to them.

The English language is my favorite languages. The English language may not one of the easiest languages to master, but it is a beautiful language. It has a wide array of words and meanings and many words that you can use to make a point. It is a wonderful thing to be able to master and be competent enough in, to be able to express and convey to the other person exactly what you have in mind. You can clearly elaborate what you think or what want the other person to comprehend.

Then comes controlled enthusiasm, the sixteenth important trait in having a pleasing personality. Why not let your enthusiasm run wild and let it go? Well, just because you will get in trouble if you do. Your enthusiasm has to be handled the way you handle your electricity. You can cook your food, wash your dishes, you can light your home, warm your house and many other uses that we know about. You can turn it on when you want, and you turn it off when you do not need it any longer.

Enthusiasm is the same way. I you are not able to turn it off as quickly as you are able to turn it on, you can be too enthusiastic with the other person where you wear him out. If you do, she pulls down the mental shades and resists you. I have met several overly-enthusiastic salespeople whom I had to avoid a second time because I did not want to defend myself against them.

The man that can turn down his enthusiasm at the right time, in the right amount, and then turn it off as quickly as he can turn it on, is considered to have a very pleasing personality. There are many times you will need enthusiasm in teaching, in speaking and in selling where you could be incredibly impactful.

Most human relations require a certain amount of enthusiasm and its one of those things that you can cultivate. I was a shy introvert most of my early years, but I learned how to cultivate enthusiasm where I have given speech and have had standing ovation of thousands of people.

Good clean sportsmanship is the seventeenth trait of a pleasing personality and a Canadian-valued personality trait. Being a good sportsman about everything in life is important because you are not going to win every time. There will be times when you lose and when you do, lose gracefully and graciously, and look for ways to get better the next time.

Losing money only gives you the chance to earn even more by the use the experience as a learning lesson. Every time, I lose something I start to look for equivalent of seeds of opportunity to get even better. Even if you lose everything like I did during my brain injury, you can always get it back and earn even more. You cannot beat a person with that mindset because every time you beat him, he will come back be even stronger.

Common courtesy is the eighteenth way to develop a pleasing personality. Just simple, clean, common courtesy toward every-body does wonderful things for your personality, especially toward the people who might be in a lower status socially, economically, or financially than yourself. It is a wonderful thing to be courteous to the people that you do not have to be courteous towards; that is, it does something to the other fellow and it does something very special to you.

Nothing gets me upset quicker than to see someone newly-rich or somebody with a big ego to come into a restaurant or a public place and start to abuse the waiter or server. I have never learned to like that, but I was fortunate to have been raised and disciplined by some strong women in my life and my mother thought me to always address people who were older than me as "Sir" or "Madame." I believe that someone who humiliates another person in public has something seriously wrong with them inside.

As far as I can remember I do not ever recall humiliating anyone without a cause intentionally. I feel good about that, and I feel great to have this attitude towards all the people because it comes back to me in multitudes and people have the same attitude towards me.

When I call someone "Sir," they usually come back with the same. You get from people what you send out. You are a human magnet. You are attracting to you the total of what goes on in your heart and soul.

Nineteenth on the list is personal care and adornment in public life, which adds to a pleasing personality. You only get one chance to make a first impression. You do not know when you are going to meet the person that you need to impress, so dressing appropriately is very important in life, business, or salesmanship.

This is based on personal taste, but good-quality clean and ironed clothes would help in showing a pleasing personality as it represents the person inside the clothes. You can be a good showman and know when to dramatize your words and manner of behavior.

Appropriate personal care helps you to become a confident performer because all of us are showmen of some sort. We are all in the business of selling, and there is a dress code for such a profession. The art of showmanship is about the dramatizing your presentation in such a way that adds to your pleasing personality and helps make you memorable in the minds of your audience.

We are coming to the concluding points of developing a pleasing personality.

Twentieth is gracefulness in the posture and care for your body. When you meet new people, your confidence can be transmuted through your posture, your handshake, and the way you carry your body.

Slump around and be careless in your posture and you will be marked a person who is not too particular about the care for their body and personal appearance, which represents the standard in your life. You must carry your body the way you want to be perceived by other people.

Temperance is the twenty-first trait that I consistently modify. It's against my personal beliefs to drink and I have very low tolerance for alcohol, and it destroys a person's body and character. Too much of anything is bad for your health; in addition, you may engage in such behaviour that repels people from you. The rule that I use in all of these is that I don't do anything that overrides the control over my own mind. I would try almost anything once, but I would never let anything ever take control of my mental faculties.

I want to be always in possession of myself. I have seen people lose themselves and do awful things to others when they are not in control of themselves. This is not what great entrepreneurs ever do. If you do like to have an occasional cocktail or drink, do it but always keep things in balance. Balance is what most seek, and some may argue against, but my personal goals is to keep all areas of my life in balance.

Then comes the important twenty-second trait of patience. You have to have patience in the world we live in today. A world of competition on all levels. We need to be patient, especially in the testing times like the pandemic when most people are bound to stay at home and wait for time to pass. This is a great time of creativity for those of us that are open-minded and aware that our own immune system is the best vaccine that has ever been developed.

Patience is also required to strengthen your relationship with new people you meet and grow the relationships you already have. You have to control yourself at all times, but unfortunately most people do not have much patience and get mad in less than few seconds.

All you have to do to get someone mad is to say the wrong thing or do the wrong thing based on their understanding. I do not want to be mad because somebody says or does the wrong thing. In fact, the only thing that would make me mad is to observe the laziness of people who have enormous potential but just sit on it and waste their time in gossip and wasteful contestations.

Humility of the heart based on a keen sense of modesty, the twenty-third trait, is one of the most important traits of a pleasing personality. I do not know anything as important as having true humility in your heart when I think about criticizing anybody, and I do have to criticize people from time-to-time.

Sometimes I criticize the people I am working with, the people that are in my team or in my family. It is always out of the goodness of my heart and with the intention of care for the person. Immediately and always, I ask God for forgiveness and the person's understanding of my words and intentions inside of me. I may have done things ten times worse and have had worse habits, but nobody can accuse me of being lazy.

I am the hardest working person I know; in fact, I am a human camel. I am always the hardest working person in the room, but I always try to maintain that sense of humility in my heart, regardless of what happens to me.

After all, everything I have done so far is due to the demanding work and friendly cooperation of some marvelous people in my life. Without them I could have never to overcome all the defeats that I have, and I could not have grown the way I did. I could not have gotten their cooperation if I did not adjust myself in the state of friendliness and the state of modest humility in my heart.

The twenty-fourth trait, is that personal magnetism that the most outstanding, leaders, clergymen, lawyer, doctors, teachers, and other professionals have been able to use to transmute their creative energy with humility in their heart. Let us find out what is it that make us tick as we go out in the world and analyse our own chances of making an impact in the lives of other people around us.

You now have the tools to do some discoveries, you can start analyzing yourself and other people. Start with yourself and find out what makes you and others tick because now you have one the most important assets anyone can wish for; that is, the awareness of the subject of developing a pleasing personality.

My greatest compensation for all this effort and years of going the extra mile in every endeavour is the finding peace of mind; the twenty-fifth trait, that I have at this stage of my life. Peace of mind is something that you must find for yourself by earning it. So many people never find peace of mind because they are looking for it in the wrong place.

They are looking for joy from what money can buy, recognition, fame, and fortune. They are waiting for somebody else to make them happy or do something to trigger their happiness.

Anyone can find that peace of the humility of their heart in that hour that you connect with your Creator. For me it is in that early morning hour when I connect with my Creator to be thankful for all the wonderful things in my life. I can always go into that secluded place of meditation with the Higher Power simply by closing my eyes and being mindful of my being where I visualize my own ideal life events.

Anyone can do that; you can do that using these principles. After going the extra mile for over twenty-five years in everything that I do, I have found that the real value anyone can get is peace of mind. I am at peace with myself, or like the poet said, "All is well with my soul."

I have had the privilege of going the extra mile with a pleasing personality most of my life. I have never had a time where I did go the extra mile without seeing major benefits that come along with it.

A Self-Determining Person

The aim of this book was to make you a self-determining person without the permission of anybody. That is one of the grandest, most glorious feelings that I know about; namely, the knowing that I can do whatever I want to do without asking anybody, to have the ability to create miracles in my own life.

To do one act of going the extra mile every day you get the chance is a wonderful tonic for your soul. It could be as simple as calling someone and wishing them the best or telling them that you appreciate them in your life.

Instead of looking for what is wrong with the rest of the world,

I look for every opportunity to find out what I can do to correct myself, to better my behaviour, because I have to live with myself. I spend the most time with myself, I have to eat and sleep with myself. I have to be comfortable with myself and have a clear conscious with peace of mind.

I have to look myself in the mirror every morning and greet myself, shave myself and live with myself twenty-four hours a day. So, I try to improve myself and I try to help my family, friends, and students through my books, speeches, and other communication.

I could have drafted novel stories or about all the scandals in the world that get so much attention, but I choose to write self-help books because I know this is where most impact is made in the life of the reader. I hope that every person that reads this book will excel in every way far beyond my own and overcome every challenge he or she may face with less pain and suffering. In fact, I am just a student, an intelligent student but I am only a student of these philosophies. The only thing that I have found as I approach the afternoon of life is having peace of mind that is worth all the effort and the struggles.

To find tranquility and joy in life as I approach the next season of my life is my greatest achievement of all. If I had the chance to live my life over again, I would live it the same way. I would make all the mistakes that I made at the time that I made them, I have no regrets.

I made my mistakes early in life and perhaps I have the chance to correct some of them in the noon hour of my life through my teaching and the opportunities that I create. To have the tranquility and peace of mind that has come out of the study of this wisdom has been one of the greatest joys of my life and compensation for all my troubles.

My suggestion is to test this miraculous formula which may bring you such overwhelming positive response in life. Starting tomorrow in whatever occupation you are engaged, in start to render more service than you are expected to. Do it with a positive mental attitude where you neither ask nor expect any compensation. Follow this habit for seven days straight and you will see how the attitude those around you changes towards you.

Do not make your plan known to anyone but do it quietly and enjoy doing it in the most natural way possible. Just greet people in a friendly manner, be more courteous and sincere, and at the end of each day, you will find yourself much happier and constantly full of joy.

We are facing and unparallel paradox that His Holiness the Dalai Lama explains beautifully. I witnessed this in my birthplace in a recent visit back, but I am paraphrasing the Dalai Lama who said:

"We have bigger homes but smaller families, more conveniences but less time. We have more degrees but less sense, more knowledge but less judgment. We have more experts, but even more problems. We have more medicines, but less healthiness. We have travelled to the moon and back but have a tough time crossing the street to meet or greet our new neighbors. We have more computers and cell phones to copy and store more information, but we have less communication. We have more quantity but less quality. We have fast foods and slow digestion. We have big men with short tempers and even shorter characters."

I did reverse this paradox because I was aware that we need to reverse this trend. We need to adopt more loving ways to interact with one another. We all belong to the same family, humanity, but we get conditioned by our own paradigm, and we need to be aware of what it is and how to break it.

You were born a miracle, but we become conditioned to live average. There is a formula to break our paradigm, which we will discuss in the final chapter of this book.

Chapter 13

Changing The Paradigm

"Small shifts in your thinking and small changes in your energy can lead to massive alterations of your end result." (Kevin Michel)

Vincent Van Gogh was asked how he painted such beautiful paintings. He answered:

"I dream my painting then I paint my dreams."

Everything starts in the mind. Your thinking habits are the results of your programmed paradigm. A paradigm is a multitude of habits that are programmed into our subconscious mind that control our behavior.

Have you ever wondered why you look like your relatives? Have you ever wondered why you have so many of your mom's and dad's traits and habits?

These are good questions to ask yourself. Have you ever wondered why you get the same results repeatedly? Have you ever asked yourself why some individuals with incredible education and degrees coming out of their business cards are not doing very well while others who may have never seen the inside of a school are earning millions of dollars, building giant businesses, and doing incredible things all over the world? I did.

As a matter of fact, I have been asking these questions for the last 25 years. I have been asking nothing but those questions. They say that if you seek you will find, and I have found some answers I want to share with you in this final chapter.

I want to explain why these things happen. I want to explain it so simple that a ten-year-old child will understand without insulting your intelligence. Let's think for a moment. By now it's obvious to you that our minds control everything and the mind has two parts: the conscious mind and the subconscious part of our mind. Your subconscious mind is programmed with something called a paradigm.

Do you know what a paradigm is? A paradigm is a multitude of habits. Now, a habit is nothing but an idea that is fixed in the subconscious mind that you act on without any conscious thinking.

We know that it's our actions that produce our results, it's out actions that causes a reaction which create our world. We are originally programmed genetically, that is why we look like our relatives, then we are programmed environmentally.

If you were born in Canada and at birth moved to a remote area in Japan, you would know nothing about the English language or culture and be totally programmed with the Japanese culture even if you had blond hair and looked totally different.

At a certain age, a physical barrier develops in our mind, and we develop what is called the conscious mind where we develop the ability to make decision based on the sensory faculties. The mind collects information through our five senses; see, hear, smell, taste, and touch.

The mind also develops our higher faculties or intellectual faculties like perception, intuition, will, reason, imagination and memory as explained in detail in previous chapters.

We have the power to think positive or negative, good, or bad, abundance or poverty thoughts. Do you know what we are going to think? We are going to think thoughts that are in harmony with the paradigm.

The paradigm controls the vibration of our body. This physical instrument we call the body is in high vibration. It is the vibration of your thoughts and body that creates your results. Vibration is the first law of the universe that states that everything in the universe is in vibration. It's the ideas that you impress on the subconscious that control the vibration. There is a power that flows into you and through you. You can think any thought that you want to think, and it our paradigm controls our results.

Accidental Reprogramming

In 2013 I my memory was wiped out after the hit-and-run accident. Having been treated by some of the best doctors and psychologists and mentors in the world, I have recorded my findings and those achievers who helped me regain my memory, rebuild my health, and reprogrammed my subconscious mind. When you change your paradigm by seeing and hearing from examples of people just like you, you will build the ability to create miracles in your own life.

The outcomes of our lives have nothing to do with how smart we are, how much formal education we have or what side of the tracks we were born on. They have everything to do with our paradigm, the programmed information and multitude of habits that dictate our conditioned behavior. The paradigm is the result of both genetic and environmental influences.

Your genetic programing can go back generations of your family history. That is how you were programmed through your DNA. Your thinking habits are a result of your environmental and physical heredity.

In this book we have extensively talked about your social-environmental heredity, which is the most important of the two but your physical heredity also plays a part in your thinking habits as well. Your physical heredity is everything that you are physically, the stature of your body, texture of your skin, the tone of your voice, color of your eyes and color of hair etc. and the makeup of your DNA, which carries the seeds of our thinking habits.

Our spiritual DNA is perfect, and we can change our paradigm, which is our environmental programming. You are the total of all your ancestors as far as you can think back. You inherit a little bit of their good habits and some of the unhealthy habits as well, but there is nothing you can do about that, it is static, its fixed at birth.

However, environmental programming can be changed and reprogrammed. The will to change gives you the ability to concentrate on reprogramming yourself through power of repetition. Far important is your thinking habits which are the result of your social heredity. Those are the environmental influences and the things that you allow to go into your mind, and you have accepted as a part of your character.

Everyone that reads this book, including myself, knows how to do better than what they are doing right now. You may wonder, "Why are we not doing it?" It is because people are habitually programmed to do what we are doing. Until we change the program nothing will change. I am constantly changing my paradigm.

Our subconscious mind was programmed when we were little babies. Everything around you went right into your subconscious mind and built the way you behave. Customs, traditions, ideals, religion, and culture are all a part of our paradigm. All the energy that goes into our subconscious mind forms our paradigm.

You and I are the products of your paradigm. It is the paradigm that controls our thinking habits and that control the vibration of our bodies, which produces our results. It is the thoughts that you think, which you impress upon your subconscious mind, that control your body vibration. Vibration is nothing but an idea which controls our results, but it also controls what we attract into our lives. That is the basis for the law of attraction.

You attract people and things that are in harmony based on your vibration. Everything works based on vibration. You and I work based on a frequency as well just like a radio station frequency as mentioned in prior chapters. The only music you can attract is the vibration that you are tuned into. It is the paradigm that controls our vibration.

"We live in an ocean of motion," Bob Proctor says.

You can change your thinking but that does not do much; rather, you must change your paradigm to change your results. It is the thoughts that you think that controls your vibration, and you are in control of what you attract. So, if you keep attracting what you don't want, understand that it's the paradigm that is causing the problem.

As we think in the conscious mind, we build ideas. We can think anything we want to think. Our thought vibration controls the way we act and the results we produce. It is how you use your mind that dictates the vibration of your body. If you are not happy with your results, you need to change who and what you attract.

Facing Fears And Changing Habits

Your intellect helps you figure out how you do things, it does not mean you are going to do them. You and I should face a new fear every day because that is how you will change the paradigm. When you go through your initial fear barrier the paradigm does not change because it takes some time to change a behavior.

Our paradigms limit our performance and get us to quit things before we get to our destination. That is why grit is a wonderful quality to develop in changing our paradigms. Grit is developed through the repetition of thoughts, ideas, and habits, and through learning new things.

Learning is consciously entertaining an idea, getting emotionally involved in the idea and stepping out to act on the idea to change our results. When that behavior becomes normal, we look for a new barrier to break, some new fears to face, and new habits to adopt.

Here are three habits to start working on immediately and every day:

1. You should study every day: Focus on the study of your subject of interest. Not a day goes by where I don't study this topic of the art of creative thinking.
2. Find a mentor: Find someone who has accomplished what you dream of and ask them. The right mentors will help you. If not, they are not the one.
3. Have written goals: Writing goals on paper is the intellectual way that materializes your goals. An idea is a spiritual seed. You must plant it on paper so it can grow.

You may be thinking, "But I don't have money to start what I want to do. Where is the money going to come from?"

Well, the money is going to come from wherever it is right now. Money is energy and it floats where it is wanted. Money is looking for a good place to stay, and you can become that good place where money wants to stay. I have been in this game for the past 25 years and it's been far from easy, but I have never been stuck because of lack of money.

Money finds its way to me when I have a clear picture of what I want. I have experienced all obstacles and every bump in the road. I have faced every moment of doubt you can imagine but I have always received money from where it was to do what I wanted to do.

The will, not money, is what gives you the ability to concentrate on developing new behaviors. It all starts with the image you want to create of what you want to accomplish. Everything you see is part of an image and everything you create is created twice, first in your mind, then in reality. Everything we see around us is an image of what was in the mind of someone first.

For instance, no painter ever paints an original painting; the picture is always created in the mind first. Similarly, we have to see ourselves how and who we want to be first before we become it. Oftentimes when we begin what we want is not in physical form yet, so we act in lack, but that's not how the formula works. That is why most people get stuck. That is the paradigm overpowering the will. Instead, you must see your future self in your imagination before you can become it. You have to live there because before you can do something you have to be something.

We all have enormous potential. Let's consider where we come from for a moment. We come from a little particle of energy from dad and a little particle of energy from mom that together constitute the nucleus of us. After gaining more energy for two hundred and eighty days, we make our debut on the planet.

When we are born, we come out programmed genetically, but our subconscious mind is like a blank page. Then our subconscious mind is conditioned environmentally. We are all the same at birth with the same possibilities and potentials because we were created in the image of our Creator. Our spiritual DNA is perfect, but then we get programmed by our environment and conditioned by our paradigms.

A culture is a paradigm. Every country has a culture, every family has a culture, every company has a culture. In changing times, we can keep hanging on to the old or we can consciously choose to change our paradigm. Think of your behaviour, think of your results and if we change the habitual things we do, we can change and keep changing our paradigms. We must realize that we are conditioned and that our knowing is what stops us from making progress. We need to look at our results and ask, "What is causing this?"

How To Change A Paradigm

A paradigm is very hard to change, but it can be done in one of two ways. The first way is through an emotional impact, and the second way is through the power of repetition. Emotional impact would be something that happens to a person that impacts them deeply, like when the doctor tells someone that if you don't quit smoking you will die within six months, or when you lose someone that is dear to you in a tragic way that impacts your behaviour.

The second way is through the power of repletion. Here is where two opposite questions have the same answer. How does the paradigm form? Through the repetition of information. How do we change the paradigm? Through the repetition of information. We change the paradigm through the power of repetition that reprograms our subconscious mind. Only when the paradigm changes do your life results start to change.

Thought is preamble to everything, including paradigms.

Thought waves are cosmic waves, they penetrate all time and space. Thoughts can be under water or in outer space and the vibration is the same.

Thoughts can be changed through visualizations or affirmations. Affirmations are things you tell yourself often about your goals. Write down the affirmation of the things that you want to change and keep repeating them to yourself daily until it becomes fixed in your mind. That is when the thing that you are afraid of doing becomes easy.

When I was developing the habit of running, I started with long walks, then I started to run soon after. Now as soon as I wake up my body is ready to get going. It's an automatic habit if the weather allows.

There are many things you do automatically today that you don't give a second thought to but once upon a time you were afraid of doing. The prime example of this is when you learned to drive a vehicle. You perhaps remember being afraid to drive a car when you first started. Today it's second nature to you, like most people.

Imagine where you could be in five or ten years if you could put these principles in practice if you let go of the past and all that is holding you back. You can revise the old story, create a new paradigm, and make miracles happen in your life. It's time to write a new story for your life. I promise you amazing things will start to happen. I get messages of blessings every day, and I continue to be a positive force in my own universe. Yes, perhaps I am talking about you as becoming that source of positive energy as well.

Whether you want to build a business, retire early, or have the freedom to spend your time however you choose, you can do it. You can turn your dreams into reality. Never forget how far you have come by exposing yourself to this wisdom, and know that if you practice this wisdom, the best is yet to come. Now that we are at the conclusion of this writing, perhaps you want to change some results in your life. If so, do not focus on your behaviour but think about the beliefs or the paradigm that drives that behaviour.

Your Heart Listens To Your Voice

What goes on in our heads is based on all our references. When someone was too talkative in a negative way my grandmother used to say, "Your heart listens to your voice." I now know that your heart is your subconscious mind, and your voice is that inner-voice or your self-talk. Self-talk, perceptions and learnt habitual behaviours locked away in the implicit part of our brains are driving those thoughts and behaviours.

Most of us have been programmed with a belief that if you live life as a "good person," after you die, you will go to heaven, this incredibility beautiful eternal life of pleasure, peace, and abundance. However, our definition of goodness is based on our environmental programming and therefore it is an individual definition. What is good to one may not be so good in the eye of another. What is fun, exciting, and empowering may have the opposite effect on another; therefore, heaven is a creative place. The real heaven or hell is inside every one of us by the thoughts we create.

Heaven is an individual place based on your own creative vision of this life and the afterlife. Heaven means different things to different people based on their definition of heaven and what is required on earth to get there. We must understand that it does not matter who becomes the president or prime minister in your country. You can navigate towards what you want in life right here on earth.

Regardless of what happens in the external world, if you believe that your heart is a canvas for miracles, you can make a turn-around or accelerate your progress. That is a belief, and beliefs are lenses by which we see the world. If you want to change your results, change your focus on the beliefs that drive your behaviours.

Science reveals that our bodies are the playing field for our creative energy. Each of us have different receptors through which we connect with that creative energy field. It is different for each person, but we all connect to this power through the six faculties of creativity. This field of creativity is within all of us, but each of us access it differently. Some access it through meditation, some through prayer, others via different means of self-realization but we all must be entuned with ourselves to connect with the field of creativity.

When we pray, we talk to the Higher Power asking for help, deliverance or seek guidance. We are consciously trying to reach that level of creativity where we turn our desires into blessings in our lives. We want to be conscious of our actions and pray for our lives to run as smoothly filled with love and compassion towards others.

When we are not completely aware of our prayer habits, it becomes a one-way communication. Sometimes it turns into complaining and griping or asking for forgiveness for our past deeds. I believe prayer should be a two-way communication where you receive instruction and messages back through your faculties of creativity on how we proceed in the direction of your burning desire.

Consider that we are already born into heaven. This is the creative place, and we can create things into existence right here on earth. When we create the right thoughts and focus on the right imagines in our mind, we are literally living in heaven. That is when miracles start to happen in our lives, and we start to act before seeing the end results.

However, when we are run by our childhood auto-program we are living in the old paradigm. We may feel low-energy, fearful, disappointed and feel defeated most days. Fear is caused by doubt, and doubt is erased by awareness and understanding. We can learn the process of reprogramming our inner-self based on principles shared here. These ideas were recorded in this manner and in the order of importance to bring us to this bottleneck so we can make a positive shift in our lives.

You may have been born into a loving, supportive family and you can step on the accelerator of building your dream life of purpose. If otherwise, it's time to take your life in your own hands by steering your thoughts in the direction you desire the most. Start with why you need to change the paradigm that is controlling your outer behaviour.

Personal growth is a decision that you will have to make for yourself; this is another learning moment. You become unbe-lievably powerful and become the power generator in your family if you tap into the power of your subconscious mind. You can cultivate this power that has been given to you at birth by the repetition of the images of your ideal life to manifest your desires.

You can create love as you can create joy, harmony, health, and peace of mind in your family life. Those are all the attributes that we associate with the idea of heaven, and you can create heaven right here, starting with adopting kindness.

Otherwise, if you are not aware of your creative field, you will give into other people's "beliefs", or live in the paradigm and be controlled by circumstance all your life. If we are living by our old, programmed set of ideals, overwhelmed by fear, eventually we could break down and become immobilized.

Every human being is programmed in childhood when the brain is in hypnosis. At that age, the brain works on a lower vibration frequency called *Theta*. This is your creative imagination frequency. For instance, when a child pretends to be an adult, for the child it is as real as it gets. When we were kids, we used to ride sunflower sticks as our imaginary horses. The horse was as real as our imagination could make it.

First nature teaches our imagination, then we learn from our parents, siblings, friends, school, and our surroundings. We have to learn thousands of rules and regulations to be able to functional as members of a family, community, and the society and to fit in the environment we are born into.

It is said that if you are born into a rich family your work is based on your childhood programming and you consciously act to acquire more wealth. On the other hand, if you are born into a poor family, you stay there based on that programming unless you consciously break that cycle and reprogram yourself with success ideas.

Ninety-five percent of our lives is the result of that early programming, so most of the day we are sabotaging ourselves. Most of us think lack, scarcity, and the fear of loss. Only five percent of our lives are lived by conscious mindfulness where creativity happens by the power of decision-making to pursue something that is of value to us. We can start to pursue the study of your own faculties of creativity.

If you want to reprogram your mind, think about your life right now and how you are living verses how you want to live. What happens in the future is based on the decisions you make right now. Growth is a normal part of life, and if we are not growing, we are dying. You have to know where you are, and you need to know where you are going

If you look at your life and check where you are struggling, you will find the roots in your childhood programming. Your life is a printout of your subconscious mind's programming. The conscious mind is the creative place where we can override that prewritten program.

We do this in one of two ways:

1. Through hypnosis that happens in childhood as we grow up.
2. You can reprogram your mind through the power of repetition of thought.

I have read some books multiple times and or listen to select audio programs hundreds of times to change my thought patterns and override childhood programming. Repetition is necessary when changing our paradigms. It's repetition that changes the base programming.

For instance, when you learn to ride a bicycle, you have to fall down and keep trying or when you learn the alphabet, you keep messing it up until you get it right through repetition. Similarly, when you set a fitness goal the number of reps and frequency of repetition is more important than the size of the weights.

You have to keep repeating the movie of your future life in your mind every single day hundreds of times until you see your future self as clear as in reality. That become a learned habit where it plays out in your daily activity and directs you in that desired direction. Repetition of thought is a habit.

Like any other habit it takes practice to change, learn, and master repetition of thought. You have to repeat new habits so much until you own them. Listening to audio programs is the best way to learn the power of repetition, just like when you listen to a song so many times that you can sing along after a while.

If your mind is wandering around all day, you are run by your subconscious programming. If you are task-oriented, you are operating on the conscious level; furthermore, you are receiving instruction and making important decisions all day.

If you let go of the wheel of your thinking, it will always drive toward the ditch. If your programming is a negative, then you will always attract negative circumstances into your life. This could be overwritten as easy as using repetition of a positive thought.

Falling In Love

Reprogramming yourself is like falling in love. No matter how hard your job, how hard your life or difficult circumstances, the minute you feel you fall in love everything changes. You cannot stop thinking about the person. You start imagining all these wonderful thoughts about your future together. You start creating happy images of your future life and your love life together.

Most of the times you think about happy images that you hold inside your imagination of you about the person you love. Suddenly, it feels like you are in heaven on earth. Life starts to feel better; the job does not seem that bad, food tastes better and roses smell sweeter, all because you are operating from the conscious mind. You are creating happy images intentionally and at will.

Oftentimes when the honeymoon is over, your mind goes back to the normal grind. You start to think about managing your life. Now you start to operate based on your old habits and old subconscious programming again. Your bills, your job and your limitations start to surface and all of a sudden, your behaviour starts to change.

We stop thinking about the images and replacing them with problems at work, our home, and our career, and suddenly you distance yourself from that happy honeymoon place. We stop being mindful of our love and become mindful of our problems. She or he may even say, "If you behaved like this on our first date, we would not even have had a second one."

To keep that honeymoon feeling with you, you can keep creating new fresh images about your ideal life as it advances. Love keeps growing by being always mindful of your feelings. The conscious mind wishes and desires while subconscious mind is run on program under disguise of reality. If you program your wishes and desires into your subconscious mind, you can create your own heaven on earth.

In the case of falling in love your brain produces a cocktail that helps increase your vitality, health, and happiness. Similarly, when you look at a person who scares you, the chemistry of your brain changes. The images we feed our mind create the chemistry in our brains, and your brain chemistry controls your behaviour.

Change your images, change your chemistry. You can change your brain chemistry by feeding it new and empowering images on daily bases. You have a choice to reprogram your brain, or you can replay the existing program. Reprogramming of your subconscious mind happens with your inner desires, goals, and dreams clarify. Remember clarity is the king of all things we do.

Changing the images you feed to your subconscious mind changes the chemistry of your brain. Only think and talk about what you want to manifest in your life. The composition of your blood cells decides the health of the cell; similarly, the composition of the chemistry of your brain decides your life outcome of failure or success, misery, or happiness.

If you can see the roadblocks along the way to your goals and prepare for overcoming the obstacles, you have a greater chance of overcoming them.

Some of the latest brain research shows that in addition to visualizing the ideal outcome for your life, if you can imagine the obstacles along the way and visualize overcoming them, it strengthens your brain patterns and builds self-confidence.

Whether it is a belief that is in your way or a story that is holding you back, look at the roadblocks, or what is holding you back in life under the surface, and change that blueprint. You may have thoughts such as, "I am not smart enough, I am too old, I am too young, I came from a poor family." Address that obstacle by the power of repetition.

Visualize that obstacle and visualize yourself going around them. The very act of acknowledging your obstacles releases neuronal tension around in your brain, and if you repeatedly do that, your brain, like mine during my brain injury, starts to see that yes there is a real struggle, and it builds a new pattern around that struggle.

The brain likes anything that makes it curious, and that is novel and challenging. Yes, the brain likes a challenge. It is all a workout for your brain. I have gone through extensive testing, multiple brain scans and other brain challenges in hospitals during my recovery to prove this point.

If you can strengthen neural patterns where you see your challenges and how to overcome them, it builds self-confidence and certainty heals and enhances your brain function at the same time. If you do this work and develop these thinking patterns in your brain, over time they become your daily habits. That is when building new habits and skills becomes a fun game. You can do this you can go around any obstacle in your life versus just having knowledge in your head and staying in bed.

Andrew Carnegie, America's first billionaire, said it best when said, "People who are unable to motivate themselves must be content with mediocrity, no matter how impressive their other talents may be."

We can reprogram our lives with wishes and real desires. We could have love, health, wealth, harmony, and happiness and once again. Nature demands balance and supports your consciously written goals, dreams, and action steps. When you implement these changes, we are no longer victims of the childhood programming but creators of our own realities. Everyone has the same desires and wishes. We all want love, happiness, success, and wonderful relationships. This is our common standard of desires and wishes.

Ask Empowering Questions

Imagine somebody gives you a hundred-million-dollar computer that answers any question about creating an ideal of life. Your brain is that computer. If you ask it empowering questions, it will give you are empowering answers. If you give disempowering questions, it will give you disempowering answers.

Allow me to simplify how the brain looks for specific answer based on the questions you ask it. For instance, if I asked you, do you like a pen or pencil? Or do you like the oceans or mountains? Similarly, if you ask for questions that are about health, wealth, and life of abundance it will seek those answers.

The brain looks for answers based on the questions you ask it. When you ask a question but do not know the answer, you say or think, "I don't know." You put the case to rest but when you ask and answer "I wonder," your brain goes into a search mode to find answers.

Can Google, YouTube, or other search engines find you the answer to all your questions? The answer is, yes, there is an answer you can find for everything. We live in 2022 and beyond, this is the decade of all the answers to all our questions. There are answers for everything, including how to live on Mars.

So, we need to get really good at asking our brain great questions. The better questions you ask, the better the answers your brain will find. We have to train ourselves at asking great questions from our own brains.

We must be great at asking better questions from ourselves. Ask questions whereby the answers you find moves you forward to act in the direction of desired results. This kind of thinking is using your higher faculty of reason. You find the answers, not the problems.

What do I need to do to act? This is a powerful Question. If we learn how to ask the right questions the brain will find the answers. Do you believe that if you are totally committed to achieve any goal, you can find an answer to achieving it? Yes, you can. The average person tiptoes through life hoping that they can make it safely to death. It is such a shame, and it does not have to be that way any longer.

If you are not committed, you will find excuses and procrastinate. Just commit to yourself to your family to whatever inspires you to act. Affirm to yourself repeatedly that: "I am a committed person to achieve my goals."

The most important asset we have is time and the most valuable attitude is the attitude of gratitude, so I thank you for spending the time to read this book. I believe it will do absolute wonders and create miracles in your life if you commit to putting this simple principle-based advice into action.

Last Words

My grandmother used to wake me up early saying, "Excessive sleep is waste of your life son, it's time to get your day started." Rest is necessary but sleep is overrated and often mistaken for laziness. You will need six to eight hours of sound sleep and take a short nap when you need it, but to sleep away your mornings is a waste of life because it is the most productive time of day.

If you could manage going to bed a little bit early and apply the principles discuss here, you could totally change your life. Growing up our mantra was Benjamin Franklin's:

"Early to bed, early to rise makes you healthy, wealthy, and wise."

Today I still go by this principle.

Some have developed habits that make their productivity peak at various times which is fine if we apply these thinking habits daily. My most productive time is early mornings before the sun rises and fills in the picture of the day. I enjoy the quiet time to think, write, work out and create.

You need a plan for each day as you do for your life. I am an early riser by nature, so I use this habit like a wedge to crack open each day like opening a treasure chest full of jewels.

Most of my great ideas come to me early morning or when I am on my fitness run, in the shower, or just driving around observing people. By the time most in my family and friends awake, I have already put in a half day's work. This is a part of my personality, character, and personal initiative that I cannot sacrifice for anything or anyone. I stick to the program wherever I may be because I enjoy each day I experienced and create miracles in my life daily.

I have found a place of peace and Godliness inside my heart that I go to be one with the source and thank the Creator for all the blessing in my life. I ask for the wisdom to obtain what want and need. I pray, talk to my Creator, meditate, and ask the angels to bring me blessings. I practice visualization and imagine having to run my day as planned. I have developed the habit of devising a plan of action for each day the night before. It helps my day run smoother.

If you study any human beings who have "failed" they will all tell you that "yes, I have failed and I suffered but that is what has made me stronger to persevere."

I was in a state of pain, panic, suffering for a long time but I used it in framing it in my mind in such a way that empowers me instead of disempowering me. We have that ability to take things and give them meaning that lift us up instead of breaking us down.

The more I am aware of what is happening within me, the more I have control over what is going on around me. The more I can respond instead of reacting, the more I can be deliberate with every forward step that I take. If you let other people's perception of you dictate your behaviour you will never grow as a person but if you leave yourself to experience despite what others think of you, you will grow and evolve as a person.

Looking In The Mirror

I hope that tomorrow when you wake up, you are a different person. The character that you build, the courage that you show, the faith that you manifest and the pride you feel will be different when you change your thinking. When you look at yourself in the mirror and see a life well-lived, it is worth the effort you will put forward in incorporating these ideas into your daily life.

Walk with a different spirit in your footstep, embrace life as a gift. We know it may be hard at first, but you are doing it right. Remember that no one can take your pain away but yourself, so do not let anyone take away your happiness either. Now you have a choice to rewrite your programming, rewrite your story and take your God-given power back. It's time to act and create your own heaven on earth.

When I look back on my life, I see pain, mistakes, and heartache. When I look in the mirror, I see strength, learned lessons, and pride in who I have become. God will feed every bird in the sky, but He will not put food in their nest. You must do the work.

There is greatness within everyone one of us. You should attempt to discover it in yourself. Don't settle for average, because one day when you are old and gray, and you will look back at your life either full of regrets or full of joy for the contribution to made to the world for being here. You only have one life to live, so go for it, because those few moments of my life when I was extraordinary are the moments when I felt most alive.

Build a picture of how you want to live and hold those images in your mind because there is a power that flows to you and through you. The imagination is the greatest nation in the world, use your imagination daily. What do you want? How do you really want to live?

Don't settle for anything less than total and utter excellence. No one will ever see you; they only see you through the great work that you do. Make certain that your work is marked with excellence. If you keep your imagination alive you are going to have a phenomenal life and it can get better every day through the proper use of your imagination.

What a wonderful world we live in, what a wonderful idea to use your God-given faculties to create a wonderful life. In the moment of decision, you can change your life forever, choose wisely, choose to change, and grow now.

If you take nothing else away, practice this concluding note and start your new journey in the next twenty-four hours with a pen and paper and map up your next twelve months. May the blessings of God start to pour down on you and your family.

Good luck.

Roots & Fruits
About The Author & The Gilany Family

"Seek the fellowship of those who enjoy the fellowship with the Lord." (Sheikh Abdul Qadir Gilany)

Arif Gilany began his career at FedEx Corporation, travelling across North America to manage various teams for peak performance and production. In 2006, using these skills, he built the third largest organization within a top financial company in Canada. In 2013 he founded The Camel Company of Canada and in 2018 expanded operations internationally managing teams in North America, the Middle East and Asia. In 2018 he authored his first book and in 2022 he launched the *Ministry Of Miracles School Of Greatness*.

Arif is an entrepreneur, author, and business consultant with superb interpersonal, team-building, negotiating and multi-lingual skills. He is an asset to any team involved in negotiations and business ventures. Currently, he is a business development advisor, contract negotiator and senior adviser at Aral Energy.

This book and all the research done has been a result of personal experience and it is copyrighted by The Morgan-Gilany Group and Arif Gilany. The information is verifiable, and stories have been recorded for future expansion of our programs.

Contact Information

www.ArifGilany.com

arifgilany@gmail.com

+14165283136

The Gilany Family

It would be a total miss if I did not close out this book as a tribute to my two wonderful children who have inspired me to author this book, and to my ancestors – who have paved the way for generations of leaders around the world for centuries – who also inspired the writing of this book.

The mystical life in the Kurdish-inhabited area as I remember it continues with the tune of the flute of nomadic shepherds tending their herds of sheep as their forefathers had done for thousands of years. Kurds are over ninety five percent Sunni Muslims. We believe that God sends the angels down before sunrise to answer our morning prayer and bring you blessings all day long.

Your habits run your day and therefore your life. You could do the same and start each day with gratitude and a plan of action. Thank the Creator for all your blessings and ask what you want through meditation, prayer, presence of mind or any other way you connect to the Higher Power.

Only when one is peaceful and present in a state of mindfulness, we can feel presence of the Creator inside our hearts. The power of visualization you can be cultivated in those early moments before the start of your busy day. The Ministry Of Miracle's special formula is to start each day with an attitude of gratitude. It is the opening of the gate for miracles.

When I was ten-years-old, I spend six months on a hospital bed recovering from my first coma and terrible injuries sustained during the Iran-Iraq war. I lay there all alone on a hospital bed with broken pieces of my body in different casts, I was scared. I missed my family and I wanted to get better fast. That is when I found peace through prayer and visualization.

They told me that God was peace, so I learned about the power of prayer, and I was never alone again. I was up before the nurses came in for work and I ask God to bring me his peace and restore my health and pull me through this traumatic experience each and every morning as I prayed in my childhood solitude.

I have kept this routine with me through all the years and when I need to resort to its power for a second time in Toronto during my recent brain injury accident and the recovery process, I repeated my formula for a second time as a proof of its legitimacy.

The first two years following my first accident while recovering my village of Jarawa, I practiced this routine subconsciously and went out walking around in our beautiful fruit garden of quite a variety each morning. My father is a fan of gardening and planting of different fruit trees, so he had planted a heavenly garden with a unique selection of vegetations on the most beautiful piece of land before the Iranian revolution of 1979.

Ours was first the house in village built with brown and red machine pressed bricks from a modern factory. It was the home of my childhood dreams. My big red dog Gorzo always followed me wherever I went like the best friends we were.

We would walk through the garden sitting and watching as grandma prepared breakfast for ten to fifteen people every day, it was quite an undertaking. Gorzo and I would sit by beehives watch the first bees leave the colony as we witnessed my mother, and the girls wake up and join grandma for the preparations. The sun would rise behind the mountain peaks and fill in the picture as it was a masterpiece of heavenly beauty. We still talk about those magical days sometimes.

When I arrived in Canada years later, I brough this love for nature with me. Since then, I have been in pursuit of establishing a business and a lifestyle based on that kind of deep love people, respect for nature and all its life forms. Canada has given me many beautiful moments that took my breath away, but mostly Canada also introduced me to my own personal Charter of Human Rights and Freedoms.

I am here to represent my new heritage in Canada and its incredible values, freedoms and the responsibilities that comes with it. My two children have been the greatest of blessings of my life in Canada. It has been my goal to introduce them to their rich heritage.

Over 90% of the Kurdish-inhabited area is a mountainous terrain and mostly about fifteen hundred meters above sea levels. It is home to some of the most fertile lands in the world. It's also home to over forty-five million people known as Kurds, the world's largest ethnic group in the without a country of their own.

Its mainland is divided between the areas covering parts of Iran, Iraq, Syria, and Turkey. The Kurds of Yerevan in Armenia had a great musical and cultural impact in my teenage years as we listened to them on the radio stations that broadcasted news and music from the former Soviet Union.

Thousands of years of deep rivers washing away at mountain peaks has created the ideal agricultural soil and most beautiful mountain hills you can imagine. Kurds have a proverb that say:

"Kurds have no friends but mountains."

Yet here I am as a Canadian-Kurd making friends from all over the world. It is time to break the mold, change the paradigm, and create a new reality based on the brotherhood of all humankind.

Over the years, I have met organizations and individual who

have been empathetic and supportive of the Kurdish cause and our people's struggles to obtain some basic human rights and freedoms. If you are one of those, I appreciate your empathy, love, and support, but let us get clear with my intentions.

In recent years we were all exposed to the treats of fanaticism by the rise-and-fall of the so-called Islamic State of Syria and Iraq otherwise known as ISIS in the western world. Kurds were instrumental in ending their reign of terror.

I wanted to mention and appreciate the sacrifices of thousands of war veterans and men and particularly brave Kurdish women who took up arms to defeat the satanic forces of evil. We also saw how political ignorance and fanaticism took to the American Senate and the White House in the election race when Joe Biden was up against Donald Trump.

This book is a tribute to all the brave Kurdish men and women of Kobani, Shengal, and Aleppo who defended our collective global freedom. They fought so courageously and sacrificed their lives to keep us safe from ISIS devastating fanatical extremist beliefs and their narrow world view. The bravery of those people is the inspiration that has created this opportunity for us to connect here.

I wanted to have their voices heard through my brief message here because it was not long ago when my beloved capital city, Ottawa and every other capital city was under ISIS treat of destruction. Every major event around the globe was put under high security, and every movement had to be carefully monitored and scrutinized due to fear and threat of ISIS. It made all of us suspicious of each other, I want to break that invisible barrier that is isolating us like the COVID-19 pandemic has done again.

The fanatical beliefs of ISIS forces ruined thousands of lives with the devastating philosophy. They beheaded thousands of men and enslaved many more women and children. The ISIS evil army captured thousands of young Zoroastrians, Christians, Jews, and Muslim women and sold them to their allies as gifts of victory like their barbaric ancestors did. They cut down thousands of olive trees that represent the peaceful and loving nature of the Kurdish people.

That is a topic of another book, but this book is an offer to you as an olive branch that empowers you to be the best you can all days of your life.

Canada has thought me to respect and appreciate the sacrifices of our veterans. I needed to recognize and appreciate the sacrifices and the effort that the veterans of my nation put forth to defend our collective freedom.

The COVID-19 global pandemic and the ongoing world crisis make the Kurds' heroic acts seem like it was a long time ago, but it is still fresh wound in the heart of thousands of Kurdish children who lost their parents and guardians.

I consider myself a peace-loving Canadian author and businessperson. I believe one of the most practical ways to lower all tensions and conflict in the Middle East and elsewhere is to promote global cooperation through commerce, trade, and business amongst all nations. We all have products, services, and values that our neighbors, friends, sisters, and brothers across all borders need, value, and appreciate.

We need to find out what those needs and wants are and fulfill the prescription. That is the job of a new immigrant entrepreneurs and those who want to make a positive change in the world.

Sheikh Abdul Qadir Gilany (also spelled Geylani -Al-Gilani) was a Sufi Sheikh and the founder of the Qadiri Sufi order (Silsila).

He was born in the month of Ramadan in 470 AH (1077-78 AD) in the Persian province of Gilan in Iran, south of the Caspian Sea. His contribution to Sufism was so immense that he became known as the spiritual pole of his time.

Sheikh Abdul Qadir Gilany left his home to study and arrived in Baghdad during the reign of the Abbasid Caliphate in 488 AH (1095 AD) at a time where there was chaos and disunity in the Islamic world. The Muslim rulers had lost all sense of duty and paid no heed to teaching of Islam. Between 496 AH and 521AH, he underwent a period of deep reflection and seclusion during which he distanced himself from all worldly affairs.

His twenty-five-year-long spiritual journey saw him travel across the barren desert and ruins in the area around Baghdad living in complete seclusion where he would experience extreme physical hardships. During this time, he would be in constant remembrance of the Almighty Creator (Allah).

During these twenty-five years, he engrossed himself in such intense spiritual exercises that, just by reading about them, one can only but marvel at the dedication of this "Great Saint" as he is known in the Muslim world. His sincerity and dedication in controlling his inner-self took him swiftly to the top of spiritual and divine levels self-awareness. He was now totally drowned in the sea of love of the Creator.

He turned himself into a strong mountain of patience and firmness that could not be moved. He began his leadership development and sent out his disciples throughout the Middle East and North Africa. The notable events that took place during this part of his life are numerous. They are recorded in the historic books of the region, and it has filled many volumes of books and movies that have been made about his fruitful life.

The Gilany family in the Kurdish regions roots dates to time when one of his descendants, the great Shamsalldin Gilany (*The light of guidance*) moved to the north, where it's now known as the Kurdistan area and settled in a place now called Shamdinan, named after him after his passing.

Shamsalldin grew his followership for a lifetime grooming other religious and community leaders. For centuries, the descendent of the family lead the spiritual guidance of the people in the Middle East and North Africa.

My great-grandfather Sheikh Abdullah Gilany, who eventually sacrificed his life for the cause of his nation, was an iconic figure that defended the human rights and freedom of his people in 1880s. He lived and studied in Istanbul in Gilany Mehalai districted named after his legacy.

I am inspired to have come from such a rich heritage, but you do not need a strong family tree to be a great leader. The most notable of this family leaders was Sheikh Obaidullah Gilany, the founder of Qaderiah (a Sunni -Muslim religious sect).

He is well-known throughout the Muslim world as "The Great One" and respected throughout Middle East, Minor Asia, and North Africa. His followers included Muslims, Christians, Jews, and other minorities that lived in peace and harmony with their brothers of different religions under his leadership.

The latest and greatest leader of Gilany Family is Sayyed Taha Gilany (1779-1826 AD), the father of great Kurdish historic figure Sheikh Abdullah Gilany. Mohammad Shah of Iran was particularly a follower and a great fan of Sayyed Taha Gilany and gifted him Mergewar (Northwestern Iran) region to settle and develop.

After his passing in Tehran the capital of Iran, his son took up the family leadership and responsibility at an early age. Later, they decided to move his people back to Eastern Turkey close to the city of Van. He then enrolled in the Turkish academy of military operations but the collapse of Ottoman Empire and the emergence of Ataturk (the reformer of Turkey.)

The change in balance of power in the region and emergence of the superpowers dissimulated the family traditional hierarchy set up. After their defeat by Turkish army where his father and two brothers we hanged for treason, they retreated to Mergewar on the border of Iran and Turkey.

That is where I was born in the small village of Jarawa, a picturesque mountain hill that backs to mount Judi where Noah's Ark has landed, a part of Zagreus Mountain ridges that expand through out the region.

Sayed Taha Gilany led the first Kurdistan national movement. He was known as the last great Gilany leader who had a deep impact on the nationalism of whole Kurdish nation. He was well-spoken in multiple languages including English, French, Arabic, Persian, Turkish and Kurdish.

I am blessed to have come from such a family that has championed leadership, entrepreneurship, and high moral values throughout the ages. My ancestors championed the cause of all people for basic human rights and freedoms for generations.

Today the Gilany family has spread out all over the world, but our family history and our resilient and exemplary way of life have never changed. I inherited the torch of leadership to help promote education, trade, and commerce amongst nations as my ancestors did.

When I arrived in Canada, I had all this rich history to live up to in the back of my mind. Social-environmental heredity is where a man builds himself based on what he allows to impact him that shapes his character.

When disaster hit in 2013, I could not just shrink into my own selfishness and pettiness. As the citizenship judge recommended, I have been trying to be an "outstanding citizen" in my new country to pave the way for the new wave of immigrant entrepreneurs that follows me. I hope you do the same.

It all begins with awareness.

In conclusion, your role as a great human being, entrepreneur and CEO of your life is to get busy living and leading yourself, your family, your business, your community, and your country. You are the pacesetter and the bridge builder for the next generation.

Now that we have reached the end of our journey here, I recommend that you read the most important parts of this book several times. We all need more reminder than we need instructions.

Good luck and see you at the top.

Lightning Source UK Ltd.
Milton Keynes UK
UKHW020640120922
408721UK00009B/829